Compensation in Public Enterprises, Private Enterprises and MNCs in India

Institute of Public Enterprise
Hyderabad

About the Authors

R.K. Mishra is ONGC Subir Raha Chair Professor on Corporate Governance and Senior Professor and Director, Institute of Public Enterprise, Hyderabad. PhD from the University of Rajasthan and a Visiting Fellow at London Business School (UK), he studied for International Teachers programme at SDA Bocconi, Milan. Dr Mishra taught at the University of Bradford, and was a Visiting Professor at Maison Des Sciences De l' Hommes, Paris and Faculty of Economics, University of Ljubljana, Slovenia. He is a member of the UN Task Force on International Standards of Excellence in Public Administration and Education. He is special invite on OECD Working Group on Privatisation and Corporate Governance of SOEs and Asian Network of Corporate Governance. He is Non-Executive Director on some public and private enterprise Boards in India. He has considerable experience of teaching and guiding research for doctoral degree in management, economics, public administration and commerce. His areas of interest include corporate governance, international management, international finance, public-private partnership, restructuring and environmental administration.

G. Sri Hari Rao retired as an Executive Director of Electronic Corporation of India Ltd. (ECIL) in November 2006, after serving the corporation for over 35 years in various capacities. He served as faculty member and resource person at the Institute of Public Enterprise after retiring from ECIL. He had experience related to MoU and their deployment as effective tool for introspection and planning. His comprehensive grasp and overview of ECIL helped him to prepare the plan documents, progress reports, presentation material, etc., for ECIL. He also assisted Justice M.J. Rao's Second Pay Revision Committee for Central Public Sector Enterprises.

K.R.S. Sastry is a postgraduate in Business Administration, a Certified Cost Analyst from the Institute of Cost Analysis Virginia (USA), a Fellow Member of the Institute of Cost and Works Accountants of India (ICWAI), an Associate Member of the Institute of Company Secretaries of India (ICSI), and an Affiliated Member of Indian Institution of Industrial Engineering (IIIE). He worked in four renowned central public sector enterprises for over 39 years. He was on the Boards of various companies and a signatory to 25 Annual Reports. He is presently working as an Advisor & Senior Faculty member in the Institute of Public Enterprise, Hyderabad. He was actively associated with the professional activities of the ICWAI. He served as President and Advisor to the South Asian Federation of Accounts, an apex body of SAARC (comprising five institutes of chartered accountants and three institutes of cost and management accountants) from South Asia.

K.S.N. Raju, graduate in Electrical Engineering from Government College of Engineering, Anantapur, is a postgraduate in Power Systems Engineering from Andhra University College of Engineering, Visakhapatnam. He worked as System Studies Engineer in APSEB and later joined Corporate R&D Division of Bharat Heavy Electricals Ltd., Hyderabad (1974); retired as General Manager in August 2007 on superannuation. He developed a number of special electrical machines, micro-machines and superconducting machines for DST, Defence and power sector applications. His areas of specialisation include mathematical modelling of electrical machines, development of superconducting machines, power electronic and renewable energy systems. He has published a number of technical papers in the area of electrical machines and superconducting machines. He also assisted Justice M.J. Rao's Second Pay Revision Committee for Central Public Sector Enterprises.

Compensation in Public Enterprises, Private Enterprises and MNCs in India

R.K. Mishra, G. Srihari Rao,
K.R.S. Sastry and K.S.N. Raju

ACADEMIC FOUNDATION
NEW DELHI

www.academicfoundation.com

First published in 2011
by

ACADEMIC FOUNDATION
4772-73 / 23 Bharat Ram Road, (23 Ansari Road),
Darya Ganj, New Delhi - 110 002 (India).
Phones : 23245001 / 02 / 03 / 04.
Fax : +91-11-23245005.
E-mail : books@academicfoundation.com
www.academicfoundation.com

in association with

Institute of Public Enterprise, Hyderabad.

Cataloging in Publication Data--DK
Courtesy: D.K. Agencies (P) Ltd. <docinfo@dkagencies.com>

Compensation in public enterprises, private enterprises and MNCs in India / R.K. Mishra ... [et al.].
p. cm.
ISBN 13: 9788171888382
ISBN 10: 8171888380

1. Compensation management--India. 2. Government business enterprises--India. 3. Corporations, Government--India. 4. Private companies--India. 5. Public-private sector cooperation--India. 6. International business enterprises--India. I. Mishra, R. K., 1948-

DDC 658.3220954 22

Typeset by Italics India, New Delhi.

Printed and bound in India.

Contents

List of Tables, Figures and Annexures

Figures

Annexures

Preface

This volume presents a study on 'Compensation in Public Enterprises, Private Enterprises and MNCs in India'. It throws light on the structure, similarities and dissimilarities, and the trends in compensation management as related to these enterprises. The volume brings out the recent innovations in compensation management and the initiatives in this realm concerning the enterprises under reference. It examines the feasibility of delinking compensation in public enterprises from the government and building up a connect with the private enterprises. In the long run, the feasibility of bringing the compensation in public enterprises in line with their counterparts in the multinational sector has also been examined by the study. The study has discussed in detail the methodology of introducing the performance related pay in public enterprises and employee stock option plan. Finally, it presents a new paradigm for the compensation management in public enterprises.

The study is based on the results obtained through a questionnaire served to the enterprises in the various sectors and information obtained through formal and informal interaction with experts in the area of compensation management. The study has also benefited from the information accessed from *www.paycheck.in* and collected by the various expert agencies in this area.

We express our gratitude to Ms J Kiranmai, Dr Pawan Kumar A and Mr A Sridhar Raj who have helped us in completing the work and shaping the study.

Overview

Background

The Institute of Public Enterprise (IPE), Hyderabad was assigned the task of taking up a study on the existing compensation of the executives and non-unionised supervisors of the central public sector enterprises (CPSE) along with the comparative pay levels of: (a) officers of the Government of India, (b) executives in the private sector and multinational corporations in India, and (c) public enterprises and private sector abroad. This study is to assist the Second Pay Revision Committee for CPSE executives headed by Hon'ble Justice M.J. Rao.

Methodology

In order to collect information for the study, IPE circulated a questionnaire to all CPSEs requesting for relevant information regarding the executive remuneration in CPSEs. The information furnished in response to the questionnaire sent out by Department of Public Enterprise (DPE) to all the CPSEs during February 2007 was also used to the extent possible. Information pertaining to the Central government salaries has been collected from the government officers of some departments and from official publications/websites. Compensation related information is treated as very confidential by the private sector companies and MNCs. Hence, IPE had to depend on multiple sources to collect data in this regard. The sources included salary studies carried out by HR and recruitment consultants, annual reports, web-based information, one-to-one contacts with company directors, heads of HR function in private companies, present and former employees of private sector companies and MNCs and HRD functionaries of CPSEs.

Coverage

Responses to the IPE questionnaire were received from 84 CPSEs and information could be logically compiled for another 42 companies based on the data furnished in response to DPE questionnaire and the known status of implementation of the earlier wage revisions. The data covers 2,09,007 executives and 50,587 non-unionised supervisors (NUS) which implies a coverage of 84 per cent of the total of 3,07,794 executives and NUS as on March 31, 2006.

With respect to the officers of the Central government, compensation details have been covered for officers in eight grades, i.e., section officer to secretary to Government of India.

The present work has drawn inputs from the salary studies carried out by Omam Consultants (102 companies spanning 14 sectors), Gallup Team (55 companies spanning 9 sectors) and *paycheck.in* (54 companies spanning 3 sectors). The coverage also includes data sourced from annual reports regarding compensation details of board level executives of about 190 private sector companies and multinational corporations (MNCs). Similarly, the data obtained by IPE during personal interaction with various senior executives relating to compensation in various industries in private sector has been suitably included in this study. The study has extensively relied upon the data on the CPSEs included in "Public Enterprises Survey", brought out by the DPE. The Institute had to essentially depend on web-based data for the wage information concerning other nations. The compensation details with regard to Canada, Singapore, Australia, USA and France form a part of the study.

Classification and Distribution of Employees

Based on performance, the CPSEs can be classified into: (a) navratna, (b) miniratna, (c) profit-making CPSEs, (d) marginally profit/loss-making CPSEs, and (e) sick CPSEs. It can broadly be stated that out of 3,07,794 executives and NUS in all the CPSEs 2,28,613 (74%) are working in 66 navratna/miniratna CPSEs. Another 36,555 are working in the 46 profit-making CPSEs. Thus, 86 per cent of the executives and NUS are working in financially healthy CPSEs. Only 18,006 (6%) are working in financially weak CPSEs (54). The rest of the executives and NUS constituting around

8 per cent are employed in other CPSEs, a majority (55) of which are making marginal profits, as depicted in Figure 1.

Figure 1

Distribution of Executives and NUS in CPSEs (Performance-based Classification)

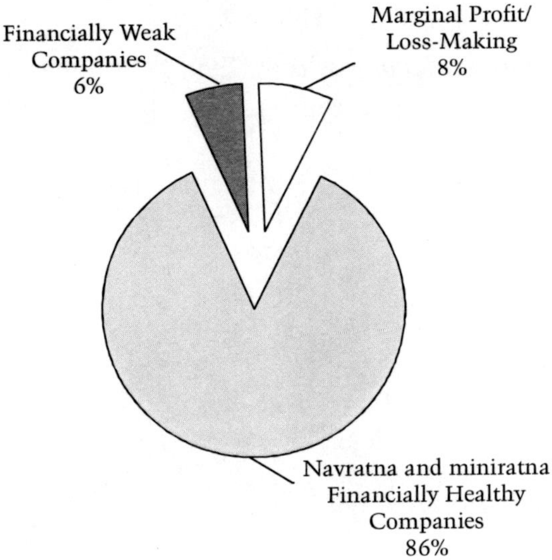

Source: Filled-in Questionnaire.

Based on the size and importance, CPSEs are categorised into four schedules namely, A, B, C, D. The number of executives and NUS working in Schedule 'A' companies is 2,39,313 which accounts for 77 per cent of the total of such employees. While 56,510 executives and NUS are working in Schedule 'B', 5923 are working in Schedule 'C' and 533 in Schedule 'D' CPSEs as depicted in Figure 2.

All-Round Improvement in the Performance of CPSEs

It is reported that in the year 2005-06, the CPSEs have contributed one-third (Rs. 1,05,853 crore) of the revenues to the Government of India, 11 per cent to the country's GDP and 27 per cent of the industrial production. The dividend paid (Rs. 22,886 crore) on a paid-up capital of Rs. 1,20,490 crore implies a 19 per cent yield to the GoI. More than one-fifth (Rs. 7,43,200 crore) of the market capitalisation of Rs. 36,00,000 crore relating to 7412 entities in the country is credited to just 44 listed CPSEs. Oil and Natural Gas Corporation (ONGC), National Thermal Power Corporation (NTPC) and Bharat Heavy Electricals Limited (BHEL) figure in the top 10 market capitalisation companies, and between them account for Rs. 4,00,000 crore market valuation forming 30 per cent of the market capitalisation of the top 10 companies as on March 31, 2007.

Figure 2

Distribution of Executives and NUS in CPSEs (Schedule A, B, C, D)

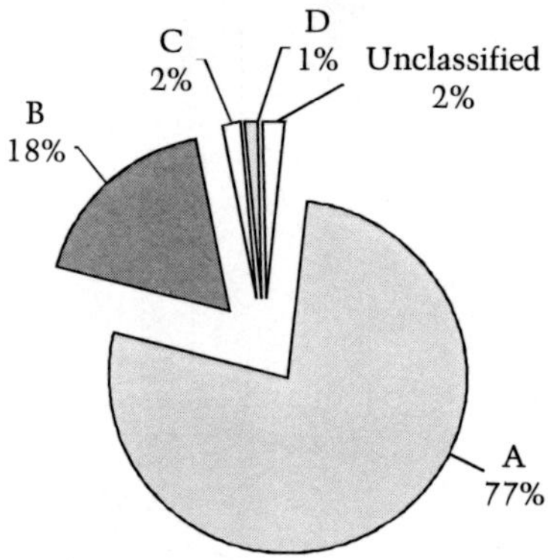

Source: Filled-in Questionnaire.

In six sectors (*viz.*, petroleum, steel, coal, power, financial services and industrial development & technical consultancy services), all the 58 CPSEs are making profits. The number of profit-making CPSEs has gone up to 157 (out of 215 operational) in 2005-06 from 138 out of 227 in the previous year. This number is expected to go up to 170 by the end of 2006-2007. The number of loss-making CPSEs has come down to 58 in 2005-06 from 79 in the previous year and by end 2006-07, the number is expected to further decline to 45 or so. Most of these loss-making CPSEs were sick companies which were functioning in the private sector and had been taken over by the GoI on humanitarian considerations.

The aggregate losses of loss-making companies have come down to Rs. 5952 crore in 2005-06 from Rs. 9356 crore in 2004-05. The turnover (Rs. 8,32,584 crore) and net profits (Rs. 70,288 crore) of CPSEs in 2005-06 signify improvements of 11.86 per cent and 8.20 per cent respectively over the previous year. The performance figures of 2006-07 are expected to be even better. This all-round improvement in the financial performance of CPSEs even under stiff competitive conditions is widely acknowledged. It is noteworthy that the shares of Gas Authority of India Limited (GAIL) and Steel Authority of India Limited (SAIL) are listed in the London Stock Exchange and those of Mahanagar Telephone Nigam Limited (MTNL) are listed in the New York Stock Exchange.

Contribution by the CPSEs to the Core Areas of Economy

The critical role being played by the CPSEs in the core areas of economy is illustrated by the contributions being made by these organisations in the fields like oil & gas, coal, steel, power generation, power generation equipment and communications. CPSEs account for 85.5 per cent production of crude oil, 85.52 per cent production of coal, 41 per cent of steel and 65 per cent of power generation equipment. The power equipment produced by BHEL supports 70 per cent of the electrical generation in the country and the company is supplying this equipment against international competitive bids (ICBs).

The impressive financial performance of CPSEs and the critical contributions being made in the vital sectors of the nation's economy have to be credited to the dedication, commitment and competence of the employees of these enterprises. These efforts have to be reckoned against the backdrop of the vast differences in the compensation levels of the executives of CPSEs and their counterparts in the private sector companies and MNCs.

Talent Erosion in CPSEs

For a long time, the institution of the Indian public sector has been the best reservoir of engineering and managerial talent for the private sector companies and MNCs to 'poach' at the junior management levels. For many bright engineering graduates, CPSEs have been excellent training schools and were the coveted destinations in the sixties and early seventies of the last century. They are no longer so, for the past 10 years or more because of the better remunerations and career growth opportunities available in the private sector and MNC enterprises. This is one of the reasons for apparent low attrition rates at the junior levels of CPSEs as the talent in demand is going elsewhere.

In the recent past, very senior level executives are leaving CPSEs to join private and MNC organisations for reasons of far superior compensation packages and perks. This is a matter of serious concern. Decades of effort in nurturing of talent will go waste unless effective steps are taken to retain talent at various key levels of engineering and managerial cadres.

A case in point is the near impossibility of nurturing high calibre software talent in CPSEs. It is ironical that some of the IT companies which developed the maximum domestic software relevant to the country's needs are unable to attract the needed talent even for the most critical and strategic applications needed by the country today because of the inability to match the paying capacity of private companies and MNCs working in the field of IT—who almost totally work for applications needed by foreign countries. The poaching of talent is not limited to Indian private sector companies and MNCs operating in the country alone. India has become an important hub for talent hunting for worldwide placements. The non-availability of high calibre talent to the CPSEs will be very keenly felt and experienced in the event of technology denials.

The attraction of India, for talent, is owing to the availability of human resources needed for intellectually intensive jobs. Several MNCs are setting up their R&D centres in India and aggressively mopping up the scarce talent.

Salaries in CPSEs

Out of the 16.45 lakh employees of CPSEs, the executive and NUS cadres account for around 3.08 lakh. Of the total salary bill of about Rs. 45,625 crore, the executive salary bill is estimated to be in the region of Rs. 13,000 crore employees' cost to turnover ratios range from 1-2 per cent in the petroleum group at one extreme and 40-50 per cent in the coal group at the other extreme. For CPSEs as a whole, the wages to turnover ratio is 5.48 per cent as on March 31, 2006 (turnover: Rs. 8,32,584 crore and wage bill: Rs. 45,625 crore).

Inter- and Intra-Group Comparison within CPSEs

Even though there are 157 profit-making CPSEs as on March 31, 2006, the maximum profitability is occurring in CPSEs belonging to petroleum, power, power generation equipment (BHEL), telecommunications, steel, coal, and minerals & metals in a large measure. These healthy CPSEs are certainly doing their best to enhance the well-being of their executives, both during service and in the retirement phase—especially in the area of health care. The intra- and inter-group differences in CPSEs essentially relate to the extent of implementation of the wage revisions recommended from time to time, better starts at the entry level, creation of intermediate scales, significant improvements in performance-related payments and making available handsome allowances and perks to the executives depending on the financial strength of the companies. In addition to improving the compensation packages of the executive cadres, the financially strong CPSEs like Hindustan Aeronautics Limited (HAL), Bharat Electronics Limited (BEL) and a few other enterprises have substantially increased the entry level emoluments by releasing a large number of additional increments to attract talent.

Though the DPE guidelines based on Hon'ble Justice Mohan Committee recommendations allowed payment of 5 per cent of the distributable profits, as performance related compensation, only a limited number of CPSEs implemented this recommendation. In some cases, the 5 per cent is shared by all employees while in some others by the executives only.

Comparative compensation details (inter-group) of select groups and select grades are indicated in Table 1 to outline the differentials across the groups.

As mentioned earlier, the employee cost to turnover in the petroleum group is the lowest hovering around 1 to 2 per cent even though they are paying handsome performance incentives. Bharat Petroleum Corporation Ltd. (BPCL) is paying 37 per cent of basic pay plus DA as performance incentive. These average annual emoluments are the highest among all the groups. The CPSEs in the power group are also giving very handsome compensation packages and probably the highest performance linked payments in 2006-07.

Comparative compensation details within select groups (intra-group) for select grades are indicated in Table 2 to outline the differentials across the groups.

Table 1

Group-wise Averages of Annual Emoluments in CPSEs

(Rs. in lakhs)

Group	*E1 (8600-14600)*	*E5 (16000-20800)*	*E8 (20500-26500)*	*CEO-Sch A (27750-31500)*
Coal and Lignite	2.68	4.73	6.74	10.05
Minerals and Metals	2.91	5.00	6.27	10.36
Steel	3.23	5.15	6.36	11.17
Petroleum	4.22	6.07	8.00	12.39
Power	3.52	5.66	7.29	11.45
Heavy Eng. (BHEL only)	3.26	4.97	6.53	11.71
Fertilisers and Chemicals	2.38	4.08	5.31	8.67
Agro-based Industries	2.27	3.71	-	
Textiles	2.69	4.56	5.60	9.58
Consumer Goods	2.73	4.87	6.12	10.27
Medium and Light Engineering	2.82	5.12	6.49	9.82
Transport Equipment	3.01	5.27	7.12	10.57
Trading and Marketing	2.65	4.61	5.82	9.51
Transportation Services	3.12	5.38	6.74	10.84
Contracts and Construction	2.51	4.71	5.85	10.03
Industrial Dev. and Tech. Consultancy Services	2.90	4.92	6.17	10.46
Financial Services	3.04	5.23	6.33	10.81
Telecommunication and Information (BSNL only)	3.10	4.87	7.45	10.62

Note: The entry level scales in respect to certain CPSEs like NTPC, petroleum enterprises, BHEL, BSNL, etc., are much higher as compared to the E1 scale indicated in the Table.
Source: Filled-in Questionnaire.

Table 2

Intra-CPSE Comparison of Compensation Packages

(Rs. in lakhs)

Group	*E1*		*E5*		*E8*	
	Highest	*Lowest*	*Highest*	*Lowest*	*Highest*	*Lowest*
Petroleum	4.72	3.15	6.34	5.83	9.19	7.28
Power	4.57	2.85	6.18	5.03	8.75	6.25
Transport Equipment	4.14	1.84	6.30	2.82	9.10	3.05
Transportation Services	4.00	2.50	6.33	4.61	8.44	5.71
Industrial Dev.	3.97	2.47	5.24	4.43	6.99	5.53
Steel	3.61	2.75	5.51	4.77	6.91	5.52
Financial Services	3.58	2.59	5.30	4.63	6.72	5.74
Minerals and Metals	3.48	1.29	5.91	1.86	7.10	2.66
Medium and Light	3.47	1.29	5.37	1.86	7.63	2.66
Trading and Marketing	3.27	1.79	5.74	2.74	7.71	2.95
Heavy Engineering	3.26	1.79	4.97	2.74	6.53	2.95
Coal and Lignite	3.25	2.57	4.94	4.66	6.90	6.55
Fertilisers	3.14	1.29	5.35	1.86	7.41	2.66
Telecommunication and Information	3.10	2.57	4.87	4.65	7.45	5.91

Source: Filled-in Questionnaire.

Intra-group variations in the emoluments are mainly on account of dissimilar scales of pays in operation. With regard to NUS, similar information could not be compiled because of data limitations.

Comparison between Central Government and CPSEs

Traditionally, parity was attempted to be maintained between the executives of CPSEs and the officers of the Central government. This parity appears to be fairly in position even now when the salaries of Central government officers are compared with the salaries of the CPSEs of the median kind characterised by lack of significant variable pays and valued perks.

The salaries of the Central government were revised in 1996 and that of the CPSEs in 1997. In respect of one-to-one remuneration parity between government officers and CPSE executives, the main difference is that there is no performance related pay to the government officers, which is applicable to CPSEs.

Another important difference is that when a wage revision takes place, it is uniformly implemented for the Central government employees whereas the implementation in CPSEs is determined by the affordability of the CPSEs concerned. As per information gathered from DPE, as on 1-1-2007, the pay scales of 14 CPSEs are still based on 1987 pay revision and those of 28 CPSE at 1992 level. Perhaps, this might be one of the reasons for the reluctance of the executives of CPSEs following the central pay scales and central dearness allowance (CDA) pattern, to switch over to industrial dearness allowance (IDA) pay scales.

In addition, the pension (for those who have joined service prior to 2004) and post-retiral medical benefits available to the Central government employees, who live in metros, state capitals and important cities are not available to a majority of the retired CPSE executives and employees.

Table 3 illustrates the parity and differences between the salary levels of Central government officers, a very healthy PSE belonging to the oil sector, a profit-making PSE and a loss-incurring PSE (which have implemented the 1997 wage revision recommendations).

Table 3

Comparison between Government Officers with the Executives of CPSEs

Central Government		*CPSEs—Annual Compensation*			
Scale and Designation	*Annual Compensation*	*Grade*	*BPCL*	*NMDC*	*ITI*
6500-200-10500 (S 12) Section Officer	2.08	E0	-	-	2.00
8000-275-13500 (S 15) Assistant Director	2.56	E1	4.72	3.16	2.55
10000-325-15200 (S 19) Under Secretary	3.13	E2	5.35	3.83	3.12
12000-375-16500 (S 21) Dy. Secretary	3.82	E3	6.34	4.59	3.89
		E4	7.03	5.39	4.30
14300-400-18300 (S 24) Director	4.49	E5	7.43	5.78	4.70
		E6	7.69	6.06	5.10
		E7	7.96	6.23	5.37
		E8	9.19	6.42	5.90
18400-500-22400 (S 29) Jt. Secretary	5.81	E9	10.31	6.73	6.78
22400-525-24500 (S 30) Additional Secretary	7.78	Sch. B	12.33	10.24	8.60
26000 Fixed (S 33) Secretary	9.04	Sch. A	13.55	11.30	9.67

Note: BPCL: Bharat Petroleum Corporation Ltd.; NMDC: National Mineral Development Corporation; ITI: Indian Telecom Industry Ltd.

Source: Filled-in Questionnaire.

Compensation in Private Sector Companies

While uniformity has been by and large the guiding principle in respect of the salary fixations in CPSEs, within and across the sectors, differentiation is the driving force with regard to the compensation levels of the private sector companies. The differentiation arises from the nature of business, profitability of business, demand and supply position of talent, the industry standards, the functions carried out by the executive and the performance of the executives at both individual and collective levels. The contribution of the executive to the wealth generation of the enterprise has a direct correlation to the compensation package in private sector companies.

While at the junior levels, the individual performance (*vis-à-vis* the agreed and assigned targets) is given higher weightage, at more and more senior levels, the section level, division level and company level performances play a key role in the fixation of compensation packages. The 'fixed' or 'assured pay' together with allowances and reimbursements, in percentage terms, is higher at the junior levels and the variable (performance based) pay, valued perks and retiral benefits are more pronounced at the senior levels. Needless to say, the productivity, responsibility and accountability standards will be in proportion to the compensation packages and they go up steeply as one goes up in the corporate ladder. Average CTC levels are reported to be ranging from Rs. 3.5-4 lakh at the junior management levels, Rs. 11 lakh at the middle management levels and Rs. 25-30 lakh at the senior management (below board) levels.

At the board level, even for the professional managers (distinct from the promoters) the commission and performance based pay set them apart by orders of magnitude, to the rest of the executive cadres. The ratio of the compensation between the junior most executive to the CEO of the company can range from 1:20 to 1:50 or more, even in the case of median class of Indian private companies.

Compensation Levels in MNCs

While the information regarding compensation packages of MNCs is included in the available survey reports, fairly reliable sources point out that the differential pay packages between a conservative MNC company and a median private sector company, at the entry level, can be in the ratio 1.3:1. The difference at the senior levels can vary from 1.5:1 and 2:1.

CPSEs *versus* Private Sector

The contrast in the compensation levels between CPSEs and private sector companies goes up asymptotically as the employees become more and more senior in the private sector. While the salaries are almost comparable with respect to healthy CPSEs at the entry level, the divergence becomes more and more pronounced as the executives go up the corporate ladder. At the middle level, the comparison between CPSEs and private sector employees will be in the ratio of 1:2, while at the senior level (say at GM and ED levels) the difference can be as much as 1:4 or 1:6. At the board level, the factorial difference (considering only professional managers and not promoters or owners), can be as much as 1:15 to 1:20—without considering other rewards like employee stock ownership plans (ESOPs).

Variable pay or performance related pay being paid by some CPSEs, comes to around 15 per cent of the total compensation. Since some of the

CPSEs are paying uniform amounts of incentives to all the executives, this percentage comes down in the case of middle and senior level executives. Conversely, this component is uniformly around 10-15 per cent in the junior and middle management cadres and much higher in the senior cadres in private sector companies. Needless to say, these higher percentages are applied on much higher base salaries compared to CPSEs.

While the average annual increases in salaries are being reported in the range of 14-15 per cent in the last one or two years (touching 30 per cent in some cases) in the private sector, the yearly hike in emoluments in CPSEs is around 8 per cent which is an in-built mechanism through increase in DA and annual increments. Such automatic year-on-year increases are inherent in the system of CPSEs compensation, which is applicable to all the enterprises irrespective of their financial status. The managements determine such annual increases in the case of private sector, which can even vary from one executive to the other, depending on their rating and performance.

Select compensation levels in different sectors below board level are indicated in Table 4.

Summary of Comparison of Compensation of the Executives of CPSEs, with Officers of the Government, Executives of Private Sector and MNCs in India

To ensure 'apple to apple' comparison, the averages of the highest payers in each group in CPSEs are considered. Since separate data in respect of MNCs is not available, these are assumed to 1.5 times private sector salaries. Based on these assumptions, the summary of comparison of compensation of the executives of CPSEs *versus* officers of the government, executives of private sector and MNCs in India is depicted in Figure 3.

Table 4

Sector Averages in CPSEs and Private Sector

(Rs. in lakhs)

Groups As per DPE	*No. of CPSEs*	*E1*	*E5*	*E8*	*Sectors BT Surveys*	*No. of Cos.*	*JMII*	*MMII*	*SMII*
Average of Coal, Minerals & Metals,					Core	9	3.50	7.49	19.30
Steel, Power, Petroleum Sectors "Core"	44	3.31	5.32	6.93	Chem. & Fertiliser Pharma.	15	4.06	11.71	31.09
Chemicals & Pharmaceuticals, Fertiliser	22	2.24	3.69	4.35	Engineering	9	2.95	6.95	17.39
Heavy & Light Engineering	35	3.26	4.97	6.53	Textiles	7	2.63	7.25	18.62
Textiles	15	2.69	4.56	5.60	FMCG	6	5.59	14.54	39.90
Consumer Goods	11	2.73	4.87	6.12	Consumer Durables	10	3.93	19.65	27.13
Trading & Marketing	13	2.65	4.61	5.82	Retail	5	2.96	11.02	26.76
Contract & Construction	11	2.51	4.71	5.85	Real Estate	8	3.13	8.32	21.66
Industrial Dev. & Tech. Consultancy	15	2.90	4.92	6.17	ITES & BPO	5	3.13	15.29	27.80
Telecommunications & IT	4	3.10	4.87	7.45	Telecom	5	4.52	13.02	28.00
Financial Services	9	3.04	5.23	6.33	IT	9	4.58	12.31	24.37
Transport Equip.	10	3.01	5.27	7.12	Banking	5	4.49	15.07	31.54
Transportation Services	11	3.12	5.38	6.74	Automotives	9	5.41	13.44	33.25
Average		2.88	4.85	6.28	Average		3.93	11.11	26.48

Source: Filled-in Questionnaire.

Figure 3

Summary Comparison of Compensation

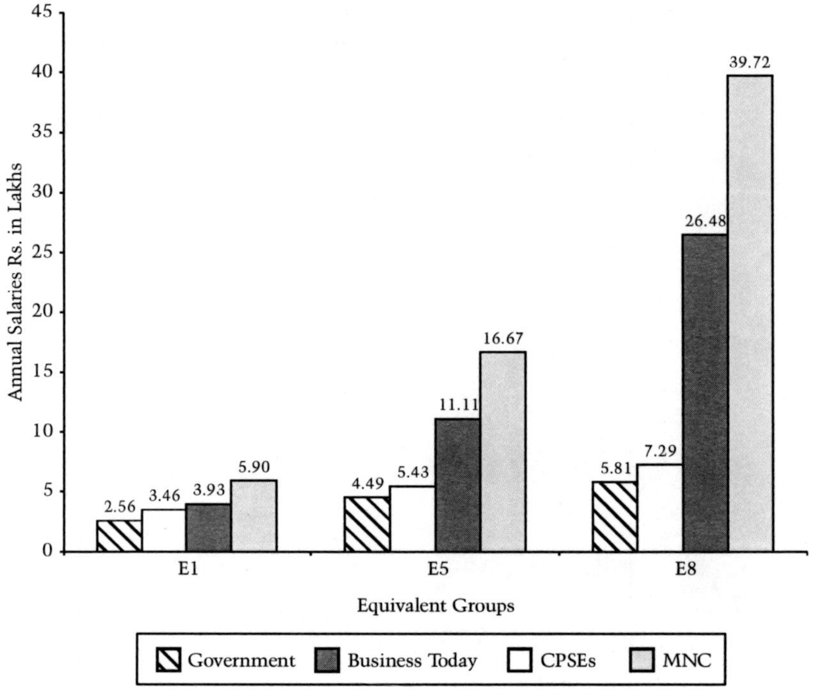

Source: Filled-in Questionnaire.

Stifled Career Prospects in CPSEs

Though the entry level salaries are by and large comparable in the CPSEs/ private companies and MNCs, the reluctance of bright talent to get into CPSEs is because of the known limitations in the increase in remuneration through periodic pay revisions, and the long gestation times in the growth paths. The factorial difference between remuneration at entry level and board level in the context of a CPSE may range from 1:3 to 1:4. In any case, everybody cannot hope to reach the board level status and even if one aspires to reach the topmost position below the board level, say to the level of GM or ED, it takes a person around 30 years to reach that position in a CPSE. The factorial difference in compensation between the two levels will be at best 1:2.5 to 1:3. Bright youngsters of today will not be willing to choose this option when the alternatives are so lucrative and promising.

Figure 4 highlights the contrast between the private sector enterprises and CPSEs in the growth profile of the executives.

Figure 4

Growth Comparisons between CPSEs and Private Sector

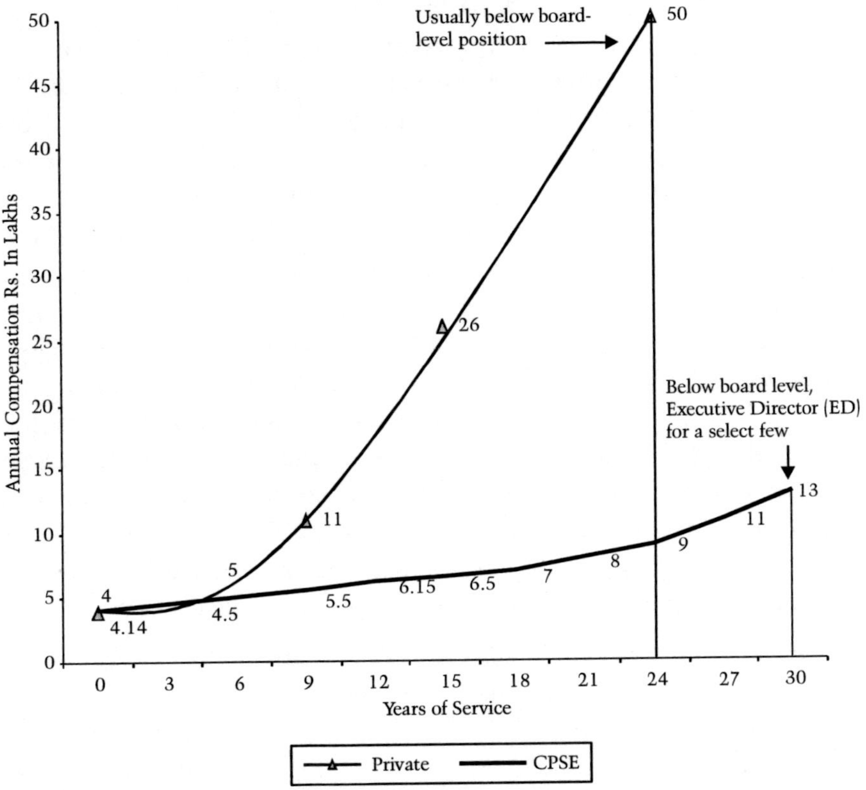

Source: Filled-in Questionnaire.

Accountability and Reward Systems in Private Sector Companies and MNCs *vis-à-vis* CPSEs

In respect of private sector companies and MNCs, the degree of accountability and responsibility, at the individual level *vis-à-vis* the goals and targets to be reached, is far more pronounced and directly linked to their reward schemes. As the individuals ascend the corporate ladder, especially to the senior management and board levels, achievement of the corporate goals related to the profitability determines the degree of their monetary benefits either in the form of variable and performance linked compensation and/or commissions. This is in sharp contrast to the uniformity principle followed in the CPSEs and general reluctance/difficulty in differentiating between 'performers' and 'non-performers' in the CPSE environment.

While it is true that the average year-on-year increase in compensations is reported to be in the range of 14-15 per cent in the executive cadres of private sector companies, it is also to be noted that these rises are directly linked to the performance standards of the personnel. Notwithstanding the differences in the nomenclature used, all executives are reported to be ranked on a scale of 1-5 i.e., 'excellent', 'very good', 'good', 'average' and 'poor'. Executives falling into the 'average' and 'poor' grades are said to receive no increase in salaries. Executives categorised as 'good' and 'very good' are reported to receive increases ranging from 8-12 per cent and 15-18 per cent respectively. Executives ranked as 'excellent' are said to receive rises as much as 20-25 per cent. It is also gathered that these rankings follow a deterministic profile like the 'excellent' category not crossing more than 5 per cent while a minimum of 5 per cent is requested to be ranked 'poor'. The category of 'good' employees is pegged at around 60 per cent whereas the 'average' and 'very good' categories of employees constitute 15 per cent each.

Figure 5 illustrates the performance and reward profits of executives in private sector companies—as generally practiced.

Affordability and Sustainability

Not withstanding the sharp differentials between private sector companies/ MNCs and CPSEs in the salary levels, the survival and growth of the CPSE will have to be the first priority of the CPSE and the government in deciding on the proposed pay revision. In the backdrop of increased and intense competition in almost every activity of the CPSEs from private sectors and MNC companies, per unit contribution or margins will sharply come down in the years to come. To improve the profitability levels or even to protect the existing levels of profits, the volume increases called for will be much higher. On the other side, the projected GDP growth rates in excess of 9 per cent offer tremendous growth opportunities and there will

Figure 5

Reward Systems in Private Sector

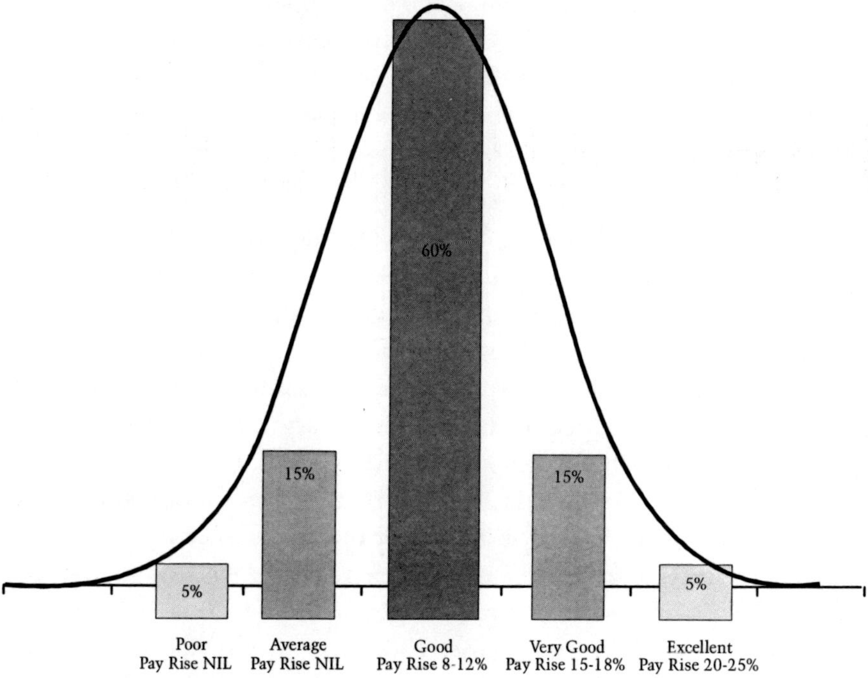

Source: Filled-in Questionnaire.

be a great demand for talent. CPSEs certainly have great opportunities ahead and have to gear up to exploit them. These issues will be sector-specific and CPSE-specific and linked greatly to the future business prospects as perceived by the CPSE concerned. Careful consideration is warranted in this regard and the CPSEs and the administrative ministry/department will be best improved to be able to come to the right conclusion.

Situation Abroad

From the limited studies that could be conducted in the time frame available, the nature of work carried out by government-run business houses abroad is fairly limited in scope and content compared to the breadth and depth of Indian CPSEs. The government business houses, in a country like Canada, called crown corporations at the federal level, are engaged in rail transport, postal services, broadcasting, air transport security, mint operations, land acquisition operations, mortgage and housing, currency trading, lottery trading, banking, and generation of nuclear power. At the provincial level, the business houses handle activities related to lotteries, gaming businesses and alcohol sales. At the local level, the activities handled include utilities like bus transport and electricity distribution.

The compensation packages are decided on a yearly basis by designated committees. The studies carried out by these committees in the labour (job) market covering various functions and various grades enable them to make recommendations on the compensation structures and packages of the executives and Deputy ministers in the government and the CEOs of the crown corporations. The salary levels of various grades (Grade 1 to Grade 10) are also systematically tracked, by the study teams and median values fixed. It is reported that 50 percentile compensation packages of the previous year in respect of the private sector companies are adopted to fix the current year's compensation levels of CEOs. This practice has commenced in the year 2005. Prior to this, 25 percentile figures were adopted for the purpose. The risk or performance related pay is said to range from 10-25 per cent of the salary at the CEO level.

The observation is that at levels—either in government or in government-run business houses—the linkage of compensation is with the labour (or job) market.

The private sector companies, on their part, will be monitoring the likely trends of the job markets for the coming years. Similar practices are adopted in a country like Singapore also. It is reported that in Singapore, the ratio of the salaries of the lowest employee to the chief executive is 1:20 and between the lowest executive and the chief executive is 1:6. At the chief executive level, the profit linked commissions far outweigh the annual salaries in a country like USA. The year-on-year increases in advanced countries are far less compared to India at the aggregate level but they are very judiciously distributed to the contributing and deserving executives.

The annual raises in compensation in most of the advanced countries range from 3-4 per cent. It is reported that considerable differentiation is practiced when the salary budgets become more and more flat, linking the rewards with individual performance.

In all the countries studied, there is a central agency functioning like a holding company to monitor and guide the functioning of the government-owned business enterprises. The remuneration levels of these business houses are continuously mapped to those of comparable private sector companies in the country irrespective of the fact whether the implementation of parity is on 1:1 basis or otherwise. These decisions are highly decentralised and board-driven, and are made based on demand-supply situations. The skills and talent are the major guiding factors and not the remuneration, in the policies of the business organisation.

The range and differentiation of compensation levels are dictated by industry type and size, location, functions to be handled and vary from country to country.

The CEO salaries are without doubt the highest in USA in large corporations even though the averages across large sample sizes are comparable to other advanced countries. Compensation levels appear to be almost equal between USA and Canada for comparable positions. The CEO/COO/CFO/President positions indicate considerable variation depending on the sample under question. The salaries in Singapore generally are 66 per cent of the levels in USA in terms of US dollars.

The variable pay, bonuses, commissions and stock options form a major part of CEO salaries in USA. There are orders of magnitude differences between the CEOs of fund managing companies and other leading listed companies in USA.

General Feedback

The feedback obtained during the one-to-one interactions IPE had with several senior executives of CPSEs can be summarised as under:

- Decisions related to employee compensation should be board-driven and shall be linked to market conditions, and the affordability and sustainability of the pay hikes as determined by the profitability of the CPSE.

- The elements of the executive compensation can be broadly divided into four parts:
  - The basic salary and allowances which can be fitted into some framework of standardisation and structure, linked again to the paying capacity of the CPSE.
  - Allowances, suitably formulated to make the compensation packages industry-specific for increased conformity to industry standards.
  - Variable and performance-based pay related to the organisation's profitability and individual performance.
  - Compensation suitably designed to offset/alleviate the occupational hazards and difficulties in working conditions.

Based on the responses received to the DPE's questionnaire, and various presentations by the officers' associations, the following observations could be made:

- Compensation is an important tool for attracting and retaining talent and the same has to conform to market trends for performing CPSEs.
- The pay scales of the CPSEs within the schedule should be uniform. Separate pay scales may be decided for performing/non-performing CPSEs.
- The number of pay scales may remain the same as at present, but the existing pay scales should be replaced by open-ended pay scales.
- More emphasis be laid on variable components of pay, which will help managements to liberally bring about variations in the pay structure to retain talent at individual or group level.
- The decisions regarding the perquisites should be left to the individual CPSEs to be decided depending upon their capacity to pay, their productivity and profit.
- The desirable ratio of pay between top level and entry level executives may be kept at 1: 6 or more; and the ratio of pay between the lowest workmen and CEO to be 1:10 or more.
- The desirable ratio of minimum and the maximum of any pay scale should be 1:2. However, it depends on the periodicity of pay

revision. Sufficient care is to be taken that employees do not stagnate at the maximum of the scale.

- A better pay package may not always be the sole factor for migration of talent. The general working environment, work culture, job satisfaction, area of operations, personnel policies are some of the intangible factors which people take into consideration before moving to another organisation.
- The individual CPSEs will have to ensure that the quality of working environment, avenues for growth and development, and empowerment to facilitate inculcating a sense of ownership amongst the executives, are taken care of, to retain the talent in the organisation.
- One of the measures to retain talent could be to revise the pay scales every five years since the economic/industry scenario changes drastically over a long period of 10 years, thus rendering the exercise of pay revision ineffective.

Limitations

Information related to remuneration and compensation is kept extremely confidential in the private sector companies and MNCs.

The reluctance to part with information is not limited to private companies and MNCs alone. Even the CPSEs have not been forthcoming in responding to the requests for information from IPE. A total of only 84 responses have been received by IPE despite several requests and reminders from IPE and DPE. Due to incomplete information available in some cases, some assumptions had to be made in the compilation of the CPSE-related data.

1 Central Public Sector Enterprises Today

During the last 50 years, the CPSEs nurtured highly competent human resources for managing their affairs. The total manpower reached a peak of 22.36 lakh by the end of March 1990. However, following the announcement of the New Industrial Policy in July 1991, the CPSEs attempted rightsizing their manpower and offered voluntary retirement schemes to their employees. These steps, coupled with privatisation of some major CPSEs like Bharat Aluminium Company Ltd. (BALCO), Hindustan Zinc Ltd. (HZL), Indian Petrochemicals Corporation Ltd. (IPCL), Videsh Sanchar Nigam Ltd. (VSNL), etc., and closure of a few sick/unviable CPSEs have caused reduction of manpower to 16.48 lakh by end of March 2006. This reduction in manpower is despite the addition of over 3 lakh employees of Bharat Sanchar Nigam Ltd. (BSNL), which was set up on corporatisation of the erstwhile Department of Telecom Services, and setting up of a number of new enterprises.

The government had made huge investments in the central public enterprises during the successive Five Year Plans. While it was just Rs. 29 crore in 5 CPSEs on the eve of the First Five Year Plan, the number of CPSEs increased to 47 with an investment of Rs. 948 crore by 31-3-1961 and further to 122 CPSEs with an investment of Rs. 6,237 crore by the end of 1973-74. The cumulative net investment as on 31st March 2006 stood at Rs. 3,93,057 crore (which includes a paid up capital of Rs. 1,20,490 crore) in 239 CPSEs. While the share of manufacturing CPSEs in investments was 51 per cent, the service sector and mining sector's share stood at 40 per cent and 7 per cent respectively. The balance relates to the CPSEs under construction.

The primary consideration for the investments in CPSEs was to accelerate the growth of core sectors of the economy and to enable the government to exert countervailing power on the operation of private monopolies and multinationals in selected and critical areas, and to provide a springboard for the economy to achieve a significant degree of self-sufficiency in the critical sectors. Intervention of government in distribution mechanisms was also consciously attempted to ensure availability of vital articles of mass consumption and to put a check on prices of important products and services.

With the opening up of the economy consequent to the policies of liberalisation, privatisation and globalisation and the upsurge in the overall industrial scenario, which is being more and more market-driven, the need for insulating the CPSEs from the controls and intervention of the government, was gradually felt in all quarters. In line with these developments, the government also initiated major steps for providing greater functional and financial autonomy to CPSEs through various schemes like recognition of financially healthy CPSEs as navratna and miniratna and entering into memoranda of understanding (MoU) with the CPSEs in regard to their performance criteria. Presently, 66 CPSEs are enjoying the status of navratnas and miniratnas. Further, 112 CPSEs have signed MoU with the Government for the year 2006-07.

Performance of CPSEs in 2005-06

The CPSEs have collectively turned in an excellent performance during the year 2005-06 as the statistics below would show:

- All-time high turnover of Rs. 8,32,584 crore during 2005-06 reflecting a growth rate of 11.86 per cent over the previous year's figure of Rs. 7,44,307 crore.
- 11.12 per cent share in the GDP, at market prices.
- Over 100 units have achieved more than 75 per cent of capacity utilisation. Some units of SAIL and Rashtriya Ispat Nigam Ltd. (RINL) in steel sector, Hindustan Petroleum Corporation Ltd. (HPCL) and Indian Oil Corporation Ltd. (IOC) in petroleum sector, Coal India Ltd. (CIL) in coal sector, Hindustan Paper Corporation Ltd. (HPC) in paper industry etc., are operating even at 100-120 per cent of rated capacities.
- 157 CPSEs (out of 215) recorded profits in the year 2005-06 as against 138 out of 227 in the year 2004-05.

- CPSEs made a net profit of Rs. 70,288 crore and paid a total dividend of Rs. 22,886 crore to the Central government representing around 20 per cent return on the paid-up capital. The reserves and surpluses of CPSEs as on 31st March 2006 stood at Rs. 3,59,077 crore.
- During the year 2005-06, the CPSEs contributed Rs. 1,05,853 crore to the exchequer by way of taxes and duties. This along with dividends represents one-third of the revenue to the Government of India.
- 102 CPSEs have signed MoUs in the year 2005-06. Out of them, 44 CPSEs achieved the rating of 'excellent', 36 'very good', 14 'good', 8 'fair' and none was 'poor'. Ten more new CPSEs have been added to this list of MoU signing enterprises, bringing the total to 112 during the year 2006-07.
- The performance of most of the CPSEs, which are listed in the stock market, has been commendable.
- The shares of GAIL and SAIL are listed in the London Stock Exchange and those of MTNL are listed in the New York Stock Exchange.
- It is expected that the performance of CPSEs in 2006-07 will still be better and about 170 CPSEs will be profitable as compared to 157 in 2005-06.

Significant Role of CPSEs in Core Sectors

Petroleum: The 12 CPSEs in petroleum sector are maintaining a near monopoly status in the exploration of crude oil (85.87%) and refining of oil (74.51%) in 2005-06. India is currently the fourth largest oil consumer in the Asia Pacific region after Japan, China and South Korea.

Coal: The 9 CPSEs in coal and lignite sector play a 'near monopoly' role with 85.52 per cent of the total production of coal in the country during the year 2005-06.

Power: The 7 CPSEs in the power sector with an installed capacity of 45,841 MW represent around 34 per cent of the total capacity at the national level. The power equipment manufacturer, BHEL, accounts for close to 70 per cent of the nation's power generation equipment—through business obtained against ICBs.

Steel: The production of steel from CPSEs amount to 41 per cent of the national production.

Minerals & Metals: The public sector is playing a dominant role in the mining of minerals and metals. The National Mineral Development Corporation (NMDC) and the Kudremukh Iron Ore Company Ltd. (KIOCL), have been dominating the iron ore sector. The National Aluminum Company Ltd. (NALCO) contributes about 35 per cent bauxite mining and aluminum production. Hindustan Copper Limited (HCL) dominates the copper ore mining sector.

Communications: CPSEs like BSNL and MTNL are still the major service providers in the communication sector in the country.

Others: CPSEs like HAL, BEL, electronic corporation of India Ltd. (ECIL), etc., have been contributing substantially in the strategic sectors. Bharat Earth Movers Ltd. (BEML) is playing an active role both in infrastructure and defence sectors.

Broad-based Contributions

Over a period of time, CPSEs have been operating in almost all the sectors of the economy. Today, 225 CPSEs including 12 CPSEs which are set up under Section 25 of the Companies Act, 1956 are operating in 21 sectors. Various CPSEs in the manufacturing sector provide enough evidence to prove the domestic capabilities not only in the manufacture and supply of capital equipment, but also in undertaking many mega projects in select sectors on commissioning basis. Indian CPSEs are offering solutions through quality products, systems and services in the fields of energy, industry, transportation, infrastructure, communications and other key areas.

The fact that the Indian CPSEs are standing their ground in the face of severe competition form the Indian private sector and multi-national corporations is noteworthy and commendable. In addition to the physical and financial contribution of the CPSEs to the nation, another significant contribution is in the nurturing of high calibre technical and managerial cadres—which today are also serving the private sector in a large measure in several industries.

Empowerment of CPSEs

The National Common Minimum Programme (NCMP) of the present government promised to give full managerial and commercial autonomy to successful profit-making companies operating in a competitive environment. The government has implemented this promise in August 2005 by delegating enhanced powers to navratna, miniratna and other profit-making CPSEs. There are 12 navratna, 54 miniratna (i) & (ii), and 55 other profit-making CPSEs (including Section 25 CPSEs). All these 121 CPSEs are presently enjoying enhanced autonomy. The navratna CPSEs can now incur capital expenditure on purchase of new items/replacement without any monetary ceiling, to enter into joint ventures or strategic alliances, to obtain technology and know-how, to effect organisational restructuring, to raise debt from the capital markets and borrowings from international markets, to establish financial joint ventures and wholly owned subsidiaries in India or abroad subject to the condition that the equity investment of the CPSE should be limited to Rs. 1000 crore or 15 per cent of the net worth, whichever is less, in one project and 30 per cent of the net worth in all such projects put together. The navratna CPSEs also have powers to take decisions on mergers and acquisitions. The miniratna CPSEs also enjoy many of these powers with lesser ceiling compared to navratnas. Other profit-making CPSEs have enhanced powers like incurring capital expenditure upto Rs. 150 crore limited to 50 per cent of the net worth.

Sick CPSEs and BRPSE

There are 54 CPSEs which are saddled with cash losses for the last 5 years and whose net worth is negative. Out of them, 17 were taken over from the private sector by government on socio-humanitarian considerations. The Board for Reconstruction of Public Sector Enterprises (BRPSE) set up in December 2004 has recommended proposals for extending a total assistance of Rs. 5,609 crore (consisting of Rs. 924.54 crore cash and Rs. 4,685 crore non-cash) which are since approved (as on 31/10/2006).

Current Trends

Increasing private participation encompassing financial, technological and managerial investments is rapidly taking place to meet the challenging growth targets in almost all the core sectors of the economy. Recognising the need for an inevitable change in the overall philosophy of the CPSEs, the Government of India had taken various initiatives in inviting private participation in core sectors also. The government policies as detailed in the public enterprise survey in respect of some of the sectors are summarised hereunder:

Steel: The steel industry has been removed from the list of industries reserved for public sector. Automatic approvals of foreign equity investment up to 100 per cent are now possible. Price and distribution controls have been removed from 1992 to make the industry efficient and competitive. Restrictions on external trade both in imports and exports have also been removed. In this process, a large capacity is being built. While 8 units with a total capacity of 5.45 MT have already been commissioned, 11 more projects have been cleared by various financial institutions and are in different stages of implementation.

Minerals & Metals: The National Mineral Policy emphasises the need for conservation and judicious exploitation of finite mineral resources through scientific methods of mining and economic utilisation. Simultaneously, it keeps in view the present and future needs of defence and development of India and strives to ensure indigenous availability of basic and strategic minerals to avoid disruption of core industrial production in times of international strife. According to the National Mineral Policy, induction of foreign technology and foreign participation in exploration and mining for high value and scarce minerals shall be pursued. Foreign equity investment in joint ventures in mining promoted by Indian companies would be encouraged. While foreign investment in equity would normally be limited to 50 per cent, this limitation would not apply to captive mines of any mineral processing industry. Enhanced equity holding can also be considered on a case-to-case basis. In respect of joint venture mining projects of minerals & metals in which India is deficient or does not have exportable surplus, a stipulated share of production would have to be made available to meet the needs of the domestic market before exports from such projects are allowed. In case of ores whose known reserves are not abundant, preference will be given to those who propose to take up their mining for captive use.

Coal: India's coal demand is expected to increase manifold within the next 5 to 10 years due to the completion of ongoing coal-based power projects and demand from metallurgical and other industries. The CPSEs are expected to increase their production by about 250 million tonnes by 2009-10, subject to their making an additional investment of US$ 8-10 billion. The unfulfilled demand will have to be met by imports in the short run and by new investments in the long run. With the advent of the economic reforms, government controls regarding pricing and distribution have been relaxed and a New Coal Policy permitting private sector participation in commercial coal mining has been announced.

Petroleum: In March 1997, the government approved the New Exploration Licensing Policy (NELP) which provides a level playing field in the upstream sector between private and public sector companies in all fiscal, financial and contractual matters. Under this policy:

- There will be no mandatory state participation through ONGC/Oil India Ltd. (OIL), nor they carry interest of the government.
- The two public sector upstream companies would compete for petroleum exploration licences, instead of the existing system of granting of licences on nomination basis.
- Government will try to attract private investment in the upstream sector.
- The public sector companies will also be able to avail the fiscal and contract benefits available to private companies.
- Freedom to the contractors for the marketing of crude oil and gas in the domestic market.

Situation Today

This changing scenario in the country is witnessing the emergence of private sector participation in every economic activity, many of which had been the sole preserve of the Indian public sector. Barring very few exceptions like nuclear power generation, uranium mining, etc., the private sector/MNC presence is visible everywhere. Annexure 1 indicates CPSEs mapped against comparable listed private sector companies, which are competing with the CPSEs. There will, naturally be many more unlisted private companies carrying out similar activities.

The skills, talent and experience required for manning the mushrooming private companies will be available as a readymade product in the CPSEs and they will be the main target for talent poaching. While the CPSEs have been the training schools for talent to be absorbed by the private sector companies after 2-3 years of grooming, the attrition is reportedly more manifest at senior levels now in various CPSEs belonging to the core and strategic sectors.

It is conceivable that if effective solutions for retention of talent are not devised and put in position, the infrastructure and investments made in the CPSEs may be deprived of some of the competent technical and managerial talent sooner than later. The dedication and commitment being displayed by the executives of CPSEs, notwithstanding the magnitude of differentials in the compensation package cannot be taken for granted in times to come. The proposed improvements have to ensure compensation packages, not only adequately attractive at the entry levels, but also compellingly so in respect of career growth opportunities in the later years both in terms of positions and monetary remuneration.

2 Classification of CPSEs

Introduction

The CPSEs are classified in different ways mainly based on their performance, size and industry group. The performance-wise classifications are navratna CPSEs, miniratna CPSEs, other profit-making CPSEs, loss-incurring CPSEs and sick CPSEs. The size and importance-wise classifications are in the nature of categorisation of CPSEs into four schedules namely Schedule A, B, C and D. This categorisation is done with reference to quantitative, qualitative and other critical factors. Based on their nature of activities, the CPSEs are broadly divided into four sectors namely mining, manufacturing, services and under construction. The first three sectors are further divided into groups like coal, steel, petroleum, trading and marketing, etc. These are discussed in the subsequent paragraphs.

Classification on Performance Basis

Navratna Enterprises: In July 1997, the government identified nine CPSEs that have comparative advantages and the potential to become global players in order to delegate higher financial and operational powers to them. These companies are named as navratnas. Subsequently, two more companies are added to this list in the same year but two of them are privatised, reducing the number of navratnas to 9 again. In the year 2007, 3 more CPSEs are included in the list of navratnas, thereby making the total number of navratna companies as 12. These are:

- Bharat Electronics Limited (BEL).
- Bharat Heavy Electricals Limited (BHEL).
- Bharat Petroleum Corporation Limited (BPCL).
- Gas authority of India Limited (GAIL).

- Hindustan Aeronautics Limited (HAL).
- Hindustan Petroleum Corporation Limited (HPCL).
- Indian Oil Corporation Limited (IOC).
- Mahanagar Telephone Nigam Limited (MTNL).
- National Thermal Power Corporation (NTPC).
- Oil and Natural Gas Corporation Limited (ONGC).
- Power Finance Corporation Limited (PFCL).
- Steel Authority of India Limited (SAIL).

The higher powers delegated to navratna CPSEs include the power to incur capital expenditure on purchase of new items/replacement, without any monetary ceiling, to enter into technology joint ventures or strategic alliances, to obtain by purchase or other arrangements technology and know-how, to effect organisational re-structuring, creation and winding up of below board level posts, powers for human resource management etc., to raise debt from the domestic capital markets and for borrowings from international markets, to establish financial joint ventures and wholly owned subsidiaries in India or abroad subject to the stipulation that the equity investment of the CPSE should be limited to Rs. 1000 crore or 15 per cent of the net worth, whichever is less, in one project (the investment in all such joint ventures/subsidiaries put together should not exceed 30 per cent of the net worth of the CPSEs), mergers and acquisitions subject to certain conditions and to approve business tours abroad of functional directors. It was also decided that the boards of the CPSEs should be professionalised by induction of eminent professionals in them. The number of such professional directors would be not less than 50 per cent of the actual strength of the board, as provided in the Securities and Exchange Board of India (SEBI) guidelines on the subject.

Miniratna-I Enterprises: Enterprises that have been making profits continuously in the preceding three years, with a pre-tax profit of Rs. 30 crore or more in any one of the three years, and fulfilling other conditions like positive net worth, non-dependence on budgetary support, not defaulting in repayments of loans and interests on loans, etc., are categorised as Miniratna-I. There are 41 Miniratna-I CPSEs. These miniratna are delegated with powers representing almost half of the financial limits specified for navratnas.

Miniratna-II Enterprises: CPSEs that have made profits during the preceding three years and have a positive net worth and fulfilling other conditions applicable to Miniratna-I are categorised as Miniratna-II. Presently there are 13 Miniratna-II companies. These CPSEs are delegated powers representing almost half of the financial limits specified for Miniratna-I.

Other Profit-Making CPSEs: There are 46 other CPSEs (excluding Section 25 companies) which are profit-making but do not qualify to become miniratna CPSEs. These companies are also delegated with enhanced powers in regard to capital expenditure and foreign tours. The powers to incur capital expenditure without government approval extends upto Rs. 150 crore or 50 per cent of the net worth, whichever is less.

Thus, the total number of navratna (12), Miniratna-I (41), Miniratna-II (13) and other profit-making CPSEs (46) is 112. These CPSEs are financially healthy and have positive net worth. This classification of the CPSEs primarily denotes the financial health of these organisations and the wider powers delegated to the board of directors. But no additional/special compensations are offered either to the employees in general or to the senior executives in particular. However, all these CPSEs being profit-making, the employees are entitled to various allowances and profit/performance related incentives which could add upto 50 per cent of basic pay, in addition to being eligible for sharing of 5 per cent of the distributable profits. The navratnas and miniratnas have been following the guidelines issued by DPE from time to time, in respect of pay and other allowances and are endeavouring to maximise the benefits to the employees through performance-related incentives, various allowances, differential increments, placement at higher scales at entry level, etc., to the extent the financial status of the enterprise permits.

Others and Sick CPSE: Of the remaining, 54 CPSEs are continuously loss-making having negative net worth which fall in the category of sick companies. The government had constituted the Board for Reconstruction of Public Sector Enterprises (BRPSE) in December 2004 to make recommendations on the revival or otherwise of such CPSEs.

Categorisation of CPSEs as Schedule A, B, C and D

The initial categorisation of CPSEs in the mid-60s was made on the basis of their importance to the economy and complexities of their operations. Over the years, the DPE had evolved norms for the purpose of categorisation/re-categorisation of CPSEs. Based on various quantitative factors (*viz.*, investment, capital employed, net sales, profit before tax, number of employees, number of units sold, value added per employee, etc.) and various qualitative factors (*viz.*, national importance, strategic importance, complexities, level of technology, etc.), and other factors like MoU ratings, navratna/miniratna classification, listing and share price, etc., CPSEs have been categorised into four schedules, *viz.*, 'A', 'B', 'C', and 'D'. As per the Annual Report of DPE 2005-06, there are 53 Schedule 'A', 88 Schedule 'B', 52 Schedule 'C' and 7 Schedule 'D' CPSEs. The remaining 37 CPSEs are yet to be categorised. It can be noted that some of the poorly performing and sick CPSEs continue to be in higher schedules while a few bigger and healthy CPSEs are in lower schedules. This probably highlights the need for a detailed review of the present system of categorisation of CPSEs. The Schedule A, B, C and D classification of CPSEs does not have a major and direct relevance for the present study, since such a classification applies only to the board level appointees, whose pay scales are linked to the schedule of the concerned enterprise. Nevertheless, the scale of pay of below board level posts in a CPSE cannot exceed the scale of pay of the board level posts in the company.

While most of the CPSEs among the Schedule 'A' category are profit-making, four CPSEs have been referred to BRPSE due to their continued losses. Heavy Engineering Corporation (HEC) and Hindustan Machine Tools Ltd. (HMT) are the two major enterprises among them. The other two are only holding companies *viz.*, Bharat Yantra Nigam Ltd. (BYN) and National Textile Corporation Limited (NTC).

Sectoral and Group-wise Classification

The DPE has categorised the CPSEs into four sectors, namely, mining, manufacturing, services and under construction. The mining sector has 19 CPSEs in two groups under it, namely, coal & lignite and minerals & metals. The manufacturing sector has 122 CPSEs in 11 groups, namely, steel, power, petroleum, fertilisers, chemicals & pharmaceuticals, heavy engineering, medium & light engineering, transport equipment, consumer goods, agro-based Industries and textiles. The services sector consists of 84 CPSEs in eight groups, namely, trading & marketing, transportation services, contract & construction services, industrial development & technical consultancy services, tourist services, financial services, telecommunications & information technology and Section 25 companies.

Distribution of Employees

As on 31st March 2006, the total number of executives working in various CPSEs was 2,39,433 and the number of NUS was 68,600, adding upto 3,08,033, representing 19 per cent of the total employees of CPSEs. Out of them, 1,93,707 executives and 45,606 NUS (total 2,39,313) are working in 52 Schedule 'A' companies. While 56,510 executives and NUS are working in Schedule 'B', 5,923 are working in Schedule 'C' and 533 in Schedule 'D' CPSEs. The details are given in Table 2.1.

Table 2.1

Distribution of Employees

Classification	*Exe.*	*NUS*	*Total*	*% to the Total of Employees*
A	193707	45606	239313	77.69
B	37680	18830	56510	18.35
C	3328	2595	5923	1.92
D	239	294	533	0.17
Unclassified	4479	1275	5754	1.87
Total	239433	68600	308033	100

Note: The table excludes 20 CPSEs under construction (942 executives and 15 NUS) and 12 Section 25 CPSEs (361 executives and 175 NUS).

Source: *Public Enterprise Survey, 2005-06.*

The above distribution is depicted in Figure 2.1.

Figure 2.1

Distribution of Employees

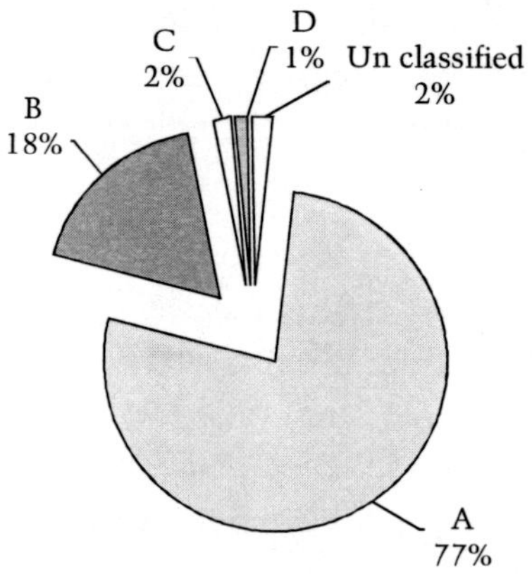

The number of employees working in 66 navratna and miniratna companies add up to 10,12,244 (representing 58 per cent of the total employees in CPSEs) and the executives and non-unionised supervisors employed in these enterprises total up to 2,28,613 representing 74 per cent of the total executives and NUS working in all the CPSEs. The number of executives and NUS working in the 46 'other profit-making' CPSEs is 36555 (excluding 9 Section 25 companies) which accounts for 12 per cent of the total executives and NUS in the CPSEs. The relevant details are provided in Annexure 2.

The number of employees working in the 54 sick companies as on March 2006 was 1,01,284, representing just around 6 per cent of the total number of employees in the CPSEs. The above include 11,904 executives and 6,102 NUS which incidentally also work out to around 6 per cent of the total number of executives and NUS working in all the CPSEs. The number of executives and NUS in the 1987 pay scale is 1017 and in the 1992 pay scales is 7842, representing around 3 per cent of the total number of the executives and NUS. The rest of the executives and NUS constituting around 8 per cent are employed in other CPSEs, a majority of which are making marginal profits.

It can be broadly stated that out of 307,794 executives and NUS in the CPSEs, 228,579 (74%) are working in 66 navratna/miniratna CPSEs. Another 36,555 are working in the 46 other profit-making PEs. Hence, 86 per cent of the executives and NUS are in financially healthy CPSEs. Only 18,006 (6%) are working in financially weak CPSEs (54). The details are given in Table 2.2.

Table 2.2

Distribution of Employees on the Basis of Classification of the CPSEs as Navratna, Miniratna, etc.

Category & No. of CPSEs	*Executives*	*NUS*	*Total*	*% of Total in all CPSEs*
Navratna (12)	77,293	26,881	104,174	34
Miniratna I (41)	101,942	19,197	121,139	39
Miniratna II (13)	2,974	292	3,266	1
Other profit-making (46)	30,049	6,506	36,555	12
Marginal profit/loss (47)	15,271	9,383	24,654	8
Sick (54)	11,904	6,102	18,006	6
Total (213)	239,433	68,361	307,794	100

Figure 2.2

Distribution of Employees

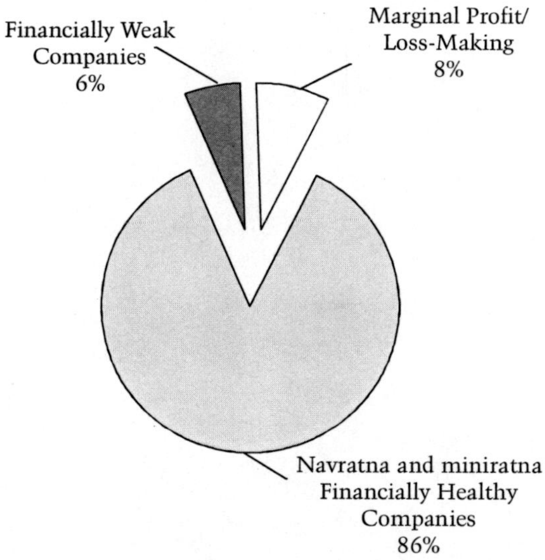

3 Methodology and Coverage

Methodology

The scope of the study covers compensation packages and their relativity in the domains of CPSEs, government, private sector companies in India, multinational corporations in India, private sector abroad and public sector abroad. Towards obtaining the relevant data and information for putting together the study report, covering all the domains, the following methodology has been adopted.

CPSEs: For obtaining the essential part of the information required for this study from the concerned organisations, a structured questionnaire was sent out to all the CPSEs with a request to furnish the details in respect of the following:

- Compensation packages scale-wise, with break-up details *viz.*, salary, various allowances, performance-related incentives and retiral benefits.
- Total number of employees grade-wise under industrial dearness allowance (IDA) and central dearness allowance (CDA) scales of pay.
- Annual expenditure on executives and non-unionised supervisors (NUS) from 2001-02 to 2005-06.
- Eligibility for promotions—qualifying years of service.
- Attritions and other employee-related information.

In addition, efforts were made to ascertain the views of some of the senior executives of the CPSEs on this subject through personal interaction. Further, some fundamental/historical data has been sourced from reliable documents like *Public Enterprise Survey* and *Annual Reports* of the DPE.

Government: The rules and regulations that govern the compensation packages of the government officers, as spelt out in authorised publications, are adopted for computing the salary data of government officers in the grades of section officer to Secretary to the Government of India, which are covered by the scales S12 to S33.

Private Sector Companies and MNCs: For obtaining information related to compensation in private sector companies and MNCs operating in the country, the following course of action was adopted:

- One-to-one interactions with company directors, present and past heads of HR functions and employees of leading private sector companies.
- Dependence on industry surveys conducted by HR/recruitment consultants.
- Dependence on specialised websites.

Situation Abroad: Dependence on various websites devoted to coverage of compensation-related information and other published documents.

Coverage

CPSEs

In response to the questionnaire, responses have been received from 77 CPSEs covering 19 industry groups out of 20 included in this study (i.e., all excepting tourism group). Further, HMT Ltd. had sent a reply stating that HMT Ltd., including the six subsidiaries *viz.,* HMT Machine Tools Ltd., HMT Watches Ltd., HMT Chinar Watches Ltd., HMT Bearings Ltd., HMT (International) Ltd. and Praga Tools Ltd., has not yet implemented revised pay and allowances for their executives in 1997 due to financial constraints, and they still continue with the 1992 pay scales. Company-wise and scale-wise details of pay and allowances of all these 7 enterprises have thus been worked out with relevant pay scales of 1992. Thus, data could be compiled in the case of 84 CPSEs.

In addition to the above, DPE had also forwarded 70 responses received by them from various CPSEs against their comprehensive questionnaire circulated in February 2007 on the subject of pay revision and related issues. These responses helped in compilation of 12 more company-wise statements of pay and allowances although replies have not been received directly by IPE on its questionnaire.

Out of the 42 companies which are yet to implement the revised pay scales of 1997 (28 operating with 1992 pay scales and 14 operating with 1987 pay scales), only 5 CPSEs have responded, besides 7 HMT units. It is understood that these organisations are finding it difficult even to make timely payment of the monthly salaries of the employees. Hence, the question of 'variable pay' representing productivity based or profit-related incentives would not arise in these cases. Based on this premise, estimated scale-wise statements of emoluments have been drawn up for these companies also and included in the study.

Thus, detailed enterprise-wise and scale-wise compensation details of 126 CPSEs, form the main database for this study, particularly for inter- and intra-group comparison of compensation packages. The group-wise CPSEs covered under this study is summarised in Table 3.1.

Table 3.1

Number of CPSEs whose Data is Compiled for the Study

Sl.No.	*Groups*	*No. of CPSEs in the Group*	*No. of CPES Covered in this Study*
1.	Steel	6	3
2.	Coal & Lignite	9	9
3.	Minerals & Metals	10	8
4.	Petroleum	12	8
5.	Power	7	4
6.	Financial Services	9	3
7.	Fertilisers	8	7
8.	Chemical & Pharmaceuticals	14	6
9.	Heavy Engineering	10	8
10.	Medium & Light Engineering	25	18
11.	Transport Equipment	10	7
12.	Consumer Goods	12	8
13.	Agro-based Industries	4	1
14.	Textiles	15	8
15.	Trading & Marketing Services	18	10
16.	Transportation Services	11	4
17.	Contract & Construction Services	11	6
18.	Industrial Development & Technical Consultancy	9	6
19.	Telecommunication & Information	4	2
20.	Tourist Services	9	0
	Total	213	126

The total number of executives and NUS working in these 126 CPSEs is 259,435 (i.e., 208,915 executives and 50,520 NUS) representing 84 per cent of the total number of such employees in all the CPSEs put together. Similarly, the total number of employees working in these 126 CPSEs amount to 14,47,866 representing 88 per cent of the total manpower in all CPSEs.

Government

As the compensation packages in the Central government are uniform, the coverage of government in this study could be considered as total.

Private Sector and MNCs

The one-to-one interactions of the IPE team have enabled collection of data pertaining to 10 sectors. The survey conducted by Omam Consultants published by *Business Today*, in three instalments, covered the cadres of junior management, middle management and senior management (below board level) across 14 sectors and 102 enterprises. The salary survey conducted by Gallup Team and published by *Business World* covered 9 sectors and 55 enterprises. The website *www.paycheck.in* covered three sectors and 54 enterprises.

Situation Abroad

The team studied websites for information pertaining to Canada, Singapore, USA and Australia. The focus was on government business enterprises and private companies. Sectors covered included manufacturing, construction, services, information and communications, financial services & trading, etc. The grades covered included entry level officers to CEOs. In addition to quantitative and qualitative data, certain policy issues related to compensation also are included.

Limitations

As already mentioned, direct responses to IPE questionnaire have been received from only 77 CPSEs. In certain cases, the information furnished was found to be inconsistent and sometimes incomplete. Eligibility figures and discretionary and selective expenditure elements, which are not universally applicable across the organisations, may lead to incorrect totals if meticulous scrutiny of the applicability is not carried out. Complete data to arrive at actual cost to the company (CTC) is not available and there are bound to be definition problems of what actually constitutes CTC at the individual executive level. Algorithms used for computing gratuity provisions etc., widely varied from company to company. Compensation details of CEOs and directors provided in the annual reports of CPSEs have not matched with the compensation details furnished in the responses.

Against this backdrop, by virtue of the experience and practical knowledge possessed by the study team, reconciliation and relevant normalisation have been carried out in respect of a few estimated components of allowances/reimbursements for logically arriving at correct and representative compensation details existing in various CPSEs as on 1.1.2007. It is gathered that some financially healthy CPSEs like HAL, ONGC, BEL and NTPC have taken several measures in the recent past to attract/retain talent. The financial implications of these measures do not figure in the current study, which are confined to the data furnished by the respective CPSEs.

The focus on compensation particulars of Central government officers has been essentially on the comparable grades with respect to CPSEs. Various occupational-specific allowances, relevant to the officers in specific designated area of work are not included in the study. Further, reimbursable/encashable components like medical claims and leave encashment are also not considered since they are not considered as allowances.

The information covered pertaining to situation abroad, regarding PSEs is limited in scope. The breadth of work carried out by government business enterprises abroad is significantly narrow compared to the tremendous depth and breadth of Indian CPSEs. While there is substantial information available in the public domain regarding compensation details, the study is limited to USA, Australia, Canada and Singapore for representative data.

4 Compensation in CPSEs

The Department of Public Enterprises (DPE) is the nodal department for 'wage policy/pay revision & other related matters' in respect of all CPSEs. While it could generally be expected that the pay and emoluments of all the employees of the CPSEs should be uniform in all respects, as in the case of government employees, there are wide variations due to a variety of reasons like:

- The financial strength of the company.
- The status of implementation of pay revision.
- The schedule in which the CPSE is categorised.

It is conceivable that executives of a lower schedule CPSE may be getting higher pay compared to an enterprise of higher schedule for the reasons mentioned above. Conversely, the compensation packages of even the best CPSEs do not match with the industry standards and the compensation packages offered by the private sector and MNC companies belonging even to the median category, especially in the middle and senior management categories. The only exception appears to be the aviation sector, where the flying crew and some specialist cadres belonging to national airlines (Air India and Indian Airlines) are said to be paid as per industry standards relevant to Southeast Asia. These cadres include pilots, stewards, airhostesses, engineers and maintenance crew. The rest of the executives belonging to the general administrative functions conform to the normal framework of CPSEs' salary structures. It is understood that similar practices are being followed in respect of specialist services in other transnational operations relating to the sailing ships and dredgers of CPSEs.

It is under this backdrop, a few financially healthy and well performing CPSEs (say around 30 per cent of the total number of CPSEs) have been constantly endeavouring to improve the levels of compensation to attract and retain talent and to improve the quality of life of its executives for motivated and higher performance levels through various measures like:

- Offering higher starts and introducing intermediate scales to the entry level executives.
- Paying handsome performance/profit linked incentives.
- Extending leased accommodation facilities to relatively junior executives posted at places where the company owned townships do not exist.
- Improving the quality of medical care to the executives during and after service.
- Liberalising the leave travel concession (LTC) schemes.
- Encouraging professional development through monetary incentives.
- Improving conveyance allowances to cope with enhanced expenditure on vehicles.
- Extending facilities to senior executives for retaining vehicles and furniture at book value at the time of superannuation.

On the other hand, some of the CPSEs which are not even in a position to pay the monthly salaries regularly, are not able to implement the 1997 pay revisions and are still operating either 1992 or 1987 pay scales. While on the subject, it is interesting to note that in a case of pay revision of sick CPSEs, a judgment was pronounced by the Supreme Court on 25th April 2003 that the employees of the government companies are not civil servants and therefore, they have no legal right to claim that government should pay their salary. It further observed that economic viability or financial capability of the employer company should be taken in to consideration in the matter of revision of pay scales of the employees. The following paragraphs outline the structure and guiding principles of the compensation packages of CPSEs.

The mix of components of compensation is categorised broadly into four groups *viz.*: (a) basic pay, (b) allowances, (c) variable pay, and (d) retirement benefits. This broad grouping of the components has been chosen, primarily to suit the available break-up of details, relating to private sector and other comparable data covered in this study. For an overall understanding, a brief on each element of the compensation is detailed hereunder.

Basic Pay

In the case of executives and NUS, the DPE formulates the structured pay scales and notifies the same to all concerned. As per DPE's guidelines dated 25th July 1999 (Pay Revision w.e.f. 1-1-1997), four scales for board level, ten scales for executives below the board level, and four scales for NUS have been specified. Further, it was clarified that in enterprises where the scales of pay are different from those prescribed in the DPE guidelines or where the rates of increments are higher than those provided had been adopted in the past, it may be necessary for such enterprises to introduce certain intermediary scales or modify the scales to be provided in the guidelines with appropriate adjustments in their span and rate of increments, and in doing so, it should be ensured that the minimum and the maximum of the individual scales prescribed are not altered and such modifications are made only in consultation with the respective administrative ministries and the DPE. Under this backdrop, most of the CPSEs in the petroleum group and a few CPSEs in other groups, introduced intermediary scales like Rs. 12,000-17,500. Nonetheless, DPE made it mandatory (through Presidential Directives) not to exceed the ceiling limits for the structured scales intimated by them. Consequently, all the CPSEs are following these structured scales intimated in DPE guidelines especially at the senior levels and board level executives.

Further, the paying capacities of the CPSEs remain the main criteria in implementation of pay revisions notified by DPE from time to time. Consequently, all the CPSEs could not implement the 'pay revisions' automatically as in the case of government employees. There are 42 CPSEs, which are yet to implement the last pay revision which came in to effect from 1-1-1997. Of them, 14 CPSEs are still operating at 1987 pay scales and 28 are operating at 1992 scales. Thus, this study covers the following three different types of pay scales for NUS and executives below board level.

All CPSEs are expected to follow the pay scales that are linked with Industrial Dearness Allowance (IDA) system. But for some historical reasons, 69 CPSEs are constrained to follow parallel scales of pay i.e., both industrial dearness allowance (IDA) and central dearness allowance (CDA). Table 4.1 indicating the comparative scales for these two different patterns of pay scales being operated by Mazagon Dock Limited (MDL) is detailed hereunder.

Table 4.1

Scales of Pay

Grades	*1987*	*1992*	*1997*
Executives			
E0	2350-100-4150	3500-150-6200	6550-200-11350
E1	2800-130-4830	4000-175-7150	8600-250-14600
E2	3450-150-5470	4800-225-8275	10750-300-16750
E3	4000-150-5950	5400-250-9050	13000-350-18250
E4	4600-160-6790	6500-275-9425	14500-350-18700
E5	5200-175-6875	7000-300-9600	16000-400-20800
E6	5800-175-7200	7500-300-9900	17500-400-22300
E7(a)	6500-175-7725	8250-300-10500	18500-450-23900
E7(b)		8500-300-10300	
E8	7250-200-8250	9500-400-11500	20500-500-26500
E9	8250-200-9250	11500-400-13500	23750-600-28550
Non-Unionised Supervisors			
S1	1750-75-3125	2800-100-4830	5200-140-8000
S2	1950-90-3420	3000-110-5055	5600-150-8600
S3	2075-100-3615	3200-120-5290	6000-160-9200
S4	2300-100-3700	3375-140-5875	6400-180-10000

Source: Complied from Questionnaire.

Table 4.2

Comparative Scales of Pay under IDA and CDA in MDL

Grades	*IDA(1/1/97)*	*CDA(1/1/96)*
E0	6550-200-11350	5500- 175-9000
E1	8600-250-14600	8000-275-13500
E2	10750-300-16750	10000-325-15200
E3	13000-350-18250	12000-375-15200
E4	14500-350-18700	12000-375-16500
E5	16000-400-20800	14300-400-18300
E6	17500-400-22300	14300-400-18300
E7	18500-450-23900	14300-400-18300
E8	20500-500-26500	16400-450-20900
E9	23750-600-28550	18400-500-22400

Source: Same as Table 4.1.

Though DPE desired that all the employees of CPSEs be covered uniformly under IDA pattern, this did not materialise though some of the employees approached the courts. However, the Hon'ble Supreme Court delivered their judgment on 3rd May 1990, allowing the employees appointed on or before 1-1-1986, an option to choose either CDA or IDA pattern. Consequently, some of the employees who joined the CPSEs on or before 1/1/86, are still continuing under CDA pattern. Thus, it is mandatory for all those who joined CPSEs after 1-1-86, to fall under IDA pattern.

In respect of pay and allowances relating to the unionised workmen, DPE only conveys the guidelines of the government, authorising the managements of the CPSEs to conduct negotiations with the trade unions, subject to certain stipulations. This would obviously end up with differential pay structure depending upon the bargaining as well as paying capacities of each CPSE. In the wake of the last pay revision which came in to effect from 1-1-1997, several dissimilarities cropped up in structuring of the scales and the rates of increments among the workmen in various CPSEs. The managements of some CPSEs agreed for operating open-ended scales with the rates of increment as a percentage of the basic pay. This lead to some unusual situations, where some of the workmen are drawing more pay and emoluments compared to the middle level managers of some CPSEs. Such cases would be more pronounced in CPSEs which have not implemented the 1997 pay revision. Therefore, there is no uniformity in the scales of pay of the workmen.

An authorisation for the 7th round of wage negotiations for unionised workers in CPSEs w.e.f. 1-1-2007, was issued by DPE vide its OM No.2 (7)2006-DPE (WC)-GL-XIV dated 9th November 2006 subject to the following stipulations:

- The managements of the CPSEs would be free to negotiate the wage structure, consistent with the generation of the resources/profits by the concerned enterprises.
- The negotiated wages would not come in conflict with the pay revision of officers and NUS of the respective CPSEs.
- For CPSEs which are monopolies/near monopolies or operate under an administered price structure, it must be ensured that any

increase in wages after negotiation does not result in increasing the administered prices of their goods and services.

- The validity period of wage settlement would be for 10 years, with 100 per cent DA neutralisation w.e.f. 1-1-2007.
- The revision shall be subject to the condition that there shall be no increase in labour cost per physical unit of output.
- In the case of sick/incipient sick CPSEs referred to Board for Reconstruction of Public Sector Enterprises (BRPSE), the wage revision would be considered on the basis of final decision on the recommendations of BRPSE.
- CPSEs which incurred net losses during any of the three financial years preceding the proposed wage negotiation, but not referred to BIFR/BRPSE may also be allowed to enter into wage negotiations, provided they give an estimate to their administrative ministry/ departments and show how resources would be generated by them to meet the extra expenditure arising out of implementation of wage revision.

Similar flexibility was not allowed in the case of pay revision of the officers and NUS, and only structured scales with specific rates of increments were framed by DPE. Consequently, all the CPSEs including the navratnas are following these scales barring a few deviations like: (a) framing of intermediary scales within the framework of the scales intimated by DPE, (b) fixing the pay with higher increments, (c) operating higher scales up to certain levels right from E1, (d) the rate of increment reckoned on a percentage basis etc. But in the case of senior management and board level appointees, no such deviations have been made. Consequently, the initial scales in the comparative enterprise-wise statements differ in the case of some of the enterprises. Nevertheless, these deviations do not substantially affect the overall grade-wise comparisons as almost all the CPSEs continue to maintain more or less the same scales notified by DPE.

NUS are far less in number compared to the executives, and some CPSEs do not have the cadre. While BHEL is operating 6 scales for their NUS supervisors (as against 4 scales notified by DPE), a majority of the CPSEs are operating only 2 or 3 scales for NUS.

Dearness Allowance

In all periodical pay revisions effected through revised pay scales, the basic pay is the core determinant in the compensation structure and the rest of the allowances become fallouts. Next to basic pay, dearness allowance (DA) is a major element in the compensation package of the employees for calculation of current and terminal benefits like provident fund (PF), gratuity etc., both basic pay and DA are considered. However, this is not considered as a part of the allowances for reckoning the quantum of perks, covered by the 50 per cent of basic pay ceiling limit specified by DPE. For the present study, DA is considered as part of the allowances, for ease of comparison with private/MNCs operating in India.

In the earlier pay revision, the IDA at AICPI-1708 as on 1-1-1997 admissible to the incumbents in these posts had been merged in the revised basic pay. The following are the salient features under IDA Scheme:

- All-India consumer price index number for industrial workers (general) based on 1960=100(AICPI) is used for grant of compensation to the employees of PSEs for price rise.
- DA instalments are released 4 times a year w.e.f. 1st January, 1st April, 1st July and 1st October.
- DA is paid for the increase in AICPI above quarterly index average to which the revised scales of pay are related.
- The percentage neutralisation for all employees is 100 per cent.
- As per the responses received from various CPSEs, 68.8 per cent of the basic pay is being paid as DA on 1-1-2007 by all the CPSEs who have implemented 1997 pay revision. However, it is observed that the IDA being paid by some of the enterprises who are still continuing on 1992 or 1987 pay scales is little higher than the basic pay, since DA merger did not take place in their cases, which is linked to the adoption of the revised scales.

The DA applicable to those CPSEs which are still on 1987 or 1992 pay scales is as follows:

- 162.4 per cent of pay subject to a minimum of Rs. 3,570 for those drawing a pay upto Rs. 3500 per month.

- 121.8 per cent of pay subject to a minimum of Rs. 5,684 for basic pay above Rs. 3,500 and upto Rs. 6,500 per month.
- 97.4 per cent of pay subject to a minimum of Rs. 7,917 for basic pay above Rs. 6,500 and upto Rs. 9,500 per month.
- 81.2 per cent of pay subject to a minimum of Rs. 9253 for basic pay above Rs. 9,500.

Dearness Pay for the Employees Covered under CDA Pattern of Scales: Consequent on the decision of the Department of Expenditure, Ministry of Finance on merger of 50 per cent of DA with basic pay to the Central government employees with effect from 01-04-2004, all the administrative ministries have been advised by DPE (vide OM No. 2(6)/2004-DPE(WC)-GLVI dated 24th May 2005, to bring to the notice of all the concerned CPSEs for merger of 50 per cent of DA with basic pay to the employees of CPSEs following CDA pattern of pay scales, and to show it distinctly as 'Dearness Pay' (DP) which would be counted for purposes like payment of allowances, transfer grant, retirement benefits, contribution to GPF/CPF, licence fee, various advances etc. It further clarified that, such portion of DA which is converted in to DP, would be deducted from the existing DA while computing the quantum of DA.

Table 4.3 indicates the comparative benefits of basic pay plus DA/DP, under CDA and IDA pattern of pay scales.

Table 4.3

IDA and CDA Pattern of Pay Scales

Grade	*IDA (Basic+DA)*	*CDA (Basic+DP+DA)*
E1	14517	16200
E2	18146	20250
E3	21944	23400
E4	24476	23400
E5	27008	28958
E6	29540	28958
E7	31228	28958
E8	34604	33210
E9	40090	37260

Source: Same as Table 4.1.

From the above details, a precise conclusion cannot be drawn as to which of the above patterns are beneficial. However, it is seen that at the lower levels of pay scales, the benefits under CDA pattern are better, mainly because of merger of 50 per cent DA. Further, the employees operating under CDA pattern can automatically expect their new scales of pay, whenever revised scales of pay are announced for the government employees.

Allowances: Apart from dearness allowance (DA) as stated above, DPE in its OM No. 2(43)/90-DPE (WC) dated 12th June 1999, spelt out in detail various perquisites. (a) The common perks cover house rent allowance, city compensatory allowance, medical facilities, LTC, etc., (b) specific perks include items like field allowance, drilling allowance, underground/mining allowance, and (c) special compensatory allowances at the specified rates, subject to the compliance with the conditions laid down by the Central government for payment of similar allowances for government servants. Primarily, these allowances are either related to the occupation, geographical locations, job hazards or compensation or reimbursement of expenses. Apart from the above, a few other perks which vary from company to company are included in this part of pay component.

Common Perks

House Rent Allowance: Historically, industrial establishments were located at remote places for a variety of reasons. Considering the advantages in providing housing facility close to the work places, industrial townships were developed by the CPSEs close to their factories. Along with these residential facilities, certain associated facilities like hospitals, schools, recreation centres etc., were also developed in these industrial townships. These integrated facilities are considered as a part of the obligations of the CPSEs to their employees. In due course of time, these small industrial townships have grown into major townships with many amenities in and around them. As per the DPE Survey 2005-06, there are 631,494 residential houses which are owned by various CPSEs and 9992 are under construction, representing 39 per cent satisfaction. Nevertheless, in due course of time, the employees felt the need of bringing up their own houses close to their factories which becomes essential for their post-retirement settlement. Consequently, a majority of the employees are living either in the industrial townships or in their own houses close to their workplace. Most of them fall under B1 and B2 class of towns.

The corporate/registered offices however might be located in A1/A class cities. As per the DPE's guidelines, HRA is payable at the following rates as a per cent of basic pay in the case of IDA and basic pay plus DP in the case of CDA pay scales.

Classification of Cities/Towns	*Rates of HRA*
'A1'	30%
'A', 'B1' & 'B2'	15%
'C'	7.5 %
Others	5%

While the above rates are generally being followed by most of the CPSEs, a deviation was allowed by DPE in the case of those CPSEs which were earlier (pre-1997 revision) entitled to 25 per cent HRA in 'A' class cities like Hyderabad. While many of the CPSEs in Hyderabad pay 25 per cent HRA, the employees of BSNL working at Hyderabad get only 15 per cent, since it came into existence as a CPSE only after 1997.

City Compensatory Allowance: DPE vide its OM No.2 (49)/98-DPE (WC) dated 25th June 1999, detailed the rates of city compensatory allowance payable to CPSEs in various cities. This ranges from Rs. 120 to Rs. 300 for the employees whose basic pay is Rs. 6500 and above.

Leave Travel Concession (LTC): As per existing rules, all the employees of CPSEs are eligible for LTC i.e., once in a block of two years to hometown and in a block of 4 years to anywhere in India subject to a maximum distance of 3000/3600 km. While a few financially strong enterprises have liberalised these LTC rules (i.e., permitting better mode of travel like air travel along with cash lumpsum assistance for senior grade executives and encashment of LTC which would be subject to tax), a few loss-making CPSEs have temporarily suspended operation of this facility to their employees.

Medical Facilities: Facilities for medical care vary in a significant measure from the financially strong CPSEs and the rest of the CPSEs. In the case of CPSEs which have full fledged townships, well equipped hospital facilities are also available and the employees receive medical attention there to the extent facilities permit. Many CPSEs have contractual relationship with corporate hospitals and the executives have the benefit of getting treated there with varying amenities depending on their grades. While some CPSEs cover the expenditure on a 100 per cent basis, some others limit the reimbursement at the rates fixed by institutions like AIIMS. With respect to the out-patient diagnosis and treatment, some CPSEs are paying lumpsum amounts in varying degrees while many CPSEs reimburse the amount spent as per the extant rules. By the very nature of this facility, there cannot be a uniformity of expenditure at the individual level and one has to go by the average expenditure of the CPSE at the aggregate levels. There are wide variations in the estimates furnished by various CPSEs under this item.

Other Perks: Various CPSEs have indicated different types of perks under the head 'allowances'. These include items like children education allowance, magazine/news paper allowance, entertainment allowance, conveyance reimbursement, professional pursuit allowance, canteen, project/field allowance, furnishing allowance, etc.

Ceiling on Payment of Perks: DPE vide its OM No.2 (49)/98-DPE (WC) dated 25th June 1999 stipulated that the payment of perquisites and allowances may be allowed up to a maximum of 50 per cent of the basic pay. Dearness allowance, HRA and CCA shall not be considered as a part of the allowances for compliance with the above ceiling limit. Payments over and above the ceiling limit of 50 per cent should be entirely in the nature of performance-related payments which should not exceed 5 per cent of the distributable profits in an enterprise.

Valued Perks: The financial value of 'valued perks' like provision of housing in the company-owned townships or provision of canteen/bus facilities etc., at subsidised rates to the executives below the board level in the CPSEs, are not easy to estimate. However, the house rent allowance has been considered for all the executives irrespective of the fact whether they stay in the company-owned township or elsewhere. Some CPSEs provide leased accommodation for some of their senior officers, where the concerned CPSE does not have their own residential facilities. Other valued perks being offered by CPSEs, which can afford them include, hard and soft furniture facilities, company transport to board level and some senior level executives, the option to retain the car at book value at the time of retirement etc. However, as a majority of the CPSEs do not follow this practice and such minute details have not been furnished by the CPSEs, 'valued perks' in the form of provision of the accommodation by some of the CPSEs either in their own townships or leased accommodation has not been considered in the case of executives below the board level.

Retiral Benefits

Provident Fund: In the case of CPSEs, the PF scheme is known as 'Contributory PF scheme (CPF)'. Currently, 12 per cent of basic pay plus DA is being contributed to this scheme both by the employee as well as the employer.

Gratuity: In terms of Payment of Gratuity Act 1972, all the employees of the CPSEs are uniformly covered under this Act, irrespective of the grade or salary drawn. No employee needs to contribute for the gratuity scheme and it is contributed entirely by the employer. At the time of separation from service (including resignation or on any count), this scheme provides for a payment of 15 days salary (basic+DA) for every completed year of service, which is reckoned after a minimum service of 5 years in the concerned CPSE or the cumulative services in other CPSEs/ service in government, provided the accumulated amount of gratuity for such earlier service gets transferred, during every change from one CPSE to the other/from government. But there is a ceiling limit for the maximum eligible amount of gratuity. While the ceiling limit for the payment of gratuity for a long time in the past was Rs. 1 lakh, it got gradually enhanced to Rs. 3.5 lakh. Considering the wage revision effected from time to time, there has been a general concern about the need for enhancing this limit. While furnishing the data, varied figures have been considered by the CPSEs in their working towards the contribution for gratuity. It is apparent that the fact of having a ceiling limit has been ignored by almost all the CPSEs while furnishing the data. As per the accounting standards, it is essential for every organisation to highlight the relevant accounting policy towards retirement benefits and provision for gratuity is allowed based on 'actuarial valuation'. Considering a minimum service of 30 years in one's life and also by assuming 8 per cent compound interest on the annual contribution to the gratuity fund, the annual contribution on this account works out to around Rs. 6000 per annum for all the employees, right from a worker to CEO's level as the limit is the same for all. Therefore, the individual figures furnished by various CPSEs towards gratuity have not been considered as mentioned above, and a uniform rate of Rs. 500 per month is adopted.

Leave Encashment: The practice of permitting encashment of 'earned leave' up to a certain limit is followed by almost all the CPSEs. However, this cannot strictly be considered as a part of retirement benefit, since in the case of CPSEs this can be availed of at anytime during the service and not necessarily at the time of retirement. In fact, many employees especially at lower levels do not utilise this facility and instead avail their earned leave. Hence, this item is not considered as an allowance or as a retiral benefit.

Pension: In the year 1971, the 'Family Pension Scheme' was introduced in CPSEs also. It entails transfer of 1/6th of the Central Pension Fund (CPF) contributions of both the employee and the employer to the pension fund. At the time of initial introduction of this scheme, the employees were given an option for joining this pension scheme. But considering the then interest rates and comparative advantages under the CPSEs *vis-a-vis* the new pension scheme, some employees at higher levels have not opted for it. In the year 1995, the 'Family Pension Scheme' was replaced by 'Employees Pension Scheme' (EPS). Under this new scheme, 8.33 per cent of both the employees' and employers' contribution to CPF (subject to a maximum of Rs. 6500 per annum) would get transferred to EPS as against 1/6th earlier. But this scheme provides a very meagre pension which works out to around Rs. 1800 per month as the maximum amount, which is fixed once for all. Only half of it shall be paid to the family members in the case of the demise of the concerned individual. DPE in its O.M. No. 2(49)/98-DPE (WC) dated 25th June 1999, clarified that the rules of the EPS 1995 should be amended so that the decisions to either choose EPS 1995 or to work out their own new contributory pension schemes must be that of, and made by the public sector enterprises themselves.

Post-Retirement Medical Benefits: A few CPSEs, which are financially strong are extending post-retiral medical facilities to their employees and executives especially for treatment in the company-owned dispensaries. Some are making attempts to introduce some schemes in association with insurance organisations as per DPE guidelines. In fact, DPE in its O.M. No. 2(49)/98-DPE (WC) dated 25th June 1999, notified that 'The Public Sector Enterprises should look into Medi-claim cover through insurance companies for their retired employees and the said policies could be funded from collateral contributions from both employees and organisations.' But many CPSEs are not following these guidelines.

Variable Pay: With the meagre pay limits fixed for eligibility under 'Bonus Act', almost none including a majority of the workmen are presently getting any bonus under this Act. However, traditionally many CPSEs are operating some performance-related 'incentives', which are either 'individual' or 'group' incentives, paid either on a monthly or on a quarterly basis. In addition to the above, annual incentives for achieving higher/targeted performance levels are also prevalent in many CPSEs. The DPE's guidelines provide for sharing of distributable profits up to 5 per cent, among the executives of profit-making CPSEs. This facility is being availed by some of the profit-making CPSEs. However, the pattern of such sharing is not uniformly followed. While some of the CPSEs are sharing the prescribed distributable profit among all the employees right from the top management to the lowest level of workmen, other CPSEs are sharing the distributable profit only among the executives.

As may be seen from the above details of components of pay and allowances, it is evident that there are bound to be differences in the overall emoluments among the executives of CPSEs.

A careful study of the pay scales reveals that, right from the first cadre (S1) of the NUS, up to the highest level including the chief executives, all the scales are very close and almost interwoven both in respect of the minimum and maximum of the scales as well as in the rates of increments, which clearly reflect that there are no distinct cadres for: (a) Junior managers, (b) Middle level managers, and (c) Senior managers. Theoretically, every entry level executive could climb the corporate ladder and reach the highest positions since there are no distinct barriers to senior cadres, as in the case of workmen who would continue in the workmen category, throughout the service, unless one gets into executive cadre on compliance with the prescribed norms/standards.

The maximum of the scale of E1 is Rs. 14,600 (Rs. 8600-250-14600) which is more than the minimum of E2 and E3 scales (i.e., 10750-300-16750 and 13000-350-18250). Similar situations can be observed in the entire pay structures of both executives below the board level and executives at board level. Unless one joins in a scale at its minimum level, and gets promoted within the specified qualifying period of say 3/4 years, there would not be any reckonable monetary gain in the normal promotions, except a marginal gain in the form of a fitment benefit in the next scale. Sometimes, even such marginal gains would also vanish at the time of implementation of pay revision, where point-to-point fixations are not allowed. The overall effect of it is perceivable in the ratio of compensation levels of managers (E5) and the junior officers (E1), which is just one and half times (1.5: 1). Considering that 10 to 12 years of service is put in for getting in to the position of a manager, with three intermediate promotions, this ratio should normally be much more. But elevation to this cadre (E5), which implies much higher responsibilities, is not compensated by any significant monetary gain. Further, stagnation for a majority occurs from this level. Similarly, in the case of E5 and E8 grades distinctive monetary differentials are not seen, in view of the very narrow gaps in the scales as well as in the rates of increments. This is the main reason for a relatively low ratio of total emoluments between even the CEOs and the first level executives in CPSEs.

In general, CPSEs strictly honour the qualifying service as the determining factor for promotions and they are linked to the vacant positions in the company especially in senior positions. It is expected that once a person is elevated to senior grade, such incumbent should effectively discharge the managerial and administrative functions befitting the position. In this process, many a time, technical experts and scientists working in research & development (R&D) divisions who are not generally familiar with administrative matters which are a pre-requisite for heading a division or occupying senior positions are not distinctly treated. In fact, in CPSEs all the functions are treated alike and it is only the grade that matters. But in private sector and in international arena, the compensation differs from one function to the other.

Increments, which are released once in a year, are too meagre and close among all the scales and in fact, they are repetitive in certain scales.

The rate of increment is Rs. 350 both in the case of E3 and E4. The annual raises do not really make a significant difference to the income of the CPSE executives.

Apart from the rate of increments, it is important to observe the span of the scale. In the case of E0 and E1, the scale provides 24 increments/ stages. In the case of E2 it is 20, in E3 it is 15 and from E4 to E8 it is 12 and for E9 it is 8.

Most of the responses received from CPSEs clearly point at the stagnation at senior levels. Considering the wider span in the E0 and E1 levels, some profit-making CPSEs are offering sizeable advance increments or operating intermediary scales with higher basics. While this leverage would help in the initial stages, it would lead to stagnation, in the later years when the executive reaches higher stages in the scales. In view of the close ranges of the scales, it is possible that once an incumbent reaches higher stages in any one scale, he would continue to be at higher stages at all the scales when promoted periodically. In such cases, the effect of promotion is not really felt in view of the low monetary benefits. In fact, this defeats the very purpose of the structured scales.

From the promotion policies of a majority of the CPSEs, it is seen that for promotion from E1 scale to E5, a qualifying service of 3 years is specified at every level and thereafter it is 4 years for further promotions to senior management scales. Consequently, it takes a minimum of 12 years for a new incumbent at E1 level to reach the manager's scale at E5 level. Likewise, it takes a minimum of around 25 years for a first line executive to reach the level of general manager (E8). These aspects in career movements of the officers are important to be understood on two counts, namely: (a) the slender variances between the emoluments of E1 compared to E5, and between E5 to E8 and (b) career prospects due to stagnation, which could seriously affect the executive's contribution to the organisation and his dedication to job.

Other Related Issues: In view of the open-ended scales made applicable to the workers, situations have cropped up wherein the worker category of employees are paid remunerations even more than middle level managers. Payments of overtime allowances, etc., also contribute to this situation. This is very pronounced in respect of CPSEs which have not implemented the 1997 pay revision recommendations and where workers have open-ended scales.

Cost of Employees and Executives in CPSEs: The total employee cost of all the CPSEs during the year 2005-06 stood at Rs. 45625 crore. The share of the executives and NUS who represent 19 per cent of the total number of employees, in the above expenditure is estimated at around Rs. 13,000 crore (considering the salaries of executives and NUS at 1.5 times of the other employees–45625×19%×1.5). Two-thirds (66%) of the above expenditure is being incurred by four groups only, namely coal (23%), telecom & IT (20%), petroleum (12%) and steel (11%). Another five groups (heavy engineering, transport equipment, medium and light engineering, power and trading and marketing) share 19 per cent of the expenditure while the rest of the 11 groups account for the balance 15 per cent of this expenditure, as detailed in Table 4.4.

Table 4.4

Cost of Employees and Executives in CPSEs

Sector	*No. of CPSEs*	*No. of Employees*	*% of No. of Employees to Total Employees*	*Salaries (Rs. in crore)*	*% of Salaries to Total Salaries*	*Per Capita (Rs. in lakhs)*
Coal	9	467422	28	10430	23	2.23
Telecom & IT	4	378274	23	9335	20	2.46
Petroleum	12	109554	7	5679	12	5.18
Steel	6	158383	10	4827	11	3.04
Heavy Engineering	10	51254	3	2016	4	3.93
Transport Equipment	10	65256	4	1800	4	2.75
Medium & Light Engineering	25	70655	4	1682	4	2.38
Power	7	53253	3	1573	3	2.95
Trading & Marketing	13	55600	3	1589	4	2.85
Other Sectors	129	238886	14	6694	15	2.80
Total	225	1648537	100	45625	100	2.77

Source: Same as Table 4.1.

5 Intra- and Inter-Group Comparisons

Introduction

Viewed from the historical evolution of the public sector set-up and nurtured under the backdrop of various Industrial Policy Resolutions of the Government of India, amended from time to time to keep pace with the changing economic scenario, the CPSEs can be broadly segregated into the following four categories:

i. CPSEs enjoying a near monopoly in respect of their products and services.

ii. CPSEs enjoying almost an assured captive consumption of their products/services by other CPSEs which are also under the administrative control of the same Ministry/Department.

iii. CPSEs which are to operate in the open market conditions facing competition from within and outside the country.

iv. CPSEs whose primary objectives are aimed at realising certain social objectives on non-commercial basis.

At a macro level, it might appear that the CPSEs in categories (i) and (ii) are enjoying many advantages including liberal pricing and least liquidity hardships, when compared to the CPSEs in the category (iii) above. But history reveals that even these CPSEs are not practically privileged and are subjected to numerous commercial and financial constraints like any other business enterprise. Further, as a result of the recent government policies in respect of various core products like Steel, coal, petroleum, etc., which were hitherto enjoying near monopoly position by the public sector are now opened up for private participation. Therefore, the emerging scenario for the future of CPSEs that fall under the categories (i) and (ii) above can rightly be perceived with the fast penetrating entry of private sector giants and MNCs. Nevertheless, the CPSEs falling under the category (iii) above are obviously more exposed to the ruthless competition from all the corners, and hence their intrinsic strength coupled with strategic administration alone could help them to remain profitable and financially sound. The excellence in management, coupled with certain entry barriers in the past have contributed for the commendable financial results of some of the CPSEs which have been classified as navratna and miniratna in recognition of their excellent track record and ability to face competition. Examples are: SAIL, BHEL, NTPC, Power Grid Corporation of India Ltd. (PGCIL), ONGC, IOC, GAIL, NMDC, NALCO, BEL, HAL, NLC, CIL, BSNL, MTNL, etc.

Significant wealth generation is still taking place in CPSEs that are engaged in core and infrastructure related areas like oil and gas, power, minerals and metals, communications, etc. Similarly, some of the CPSEs like BEL, HAL, BEML have not only taken advantage of their strategic position in the defence sector, but also demonstrated their managerial acumen. The contribution made by the employees of the CPSEs as a whole is most commendable, despite their varying compensation levels. Although it is gratifying that year after year, many CPSEs are getting added to the list of profit-making enterprises, which now crossed a mark of $3/4^{th}$ of the existing CPSEs, many of them are unable to match in offering handsome compensation packages to their employees like the private sector giants/ MNCs. Yet attempts are being made by some of the financially healthy CPSEs to offer the best compensation packages, by offering higher scales of pay to attract and retain talent at the entry level, granting of additional increments, rates of increments as a percentage to the basic pay, better allowances and reimbursements apart from performance linked incentives in the form of variable pay. For example, HAL had announced 12 advance increments to the Grade 1 executives (E1), 9 to Grade 2 executives (E2) and so on up to Grade 10. Recently, NTPC announced a substantial variable pay linked to its performance relating to the financial year 2006-07 which ranged from Rs. 1.03 lakh at E1 level (8600-14600 scale) to Rs. 2.75 lakh at E9 level (ED in the scale of 23750-28550). Similarly, BHEL announced variable pay of Rs. 0.59 lakh at E1 level which ranged up to Rs. 0.91 lakh at E9 level for the year 2006-07.

Intra-Group Comparison

DPE classified the operating CPSEs into three broad sectors consisting of 20 cognate groups (excluding Section 25 CPSEs) *viz.*: (a) Mining sector with 2 groups, (b) Manufacturing sector with 11 groups, and (c) Service sector with 7 groups. Table 5.1 showing highlights sourced from DPE's annual survey relating to the results for the year 2005-06 are noteworthy.

Table 5.1

Sector-wise Results, 2005-06

Sector	*No. of Cognate Groups & CPSEs*	*Turnover (Rs. crore)*	*Profit (Rs. crore)*	*No. of Employees*	*Manpower Cost (Rs. crore)*
Mining % to Total	2 Groups & 19 CPSEs	46874 (5.63%)	12255 (17.49%)	503744 (30.69%)	11446 (25.12%)
Manufacturing % to Total	11 Groups & 122 CPSES	622798 (74.83%)	41917 (59.83%)	591084 (36.01%)	18972 (41.64%)
Service % to Total	7 Groups & 72 CPSEs	162635 (19.54%)	15879 (22.67%)	546619 (33.30%)	15081 (33.24%)
Total	20 groups & 213 CPSEs	832307 (100%)	70051 (100%)	1641447 (100%)	45499 (100%)

As may be seen from the above, across the sectors and the groups there are wide variations in the number of CPSEs. For example, in the telecommunication & IT group in service sector, there are only 4 CPSEs compared to 25 CPSEs in the medium and light engineering group in manufacturing sector. Similarly, there is heterogeneity in the magnitude of the CPSEs in terms of capacity, turnover, number of employees etc. In the telecom group, only 2 CPSEs (BSNL and MTNL) are reckonable as the other two (Millennium Telecom Ltd. and RailTel Corporation) are too small for any comparative purposes. In terms of employment, BSNL tops the list among all the CPSEs with a manpower of 3,26,948 (i.e., around 20 per cent of the total employees in all the CPSEs) which includes 61,857 executives. Its turnover during the year 2005-06 was Rs. 36,139 crore, with a profit of Rs. 8,939 crore. Therefore, comparing it with RailTel Corporation is considered inapt since the turnover of the latter is just Rs. 56 crore with a manpower of 193. Similar cases can be seen in other groups also. Keeping in view these inherent limitations in this study of intra-group, it is essential to understand the heterogeneity among the CPSEs in each group in respect of the following:

- The financial strength of the company.
- The size of the company in terms of capacity, turnover, number of employees etc.
- The status of implementation of 1997 pay revision.

For comparison of compensation of the executives of the CPSEs with that of the officers of the government, the data relating to those CPSEs who are operating 1997 pay scales only is considered. Similarly, for comparison of compensation levels of CPSEs with that of the executives in private sector/MNCs, the group averages have been arrived at, by considering the data relating to 1997 pay scales. However, for intra- and inter-group comparisons, the compensation data in regard to the CPSEs which are operating 1992 and 1987 scales of pay (as on 1/1/2007) have also been included as the study covers the existing compensation of all the CPSEs and are shown separately at the bottom of the group-wise analysis.

As elaborated earlier, for various reasons some of the CPSEs have made some deviations in the initial scales of pay (specifically in entry level-junior management cadre) compared to those contained in the DPE's OM No.2 (49)/98-DPE(WC) dated 25th June 1999. In view of the same, the induction level of the first level executives as given by the concerned CPSEs have been considered irrespective of their scale, for the purposes of intra- and inter-group analysis. Further, for sketching the comparative analysis of CPSEs, two more scales at below the board level i.e.: (a) the scale of Rs. 16000-20800 at middle management cadre and (b) the scale of Rs. 20500-26500 at the senior management cadre have been identified. At the board level, the group-wise and sector-wise averages are made in respect of CEOs only, as not all CPSEs are operating the posts of functional directors and the averages with a few entries would vitiate the comparative analysis. The brief group-wise details are as follows.

Mining Sector

Coal & Lignite Group: This group tops in total manpower strength as well as manpower cost in the entire gamut of the CPSE establishment. The total manpower of this group as on 31st March 2006 stood at 4,67,422 (representing 28 per cent of the total manpower in all the CPSEs) with a manpower cost of Rs. 10,430 crore (representing 23 per cent of the total man-power cost of all CPSEs (Rs. 45,625 crore) for the year 2005-06). In addition to these regular employees, 60,428 casual/daily rated workers are also engaged in this group. Coal India Ltd. (CIL), along with its subsidiaries and Neyveli Lignite Corporation (NLC) are the only two entities in this group. As CIL is a holding company with very marginal earnings of its own, all its subsidiaries are treated as separate CPSEs. Consequently, there are 9 CPSEs in this group. Out of the 9 CPSEs, 3 subsidiaries of CIL and NLC have responded directly to the IPE's questionnaire. CIL had however furnished the required compensation details including all its subsidiaries in response to DPE's questionnaire. Further, it is observed that all the subsidiaries of CIL have almost uniform pattern of pay and allowances including the variable pay (incentives). Based on this premise, data sheets in respect to CIL and all its subsidiaries have been worked out. Thus, all the CPSEs in this group have been covered in this exercise.

In the coal and lignite group, NLC is paying higher emoluments to their executives compared to CIL and its subsidiaries. While the variable pay of NLC is around Rs. 1,750 per month, it is only Rs. 460 per month in the case of Bharat Coking Coal Limited (BCCL). Also, the other allowances are more in the case of NLC. At this juncture, it is essential to note that NLC with its staff strength of 19,023 is engaged not only in mining of lignite, but also is generating 14,622 MU power, which helped it in achieving a turnover of Rs. 2,201 crore during the year 2005-06. It is also pertinent to note the disproportionate manpower distribution and the consequential productivity levels in some of the subsidiaries of CIL. While Northern Coalfields Limited (NCL) which is engaged in coal extraction from its 8 operating mining projects with a turnover of Rs. 4,547 crore during the year 2005-06 is driven by a workforce of 16,914, Eastern Coalfields Limited (ECL) which has a lesser turnover of only Rs. 3,418 crore has a workforce of 1,01,474 employees, almost six times more than NCL.

CPSE-wise annual compensation is summarised in Table 5.2.

Table 5.2

CPSE-wise Annual Compensation: Coal & Lignite Group

(Rs. lakhs)

Coal and Lignite (Operating in 1997 Pay Revision)	*Junior Mgt.*	*Middle Mgt.*	*Senior Mgt.*	*Director*	*CEO*
Neyveli Lignite Corp. Ltd. (Highest)	3.25	4.94	6.90	10.05	11.12
Central Coalfields Ltd.	2.61	4.70	6.76	8.50	9.83
Eastern Coalfields Ltd.	2.61	4.70	6.76	8.50	9.83
Mahanadi Coalfields Ltd.	2.61	4.70	6.76	8.50	9.83
Northern Coalfields Ltd.	2.61	4.70	6.76	8.50	9.83
South Eastern Coalfields Ltd.	2.61	4.70	6.76	8.50	9.83
Western Coalfields Ltd.	2.61	4.70	6.76	8.50	9.83
Coal India Ltd.	2.62	4.78	6.66	9.83	10.89
Bharat Coking Coal Ltd. (Lowest)	2.57	4.66	6.55	8.44	9.42
Average	2.68	4.73	6.74	-	10.05

Minerals & Metals Group: The total turnover of this group in the year 2005-06 was Rs. 12384 crore with a net profit of Rs. 4039 crore. Out of 10 CPSEs in this group, NMDC with a turnover of Rs. 3711 crore, NALCO with a turnover of Rs. 4852 crore and Kudremukh Iron Ore Co. with a turnover of Rs. 1180 crore are the three major CPSEs with a profit of Rs. 1828 crore, Rs. 1562 crore and Rs. 356 crore respectively. Out of the 10 CPSEs' eight are profit-making while the other two are loss-making. Six out of the eight profit-making and one out of the two loss-making CPSEs have responded to IPE questionnaire.

In Minerals & Metals group, NALCO pays the highest emoluments and FCI Aravali is the lowest payer among the CPSEs operating the pay revision of 1997. However, if the entire group including those which could not implement 1997 pay revision are considered, J&K Mineral Development Corporation Ltd., is the lowest payer. J&K Mineral Development Corporation Ltd., which is a loss-making company is still operating 1987 pay scales, where the entry level scale for officers is only Rs. 2800-4830. Apart from higher allowances, NALCO is also paying 4 per cent annual increments and a variable pay of Rs. 5,526 per month which is the highest in this group.

CPSE-wise annual compensation is summarised in Table 5.3.

Table 5.3

CPSE-wise Annual Compensation: Minerals & Metals Group

(Rs. lakhs)

Minerals and Metals (1997 Scales)	*Junior Mgt.*	*Middle Mgt.*	*Senior Mgt.*	*Director*	*CEO*
National Aluminium Co. Ltd. (Highest)	3.48	5.91	7.1	10.76	11.67
National Mineral Devp. Corpn. Ltd.	3.16	5.39	6.73	10.25	11.30
Kudremukh Iron Ore Co. Ltd.	2.92	4.89	6.19	9.89	10.96
Indian Rare Earths Ltd.	2.60	4.63	5.73	8.50	9.84
Uranium Corp. of India Ltd.	2.70	4.60	5.61	8.56	9.92
FCI Aravali Gypsum & Minerals (India) Limited (Lowest)	2.59	4.55	-	-	8.49
Average	2.91	5.00	6.27	-	10.36
1992/1987 Pay Revision					
Bharat Refractories Limited	1.84	2.82	3.05	-	5.06
J&K Minerals Development Corp. Ltd.	1.29	1.86	2.66	-	4.66

Manufacturing Sector

Petroleum Group: The turnover of this group during the year 2005-06 was Rs. 4,99,555 crore with a net profit of Rs. 26,181 crore. All the 12 CPSEs in this group have a good quantum of turnover and are making profits. However, in the last couple of years, some of the downstream units are unable to maintain their profitability as in the past. The total manpower in this group is 1,09,554 (including 43,835 executives and 4,499 NUS). Out of 12 CPSEs in this group, responses have been received from seven (*viz.*, ONGC, BPCL, GAIL, IOCL, HPCL, Chennai Petroleum Corp. Ltd. and Bongaigaon Refinery and Petrochemicals Limited). ONGC Videsh had clarified that their pay and allowances are in line with their parent organisation ONGC. Out of the four CPSEs from whom responses have not been received, three CPSEs *viz.*, IBP, Mangalore Refinery & Petrochemicals Ltd. and Numaligarh Refinery Ltd. (all subsidiary companies) are considered comparatively smaller, and Oil India Ltd. is the only major enterprise.

Among the responses received, BPCL is paying highest emoluments for their executives, and Bongaigaon Refinery the lowest. It is observed that only BRPL is operating the DPE's prescribed scale of Rs. 8600-14600 for their first level executives. CPCL, BPCL, IOC, HPCL are operating an intermediary scale of Rs. 12000-17500 for their first level officers. On the other hand, ONGC is operating the scale of Rs. 10750-16750 as the starting scale for their officers. Apart from the above, BPCL is also paying higher variable pay of Rs. 5,836 per month as compared to Rs. 3,000 per month by BRPL.

CPSE-wise annual compensation is summarised in Table 5.4.

Table 5.4

CPSE-wise Annual Compensation: Petroleum Group

(Rs. in lakhs)

Petroleum (Operating in 1997 Pay Revision)	*Junior Mgt.*	*Middle Mgt.*	*Senior Mgt.*	*Director*	*CEO*
Bharat Petroleum Corp. Ltd. (Highest)	4.72	6.34	9.19	12.33	13.55
Chennai Petroleum Corpn. Ltd.	4.64	6.12	8.46	10.89	11.75
GAIL (India) Ltd.	4.33	6.57	8.39	11.82	13.01
Hindustan Petroleum Corpn. Ltd.	4.33	5.77	7.64	11.26	12.47
Indian Oil Corpn. Ltd.	4.33	5.77	7.64	11.26	12.47
Oil & Natural Gas Corpn. Ltd.	4.05	6.09	7.38	11.37	12.42
Bongaigaon Refinery & Petrochemicals Ltd. (Lowest)	3.15	5.83	7.28	9.64	11.05
Average	4.22	6.07	8.00	-	12.39

Power Group: The turnover of this group during the year 2005-2006 was Rs. 34,305 crore with a net profit of Rs. 9,082 crore. Out of 7 CPSEs in this group, NTPC with a turnover of Rs. 26,142 crore and NPCIL with a turnover of Rs. 3,567 crore, are the two major CPSEs with profit of Rs. 5820 crore and Rs. 1712 crore respectively. All the 7 CPSEs in the group are making profits. Responses have been received from four CPSEs (i.e., NTPC, Northeastern Hydro Electric Power Corp. Ltd., Northeastern Electric Power Corpn. Ltd., and Satluj Jal Vidyut Nigam Ltd.). Among the CPSEs from whom responses have not been received, Nuclear Power Corporation is the major one. During the deliberations with their senior officials, it is ascertained that they are following CDA pattern of scales for all their employees. The other two CPSEs from whom responses have not been received are smaller companies.

From among the responses received, it is seen that NTPC is paying higher emoluments to their officers in the form of allowances and a sizeable variable pay of Rs. 4,260 per month. Also, NTPC is the only company among the CPSEs in this group, which is paying, 4 per cent of the basic pay as annual increment, as against specific rates existing in various scales intimated by DPE.

CPSE-wise annual compensation is summarised in Table 5.5.

Table 5.5

CPSE-wise Annual Compensation: Power Group

(Rs. in lakhs)

Power (Operating in 1997 Pay Revision)	*Junior Mgt.*	*Middle Mgt.*	*Senior Mgt.*	*Director*	*CEO*
NTPC Ltd. (Highest)	4.57	6.18	8.75	11.92	12.97
Satluj Jal Vidyut Nigam Limited	3.61	6.11	7.59	9.91	11.35
North Eastern Electric Power Corp. Ltd.	3.06	5.32	6.55	9.10	10.47
National Hydroelectric Power Corpn. Ltd. (Lowest)	2.85	5.03	6.25	9.93	11.00
Average	3.52	5.66	7.29	-	11.45

Steel Group: The turnover of this group in the year 2005-06 was Rs. 41,742 crore, with a net profit of Rs. 5,307 crore SAIL with its major production units located at Bhilai, Rourkela, Durgapur and Bokaro is the biggest CPSE in this group with a turnover of Rs. 28,266 crore during the year 2005-06, driven by a manpower strength of 1,38,211 (including 10,672 executives and 4,534 NUS). The only other major CPSE in this group is RINL which had a turnover of Rs. 7,306 crore during the year with staff strength of 16,575 (including 3,532 executives). The other four CPSEs in this group are smaller as compared to these two major CPSEs. But all the six CPSEs in this group are making profits.

Responses have been received from three CPSEs in this group including the two major steel giants SAIL and RINL. Apart from the above, Mishra Dhatu Nigam Ltd. (MIDHANI) had responded.

It is observed that the pay and emoluments of the executives working both in RINL and SAIL are almost similar except in respect of performance linked variable pay. While RINL pays the highest compensation in this group, MIDHANI is the lowest payer. RINL after its turnaround had emerged financially strong, and is able to operate at 122 per cent capacity, compared to SAIL and MIDHANI which are operating at 109 per cent and 45 per cent capacity respectively. Apart from higher allowances, RINL is also paying around Rs. 6,500 per month as incentive, as against around Rs. 3,800 per month by SAIL and Rs. 775 per month by MIDHANI as variable pay:

CPSE-wise annual compensation is summarised in Table 5.6.

Table 5.6

CPSE-wise Annual Compensation: Steel Group

(Rs. in lakhs)

Steel (Operating in 1997 Pay Revision)	*Junior Mgt.*	*Middle Mgt.*	*Senior Mgt.*	*Director*	*CEO*
Rashtriya Ispat Nigam Ltd. (Highest)	3.61	5.51	6.91	10.73	11.78
Steel Authority Of India Ltd.	3.33	5.18	6.64	10.48	11.53
Mishra Dhatu Nigam Ltd. (Lowest)	2.75	4.77	5.52	8.85	10.19
Average	3.23	5.15	6.36	-	11.17

Transport Equipment Group: The turnover of this group during the year 2005-06 was Rs. 9,619 crore with a net profit of Rs. 1,044 crore. Out of 10 CPSEs in this group, HAL with a turnover of Rs. 5,341 crore, and BEML with a turnover of Rs. 2,059 crore, are the two major CPSEs with a profit of Rs. 1,440 crore and Rs. 186 crore respectively. Out of 10 CPSEs in this group, eight are profit-making and two are loss-making. Responses from six profit-making companies have been received. It is noticed that all these six CPSEs have uniformly followed the scales contained in DPE guidelines commencing from E0 scale of Rs. 6500-11350. Data sheets have been compiled in respect of Hoogly Dock & Port Engineers Ltd. based on the data contained in the replies to the DPE questionnaire and observed that it is operating in 1992 pay scales i.e., Rs. 4000-7500 at the entry level.

HAL is the highest payer in this group and Hindustan Shipyard Ltd., is the lowest payer among the CPSEs which have implemented 1997 pay revision. However, Hoogly Dock & Port Engineers Ltd. which is still operating 1992 pay scales is the lowest payer in this group.

CPSE-wise annual compensation is summarised in Table 5.7.

Table 5.7

CPSE-wise Annual Compensation: Transport Equipment Group

(Rs. in lakhs)

Transport Equipment (Operating in 1997 Pay Revision)	*Junior Mgt.*	*Middle Mgt.*	*Senior Mgt.*	*Director*	*CEO*
Hindustan Aeronautics Ltd. (Highest)	4.14	6.30	9.10	11.06	12.16
Mazagon Dock Ltd.	3.14	5.52	6.77	10.26	11.35
Goa Shipyard Ltd.	2.80	4.94	7.17	9.06	10.46
Garden Reach Shipbuilders & Engineers Ltd.	2.77	5.03	7.35	8.68	10.05
Bharat Earth Movers Ltd.	2.75	4.93	6.12	9.87	10.93
Hindustan Shipyard Ltd. (Lowest)	2.47	4.44	5.96	7.75	8.47
Average (Operating in 1992 Pay Revision)	3.01	5.27	7.12	-	10.57
Hooghly Dock & Port Engineers Ltd. (Estimated)	1.84	2.82	3.05	-	5.06

Medium & Light Engineering Group: The turnover of this group during the year 2005-06 was Rs. 9,559 crore with a net loss of Rs. 25 crore. Out of the 25 CPSEs in this group, 15 are profit-making and 10 are loss-making. However, only BEL with a turnover of Rs. 3,502 crore and Balmer Lawrie & Co. with a turnover of Rs. 1,234 crore are the two major units in this group, followed by ECIL, BDL, Antrix Corp. Ltd. Some of the subsidiaries of HMT and ITI are making losses. Apart from six responses received, six more could be added for this comparative study based on the letter received from HMT Ltd. intimating its status of non-implementation of 1997 pay revision along with its subsidiaries. Out of 15 profit-making CPSEs, only three have responded. But data in respect to all the 10 loss-making units could be estimated and included in this comparative study. BEL is the best payer in this group.

CPSE-wise annual compensation is summarised in Table 5.8.

Table 5.8

CPSE-wise Annual Compensation: Medium & Light Engineering Group

(Rs. in lakhs)

Medium and Light (Operating in 1997 Pay Revision)	*Junior Mgt.*	*Middle Mgt.*	*Senior Mgt.*	*Director*	*CEO*
Bharat Electronics Ltd. (Highest)	3.47	5.73	7.63	10.20	11.29
Balmer Lawrie & Co. Ltd.	3.43	5.67	7.80	9.09	10.43
Bharat Dynamics Limited	2.89	5.85	6.37	8.27	10.06
Electronics Corporation Of India Ltd.	2.68	4.71	6.34	9.80	10.86
ITI Ltd.	2.55	4.70	5.90	8.60	9.67
Hindustan Cables Ltd.	2.54	4.84	5.57	7.84	9.19
Andrew Yule & Co. Ltd.	2.51	4.85	5.76	7.84	9.18
Biecco Lawrie	2.46	4.59	6.53	0	7.84
Average	2.82	5.12	6.49	-	9.82
(Operating in 1987/1992 Pay Revision)					
Vignyan Industries Ltd. (Estimated)	1.79	2.74	2.95	-	5.66
Instrumentation Ltd. (Estimated)	1.79	2.74	2.95	-	5.66
Praga Tools Ltd. (Estimated)	1.84	2.82	3.05	-	5.06
HMT Bearings Ltd. (Estimated)	1.84	2.82	3.05	-	5.06
HMT Chinar Watches Ltd. (Estimated)	1.84	2.82	3.05	-	5.66
HMT Ltd. (Estimated)	1.84	2.82	3.05	-	6.09
HMT Machine Tools Ltd. (Estimated)	1.84	2.82	3.05	-	5.66
HMT Watches Ltd. (Estimated)	1.84	2.82	3.05	-	5.66
Richardson & Cruddas (1972) Ltd. (Estimated)	1.84	2.82	3.05	-	5.06
Bharat Pumps and Compressors Limited (Estimated)	1.79	2.74	2.95	-	5.66
National Instruments Ltd. (Estimated)	1.29	1.86	2.66	-	4.36

Chemicals & Pharmaceuticals Group: The turnover of this group during the year 2005-06 was Rs. 976 crore with a net loss of Rs. 74 crore. Out of 14 CPSEs in this group, seven are making profits and seven are loss-making. Only Hindustan Fluorocarbons which is a loss-making unit has responded. This unit is still operating on 1992 pay scales. However, it is ascertained that Hindustan Organic Chemicals, Hindustan Antibiotics, Hindustan Insecticides, Bengal Chemicals are close to profit-making zone and are in the process of implementation of 1997 pay revision. But in the absence of any responses from them, the same could not be included in the comparative analysis. Hence, estimated compensation details in respect of all of them with 1992 pay revision have been made. Consequently, the comparative average compensation with 1997 pay scales could not be made for this group.

CPSE-wise annual compensation is summarised in Table 5.9.

Table 5.9

CPSE-wise Annual Compensation: Chemicals & Pharmaceuticals Group

(Rs. in lakhs)

Chemicals and Pharmaceuticals (Operating in 1992/1987 Revision)	*Junior Mgt.*	*Middle Mgt.*	*Senior Mgt.*	*Director*	*CEO*
Bengal Chemicals and Pharmaceuticals Limited	1.84	2.82	3.05	-	5.06
Hindustan Fluorocarbons Ltd.	1.84	2.82	3.05	-	4.56
Hindustan Salts Ltd.	1.79	2.74	2.95	-	5.06
Sambhar Salts Ltd.	1.79	2.74	2.95	-	5.06
Indian Drugs and Pharmaceuticals Ltd. (Estimated)	1.29	1.86	2.66	-	4.66
Orissa Drugs and Chemicals Limited (Estimated)	1.29	1.86	2.66	-	4.66

Fertiliser Group: The turnover of this group during the financial year 2005-06 was Rs. 9,364 crore with a net loss of Rs. 1,990 crore. Rashtriya Chemicals and Fertilisers Ltd. (RCF) with a turnover of Rs. 3,045 crore. National Fertilisers Ltd. (NFL) with a turnover of Rs. 3,590 crore and Fertilisers and Chemicals (Travancore) Ltd. (FACT), with a turnover of Rs. 1,394 crore, are the three major units in this group and are making profits. The other five CPSEs in this group are incurring losses. While five responses have been received, two more have been compiled based on the information furnished against the DPE questionnaire. The data covers all the three major fertiliser units. Out of the loss-making units, responses have been received from Brahmaputra Valley Corp. Ltd., Fertiliser Corp. of India Ltd., Madras Fertilisers Ltd. and Hindustan Fertilisers Corporation Ltd. From the responses received, it is observed that all these CPSEs have implemented 1997 pay scales, except Fertiliser Corporation of India Ltd., and Hindustan Fertiliser Corpn. Ltd. which are under winding-up stage.

Among the responses received, National Fertilisers Ltd. pays higher emoluments in this group, compared to Fertiliser Corp. of India Ltd. which pays the lowest.

CPSE-wise annual compensation is summarised in Table 5.10.

Table 5.10

CPSE-wise Annual Compensation: Fertiliser Group

(Rs. in lakhs)

Fertilisers (Operating in 1997 Pay Revision)	*Junior Mgt.*	*Middle Mgt.*	*Senior Mgt.*	*Director*	*CEO*
National Fertilisers Ltd. (Highest)	3.14	5.35	7.41	9.69	10.75
Rashtriya Chemicals & Fertilisers Ltd.	3.11	5.50	6.95	9.74	10.8
Madras Fertilisers Ltd.	2.93	5.35	6.77	-	8.82
Brahmaputra Valley Fertiliser Corpn. Ltd.	2.68	4.71	5.95	8.31	9.60
Fertilisers & Chemicals (Travancore) Ltd.	2.63	4.55	5.65	8.63	9.68
Fertilisers and Chemicals Average	2.38	4.08	5.31	-	8.67
(Operating in 1987 Pay Revision)					
Fertiliser Corpn. Of India Ltd. (Lowest)	1.29	1.86	2.66	-	4.66
Hindustan Fertiliser Corpn. Ltd.	1.29	1.86	2.66	-	4.66

Heavy Engineering Group: The turnover of this group during the year 2005-06 was Rs. 15,042 crore with a net profit of Rs. 977 crore. BHEL with a turnover of Rs. 13,374 crore and with a net profit of Rs. 1,679 crore is the only major unit in this group. Out of 10 CPSEs in this group, three more CPSEs apart from BHEL, are making profits and the balance six are loss-making units. Apart from BHEL, responses have been received from three loss-making units *viz.*, Burn Standard Co. Bharat Heavy Plate and Vessels Ltd. and Tungabhadra Steel Products Ltd. All these loss-making units have yet to implement 1997 pay revision. Therefore, it is obvious that the pay and allowances of BHEL are far superior compared to the loss-making units from whom responses have been received.

CPSE-wise annual compensation is summarised in Table 5.11.

Table 5.11

CPSE-wise Annual Compensation: Heavy Engineering Group

(Rs. in lakhs)

Heavy Engineering (Operating in 1997 Pay Revision)	*Junior Mgt.*	*Middle Mgt.*	*Senior Mgt.*	*Director*	*CEO*
Bharat Heavy Electricals Ltd. (Highest)	3.26	4.97	6.53	10.65	11.71
Average (BHEL Only)	3.26	4.97	6.53	-	11.71
(Operating in 1992 Pay Revision)					
Heavy Engineering Corporation Ltd.	1.79	2.74	2.95	-	6.09
Braithwaite and Company Ltd.	1.84	2.82	3.05	-	5.66
Bharat Wagon & Engg. Co. Ltd.	1.84	2.82	3.05	-	5.06
Triveni Structural Ltd.	1.79	2.74	2.95	-	5.06
Bharat Heavy Plate and Vessels Ltd.	1.79	2.74	2.95	-	5.66
Tungabhadra Steel Products Ltd.	1.79	2.74	2.95	-	5.06
Burn Standard Co. Ltd. (Lowest)	1.75	2.50	2.71	-	5.93

Agro-based Industries: The turnover of this group during the year 2005-06 was Rs. 173 crore with a net loss of Rs. 21 crore. Out of 4 CPSEs in this group, National Seeds Corp. Ltd. (NSC), with a turnover of Rs. 105 crore and with profit of Rs. 4 crore, is the only major CPSE. IPE received response from NSC. There is no response from the other three loss-making units *viz.*, State Farm Corp., Andaman & Nicobar Islands Forest and Plantation Corp. and North Eastern Regional Agri-Marketing Corp.

Table 5.12

CPSE-wise Annual Compensation: Agro-based Industries Group

(Rs. in lakhs)

Agro-based Industries (Operating in 1997 Pay Revision)	*Junior Mgt.*	*Middle Mgt.*	*Senior Mgt.*	*Director*	*CEO*
National Seeds Corporation Limited	2.27	3.71	-	-	8.23
Average	2.27	3.71	-	-	8.23

Textile Group: The turnover of this group during the year 2005-06 was Rs. 856 crore with a net loss of Rs. 801 crore before extraordinary and prior period adjustments. Out of 15 CPSEs in this group, only four have made profit (primarily due to extraordinary/prior period adjustments) and the balance 11 are loss-making units. Responses have been received from

NTC (Maharashtra North), NTC (South Maharashtra), National Handloom Development Corp. Ltd., Jute Corp. of India Ltd. and NTC-Holding Company which is a loss-making unit. Further, data have been estimated in respect to five CPSEs which are loss-making and are in the 1992 pay scales. NTC (Maharashtra North) is the highest payer in this group.

CPSE-wise annual compensation is summarised in Table 5.13.

Table 5.13

CPSE-wise Annual Compensation: Textiles Group

(Rs. in lakhs)

Textiles (Operating in 1997 Pay Revision)	*Junior Mgt.*	*Middle Mgt.*	*Senior Mgt.*	*Director*	*CEO*
National Textile Corp.	2.91	3.95	4.93	9.78	10.83
National Textile Corpn. (Maharashtra North) Ltd. (Highest)	2.90	5.27	6.62	8.63	9.48
National Textile Corp. (South Maharashtra)	2.54	4.61	5.26	-	-
National Handlooms Development Corporation Limited	2.42	4.41	5.57	-	8.44
Average	2.69	4.56	5.60	-	9.58
(Operating in 1987 Pay Revision)					
National Jute Manufacturers Corporation Limited (Estimated)	1.29	1.86	2.66	-	4.66
British India Company Ltd. (Estimated)	1.29	1.86	2.66	-	4.66
Birds, Jute and Exports Ltd. (Estimated)	1.29	1.86	2.66	-	4.66
Brushware Limited (Estimated)	1.29	1.86	2.66	-	4.66

Consumer Goods Industries: The turnover of this group during the year 2005-06 was Rs. 1,606 crore with a net profit of Rs. 225 crore. Out of 11 CPSEs in this group, Hindustan Paper Corporation Ltd. (HPC) with a turnover of 699 crore, Hindustan News Print (HNL) with a turnover of Rs. 303 crore, Hindustan Latex Ltd. (HLL) with a turnover of Rs. 211 crore and Cement Corporation of India Ltd. (CCI) with a turnover of Rs. 195 crore are the four major CPSEs. While the first three CPSEs have been making profits, Cement Corporation recorded a profit of Rs. 832 crore during 2005-2006 only on account of extraordinary/prior period adjustments. Responses have been received from only two CPSEs *viz.*, Hindustan Latex Ltd. and Hindustan Paper Corpn. Ltd. Between these two, emoluments of Hindustan Paper Corpn. Ltd. are higher.

CPSE-wise annual compensation is summarised in Table 5.14.

Table 5.14

CPSE-wise Annual Compensation: Consumer Goods Group

(Rs. in lakhs)

Consumer Goods (Operating in 1997 Pay Revision)	*Junior Mgt.*	*Middle Mgt.*	*Senior Mgt.*	*Director*	*CEO*
Hindustan Paper Corp. Ltd. (Highest)	2.72	5.06	6.44	9.19	10.63
Hindustan Latex Ltd.	2.73	4.67	5.80	8.85	9.90
Average	2.73	4.87	6.12	-	10.27
(Operating in 1992/1987 Pay Revision)					
Hindustan Vegetable Oil Corporation Ltd.	1.79	2.74	2.95	-	5.66
Nepa Ltd.	1.79	2.74	2.95	-	5.06
Bharat Opthalmic Glass Ltd.	1.29	1.86	2.66	-	4.36
Hindustan Photo Films Mfg. Co. Ltd.	1.29	1.86	2.66	-	4.36
Nagaland Pulp & Paper Co. Ltd.	1.29	1.86	2.66	-	4.36
Tyre Corporation of India Limited	1.29	1.86	2.66	-	4.66

Service Sector

Financial Services Group: The operating income of this group during the year 2005-06 was Rs. 10,108 crore with a net profit of Rs. 2,469 crore. All the nine CPSEs in the group are making profits. Power Finance Corp. Ltd. (PFC), Rural Electrification Corp. Ltd. (REC), Indian Railway Finance Corp. Ltd. (IRFC), Indian Renewable Energy Dev. Agency (IREDA), Housing and Urban Dev. Corp. Ltd. (HUDCO) and Export Credit Guarantee Corp. of India Ltd. (ECGC) are the five major CPSEs. Responses have been received from three CPSEs *viz.*, HUDCO, PFC and IREDA. Among the 3 responses received, HUDCO is paying higher emoluments and IREDA the lowest.

CPSE-wise annual compensation is summarised in Table 5.15.

Table 5.15

CPSE-wise Annual Compensation: Financial Services Group

(Rs. in lakhs)

Financial Services (Operating in 1997 Pay Revision)	*Junior Mgt.*	*Middle Mgt.*	*Senior Mgt.*	*Director*	*CEO*
Housing & Urban Development Corpn. Ltd. (Highest)	2.96	5.82	6.72	10.49	11.58
Power Finance Corpn. Ltd.	3.58	5.24	6.52	9.96	11.02
Indian Renewable Energy Devp. Agency Ltd. (Lowest)	2.59	4.63	5.74	8.51	9.84
Average	3.04	5.23	6.33	-	10.81

Industrial Development & Technical Consultancy Services Group: The operating income of this group during the year 2005-06 was Rs. 6,314 crore with a net profit of Rs. 1,340 crore. All the 15 CPSEs in the group have made profits during the year 2005-06. Power Grid Corp. of India Ltd. (POWERGRID), Engineers India Ltd. (EIL), RITES Ltd., Telecommunications Consultants (India) Ltd. (TCIL) are the four major CPSEs. MECON and Engineering Projects (India) Ltd. (EPI) are the other renowned CPSEs. Only four CPSEs have responded *viz.*, EIL, HSCC, National Small Industries Corp (NSIC) and Water & Power Consultancy Services (India) Ltd. (WAPCOS). Further, data sheets have been compiled in respect of MECON Ltd. and TCIL based on the data contained in the replies to the DPE questionnaire.

From among the responses received, EIL is paying higher emoluments, and NSIC the lowest. It is seen that EIL is the only CPSE which is operating an intermediary scale of Rs. 12000-17500 for their first level officers. Also, it is paying a variable pay of Rs. 2,060 per month, while no such variable pay exists in NSIC.

CPSE-wise annual compensation is summarised in Table 5.16.

Table 5.16

CPSE-wise Annual Compensation: Industrial Development and Technical Consultancy Services Group

(Rs. in lakhs)

Industrial Development and Tech. Consul. (Operating in 1997 Pay Revision)	*Junior Mgt.*	*Middle Mgt.*	*Senior Mgt.*	*Director*	*CEO*
Engineers India Ltd. (Highest)	3.97	5.24	6.99	10.29	11.38
HSCC (India) Ltd.	3.00	5.19	6.41	7.82	9.14
Telecommunications Consultants India Ltd.	2.70	5.08	6.31	10.56	11.67
Mecon Ltd.	2.63	4.78	5.88	9.97	11.02
Water and Power Consultancy Ltd.	2.62	4.77	5.92		9.78
National Small Inds. Corpn. Ltd. (Lowest)	2.47	4.43	5.53	8.44	9.78
Average	2.90	4.92	6.17	-	10.46

Transportation Services Group: The operating income of this group during the year 2005-06 was Rs. 19,326 crore with a net profit of Rs. 2,490 crore. Shipping Corporation of India Ltd. (SCI), Airports Authority of India

(AAI), Container Corporation of India Ltd. (CONCOR), Air India (AI), Indian Airlines (IA) and Dredging Corporation of India Ltd. (DCI) are the major CPSEs. Out of 11 CPSEs in this group, eight are profit-making and three are loss-making. Only three responses (AAI, CONCOR and DCI) have been received from this group for IPE questionnaire. Further, data sheets have been compiled in respect of Ennore Port Ltd. (EPL) based on the data contained in the replies to the DPE questionnaire. In view of higher allowances and higher variable pay, the emoluments of CONCOR are more when compared to others.

CPSE-wise annual compensation is summarised in Table 5.17.

Table 5.17

CPSE-wise Annual Compensation: Transportation Services Group

(Rs. in lakhs)

Transportation Services (Operating in 1997 Pay Revision)	*Junior Mgt.*	*Middle Mgt.*	*Senior Mgt.*	*Director*	*CEO*
Container Corpn. of India Ltd. (Highest)	4.00	6.33	8.44	11.37	12.48
Dredging Corpn. of India Ltd.	3.01	5.32	6.08	8.56	9.90
Airports Authority of India	2.96	5.27	6.71	10.08	11.15
Ennore Port Ltd.	2.50	4.61	5.71	8.49	9.83
Average	3.12	5.38	6.74	-	10.84

Trading & Marketing Services: The turnover of this group during the year 2005-06 was Rs. 79,923 crore with a net profit of Rs. 288 crore. MMTC Ltd., Central Warehousing Corp. (CWC), MSTC Ltd., State Trading Corporation India (STC) are the major CPSEs. Cotton Corp. of India Ltd. (CCI) and PEC Ltd. are the other well known CPSEs. Out of 13 CPSEs in this group, nine are profit-making and four are loss-making. Responses have been received from five profit-making and one loss-making CPSEs. Among the responses received, STC pays the highest emoluments compared to the lowest emoluments by North Eastern Handicrafts and Handlooms Development Corporation Ltd. (NEHHDC) which is still on 1992 pay scales.

CPSE-wise annual compensation is summarised in Table 5.18.

Table 5.18

CPSE-wise Annual Compensation: Trading & Marketing Services Group

(Rs. in lakhs)

Trading and Marketing (Operating in 1997 Pay Revision)	*Junior Mgt.*	*Middle Mgt.*	*Senior Mgt.*	*Director*	*CEO*
State Trading Corp. of India Ltd. (Highest)	3.27	5.74	7.71	10.52	11.70
MMTC Ltd.	3.11	5.50	6.95	9.74	10.79
MSTC Ltd.	2.70	5.08	0	0	9.12
Central Cottage Industries	2.69	4.77	0	0	8.47
Central Warehousing Corpn.	2.61	0	6.10	0	8.51
The Jute Corp. of India	2.54	4.29	0	0	7.84
Food Corpn. of India	2.51	4.42	5.54	0	9.76
Cotton Corporation of India Ltd.	3.00	4.28	5.55	8.51	9.86
Average	2.65	4.61	5.82	-	9.51
(Operating in 1992 Pay Revision)					
Northern Eastern Handicrafts & Handloom Dev. Corp. Ltd. (Estimated)	1.79	2.74	2.95	0	5.06
HMT (International) Ltd. (Estimated)	1.84	2.82	3.05	-	5.66

Contract & Construction Services: The operating income of this group during the year 2005-06 was Rs. 4453 crore with a net loss of Rs. 190 crore. IRCON International Ltd. (IRCON) and National Building Construction Corporation Ltd. (NBCC) are the two major CPSEs. The other renowned CPSEs are National Projects Construction Corp. Ltd. (NPCC), Konkan Railway Corporation Ltd. (KRCL), Bridge & Roof Co. (India) Ltd. (B&R), and Hindustan Steel Works Construction Ltd. (HSCL). Out of 11 CPSEs in this group, eight are profit-making and three are loss-making. Responses from one profit-making and one loss-making CPSEs have been received. Further, data sheets have been compiled in respect of NBCC and Mineral Exploration Corporation Ltd. (MECL), based on the data contained in the replies to the DPE questionnaire. Further, estimates have been made in regard to HSCL which is still on 1992 pay scales IRCON is paying higher compared to HSCL which is a loss-making unit.

CPSE-wise annual compensation is summarised in Table 5.19.

Table 5.19

CPSE-wise Annual Compensation: Contract & Construction Services Group

(Rs. in lakhs)

Contract and Construction Services (Operating in 1997 Pay Revision)	*Junior Mgt.*	*Middle Mgt.*	*Senior Mgt.*	*Director*	*CEO*
IRCON International Ltd. (Highest)	2.71	5.40	6.62	10.33	11.46
National Buildings Construction Corp. Ltd.	2.50	4.65	5.75	8.50	9.84
Mineral Exploration Corp. Ltd.	2.45	4.48	5.64	8.45	9.78
Konkan Railway Corpn. Ltd.	2.36	4.29	5.39	8.58	9.03
Average	2.51	4.71	5.85	-	10.03
(Operating in 1992 Pay Revision)					
Hindustan Steelworks Construction Ltd. (Estimated)	1.79	2.74	2.95	-	5.66
Hindustan Prefab Ltd. (Estimated)	1.79	2.74	2.95	-	4.56

Telecommunication & IT Services: The operating income of this group during the year 2005-06 was Rs. 41,817 crore with a net profit of Rs. 9,534 crore. BSNL with an operating income of Rs. 36,139 crore and MTNL with an operating income of Rs. 5,561 crore are the major CPSEs. While BSNL made a profit of Rs. 8,940 crore during the year 2005-06, MTNL made a profit of Rs. 580 crore. BSNL is the highest payer compared to RailTel Corporation India Ltd.

CPSE-wise annual compensation is summarised in Table 5.20.

Table 5.20

CPSE-wise Annual Compensation: Telecommunication & IT Services

(Rs. in lakhs)

Telecommunication and Information (Operating in 1997 Pay Revision)	*Junior Mgt.*	*Middle Mgt.*	*Senior Mgt.*	*Director*	*CEO*
Bharat Sanchar Nigam Ltd. (Highest)	3.10	4.87	7.45	9.56	10.62
RailTel Corpn.	2.57	4.65	5.91	0	0
Average (BSNL Only)	3.10	4.87	7.45	-	10.62

Tourist Services Group: Data in respect of tourist services could not be included as none of the CPSEs from this sector has responded. Similarly, this study excludes the CPSEs falling under Section 25 of the Companies Act.

Summary of Intra-Group Comparisons

As may be observed from the above, scale to scale variations within CPSEs which are following the same pay revision are not significant excepting for: (a) variations in the variable pay and (b) operation of higher scales of pay or intermediary scales at the induction levels. Granting advance increments by some of the CPSEs could not be highlighted in this exercise since the data has been developed for the comparative purposes only at the minimum and maximum of the scales. But wide variations are seen from those who are following different pay revisions.

For example, the annual emoluments of E1 grade in JK Minerals Development Corporation (a CPSE which is following pay scales of 1987) is only Rs. 1.29 lakh as against Rs 3.48 lakh in National Aluminum Co. Ltd. (operating on 1997 pay revision + performance incentives and higher allowances).

Table 5.21

Scale of Rating: Compensation Levels

Compensation	*Relative Ranking*	*Relevant Groups (No. of Cos.)*		*Total (Entry level) (No. of Cos.)*
Above Rs. 4 Lakh pa	Excellent	Petroleum	6	
		Power	1	
		Transport Eqp.	1	
		Transport Service	1	9
Rs. 3-4 Lakh pa	Very Good	Coal & Lignite	1	
		Minerals & Metals	2	
		Steel	2	
		Petroleum	1	
		Power	2	
		Heavy Eng.	1	
		Fertilisers	2	
		Medium & Light Engg.	2	
		Transport Equipment	1	
		Trading & Marketing	2	
		Transport Services	1	
		Industrial Dev.	2	
		Financial Services	1	20
Rs. 2–3 Lakh pa	Good	From All Groups (Comparatively Smaller Cos.)		51
Less than Rs. 2 Lakh pa	Poor	All CPSEs which are yet in 1987/1992 pay scales (Very Smaller Sick PSEs)		46
		Total		126

To appreciate the relative variations in the compensation levels among those CPSEs operating 1997 pay scales, the scale of rating shown in Table 5.21 has been adopted. Since a good correlation exists among the corresponding scales within the CPSEs in most of the cases, only the initial scale (entry level) of the executives is considered for this purpose.

Inter-Group Comparisons

The per capita manpower cost varies among the three major sectors. It is Rs. 2.27 lakh in mining sector, Rs. 3.20 lakh in manufacturing sector and Rs. 2.76 lakh in service sector. But it is gratifying that the overall ratio of employees cost to turnover of all the CPSEs put together, during the financial year 2005-06, came down to 5.48 per cent (total employees cost of Rs. 45,625 cr. compared to a turnover of Rs. 8,32,584) from 11.73 per cent in the year 1996-97. This ratio works out to only 3.05 in the case of manufacturing sector. This significant fall in this ratio is due to the quantum jumps in the production/turnovers of some of the CPSEs, year after year. But it is equally important to recognise that, this ratio does not truly reflect any reliable trends or uniformity among various groups covered in the study. The group-wise ratio of manpower cost to total turnover during the year 2005-06 is detailed in Table 5.22.

The other important aspect in inter-group comparison is the analysis relating to the existing compensation differentials among various groups. The group average comparisons are considered as one familiar approach, despite some limitations in compilation of a more precise data for various reasons as explained earlier. To obviate such limitations to the extent possible, the averages of each group is limited only to those CPSEs which are operating 1997 pay scales. Accordingly, the group-wise average compensation in the three selected grades (E1, E5 and E8 at below the board level) is summarised here under for a ready comparison. In the case of the executives at board level, such comparisons are not considered possible, as their compensation levels depend on the schedule in which the concerned CPSE is categorised. Therefore, the comparative details of the CEOs are dealt with separately in this chapter.

Table 5.22

Group-wise Ratio of Manpower Cost to Total Turnover, 2005-06

Group	*Manpower Cost (Rs. Cr)*	*Net Sales (Rs. Cr)*	*Man Power Cost to Net Sales (%)*
Coal and Lignite	10430	30946	33.70
Minerals and Metals	1015	11730	8.65
Steel	4826	36056	13.38
Power	1572	34305	4.58
Petroleum	5679	457743	1.24
Fertilisers	516	9247	5.58
Chemicals and Pharma.	189	857	22.05
Heavy Engineering	2016	13849	14.56
Medium and Light Engg.	1682	9215	18.25
Transport Equipment	1799	9437	19.06
Consumer Goods	264	1524	17.32
Agro-based	56	172	32.56
Textiles	366	853	42.91
Trading and Marketing	1588	79923	1.99
Transport Services	2696	19325	13.95
Contract and Construction	331	4452	7.43
Industrial Development and Tech. Consultancy Services	893	6314	14.14
Tourist Services	156	672	23.21
Financial Services	141	10107	1.40
Telecom & IT	9336	41816	22.33

As seen from the above, the three best paying groups among all the groups are petroleum followed by power and steel, whose strength of executives and NUS constitutes around 30 per cent of the total number covered in this study (91,338 out of 307794). A similar number of executives and NUS (91,829) are engaged in two other groups—telecommunication & IT and coal & lignite, in which almost all the CPSEs are making profits and are operating 1997 pay scales. The compensation levels in these two groups are comparably better. Thus, these five groups predominate in many respects among all the groups covered in this study.

Table 5.23

Group-wise Average Compensation
(Arranged in Descending Order of the Number of Executives and NUS Engaged in the Group)

(Rs. in lakh per annum)

Groups	*Junior Mgt. (E1)*	*Middle Mgt. (E5)*	*Senior Mgt. (E8)*	*No. of Executives and NUS*
Telecommunication and Information	3.10	4.87	7.45	63839
Petroleum	4.22	6.07	8.00	48334
Coal	2.68	4.73	6.74	27990
Power	3.52	5.66	7.29	23548
Medium & Light Engg.	2.82	5.12	6.49	20580
Heavy Engg.	3.26	4.97	6.53	20020
Steel	3.23	5.15	6.36	19456
Transportation Services	3.12	5.38	6.74	15706
Industrial Dev. & Tech. Consul. Services	2.90	4.92	6.17	12596
Transport Equipment	3.01	5.27	7.12	9831
Trading & Marketing	2.65	4.61	5.82	9503
Contracts & Construction	2.51	4.71	5.85	6698
Minerals & Metals	2.91	5.00	6.27	5789
Fertilisers	2.38	4.08	5.31	4347
Textiles	2.69	4.56	5.60	2417
Financial Services	3.04	5.06	6.33	1723
Consumer Goods	2.73	4.87	6.12	1721
Agro-based Industries	2.27	3.71	-	371

Note: (a) Since none of the CPSEs in the chemical & pharmaceuticals group has apparently implemented 1997 pay revision as on 1/1/2007, their group average is not included. The total number of executives and NUS engaged in this group is 2,407 in 14 CPSEs. (b) Since no responses have been received from any CPSEs in the tourist services, the data for this group could not be included. The total number of executives and NUS engaged in this group is 2085 in 9 CPSEs. (c) Sec.25 CPSEs are excluded from the study.

In the heavy engineering group, BHEL is an exceptionally bigger unit, with more than 85 per cent of the executives and NUS engaged in this group are in this company. While a majority of the CPSEs in the transport equipment group, financial services group and industrial development & tech. consultancy services group are profit-making, only a few are making profits in the medium and light engineering, and other groups as explained earlier. The compensation levels in these groups are reasonably comparable.

To appreciate the aspect of performance-related incentives including profit sharing, a distinctive element of pay allowed in the case of CPSEs when compared to the officers of the government, it is essential to review the component mix constituting the overall compensation package. To facilitate the inter-group comparison of components of pay, the highest paying CPSE in each group is considered. Similarly, only three grades have been identified for this purpose. While the summary contained in Table 5.24 contains the absolute monthly figures, the percentage of each of the component of the total pay is depicted in Figures 5.1-5.3.

As may be seen from the table, excepting in the case of telecommunication and IT group and textile group, in all other groups, variable pay exists. While in some groups the variable pay varies with the grade, it is seen that in the case of coal & lignite, steel, heavy engineering (BHEL), fertilisers groups, almost similar amount of variable pay is being paid to the executives in all the grades. Consequently, a major variation in the quantum of variable pay as a percentage in the component mix can be seen in these cases. For example in the steel group, the component of variable pay in the case of entry-level executives constitute 21 per cent of the total pay, the same comes down to 14 per cent for middle level and to 11 per cent for senior level managers. But in the case of petroleum, power, transport equipment and consumer goods groups in the manufacturing sector, almost a uniform percentage of variable pay can be seen, as depicted in the Figures.

As the above analysis is restricted only to the CPSEs, which are operating the 1997 pay scales, the study of the existing compensation levels in all the CPSEs which form part of this exercise remain incomplete. Therefore, to appreciate the wide variations in the compensation packages among all the CPSEs within a group with dissimilar scales of pay and allowances in some groups, as well as their comparison with other groups, the method of comparison of the highest pay with the lowest pay in each group is considered. In the case of coal & lignite, petroleum, steel, financial services, industrial development & consultancy service groups, the variations between the lowest and the highest pay is much lesser, compared to all other groups which have a number of CPSEs which are operating with 1992/1987 pay scales as on 1/1/2007. Apart from two groups from mining sector, eight more groups from the manufacturing sector and four from service sector are included in Figures 5.4-5.6.

Table 5.24

Component Mix of the Highest Paying CPSE in Each Group

(in Rs.)

CPSEs	Scale	Basic Pay	Allowances	Retiral Benefits	Variable Pay	Total Pay (pm)
MINING SECTOR						
Coal & Lignite Group						
NLC	E2 (9850-250-14600)	9850	12474	3036	1754	27115
	E5 (16000-400-20800)	16000	19163	4282	1754	41199
	M5(20500-500-26500)	20500	30114	5193	1754	57561
Minerals & Metals Group						
NALCO	E0 (8600-4%-14600)	8600	12118	2782	5526	29026
	E3 (16000-4%-20800)	16000	23382	4281	5597	49260
	E8 (20500-4%-26500)	20500	27670	5192	5851	59213
MANUFACTURING SECTOR						
Petroleum Group						
BPCL	E1 (12000-17500)	12000	18089	3471	5836	39396
	E3 (16000-20800)	16000	24341	4281	8268	52890
	E8 (20500-26500)	20500	37507	5192	13399	76598
Power Group						
NTPC	E1(10750-4%-16750)	10750	17891	5218	4262	38121
	E4 (16000-4%-20800)	16000	23160	6281	6100	51541
	E8 (20500-4%-26500)	20500	37088	7692	7675	72956
Steel Group						
RINL	E0 (8600-250-14600)	8600	12395	2782	6328	30105
	E3 (16000-400-20800)	16000	19146	4281	6528	45955
	E8 (20500-500-26500)	20500	25767	5192	6188	57647
Transport Equipment Group						
HAL	E1 (8600-250-14600)	8600	17739	2782	5433	34554
	E5 (16000-400-20800)	16000	27843	4281	8167	56291
	E8 (20500-500-26500)	20500	41939	5192	10417	78048
Medium & Light Engineering Group						
BEL	E1 (8600-250-14600)	8600	14459	2782	1633	27474
	E5 (16000-400-20800)	16000	24483	4281	2867	47631
	E8 (20500-500-26500)	20500	34329	5192	3617	63638
Heavy Engineering Group						
BHEL	E1 (10750-450-16750)	10750	10629	3218	2583	27179
	E3 (16000-640-20800)	16000	18628	4281	2583	41492
	E7 (20000-800-25700)	20000	23410	5091	2916	51417
Fertilisers Group						
RCF	E1(8600-250-14600)	8600	13097	2782	1470	25949
	E5 (16000-400-20800)	16000	24108	4281	1470	45859
	E8 (20500-500-25000)	20500	30804	5192	1470	57966

contd...

...contd...

CPSEs	*Scale*	*Basic Pay*	*Allowances*	*Retiral Benefits*	*Variable Pay*	*Total Pay (pm)*
Textiles Group						
NTC (North Maharashtra)	E1(8600-250-14600)	8600	12835	2782	-	24217
	E5 (16000-400-20800)	16000	23657	4281	-	43938
	E8 (20500-500-26500)	20500	29521	5192	-	55213
Consumer Goods Group						
Hindustan Paper Corp.	E1(8600-250-14600)	8600	9187	2782	2150	22719
	E5 (16000-400-20800)	16000	17928	4281	4000	42209
	E8 (20500-500-26500)	20500	22899	5192	5125	53716
SERVICE SECTOR						
Trading & Marketing Group						
State Trading Corp.	E1(8600-250-14600)	8600	14403	3030	1290	27323
	E5 (16000-400-20800)	16000	24375	5113	2400	47888
	E8(20500-500-26500)	20500	34285	6391	3075	64251
Transportation Services Group						
Container Corporation	E0 (8600-250-14600)	8600	19899	2783	2124	33406
	E4 (16000-400-20800)	16000	28559	4282	3952	52793
	E8 (20500-500-26500)	20500	39614	5193	5064	70371
Contract & Construction Services Group						
IRCON	E1 (8600-250-14600)	8600	9228	2782	2041	22651
	E6 (17500-400-22300)	17500	19435	4585	3502	45022
	E8 (20500-500-22400)	20500	25379	5192	4136	55207
Industrial Development & Technical Consultancy Group						
Engineers India Ltd.	E1 (12000-17500)	12000	15613	3471	2062	33146
	E3 (16000-20800)	16000	20838	4281	2583	43702
	E8 (20500-26500)	20500	29429	5192	3169	58290
Financial Services Group						
HUDCO	E1(8600-250-14600)	8600	12910	2783	450	24733
	E5 (16000-400-20800)	16000	23215	4282	692	44189
	E7 (20500-500-25000)	20500	29561	5193	822	56077
Telecom & IT Group						
BSNL	E1A (9850-250-14600)	9850	13002	3035	-	25887
	E5 (16000-400-20800)	16000	20308	4281	-	40589
	E9 (23750-600-28550)	23750	29515	5851	-	59116

Figure 5.1

Junior Management

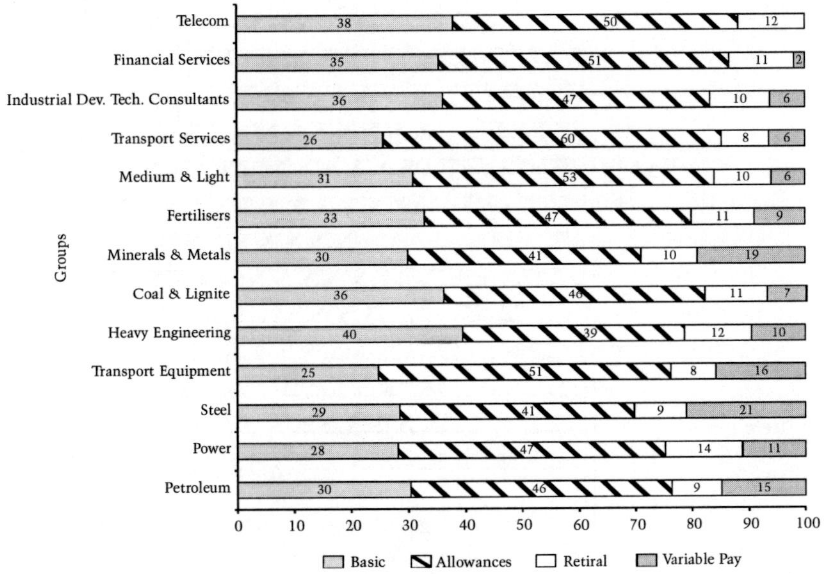

Figure 5.2

Middle Management

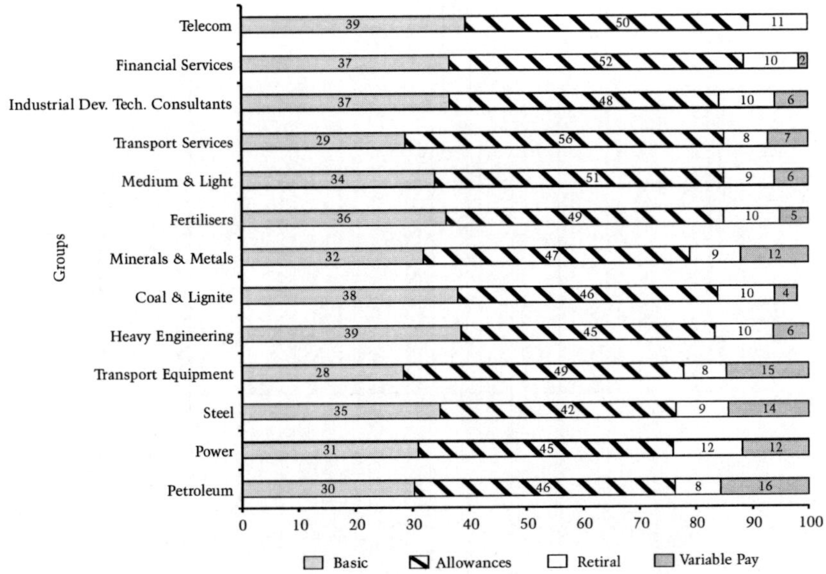

Figure 5.3

Senior Management

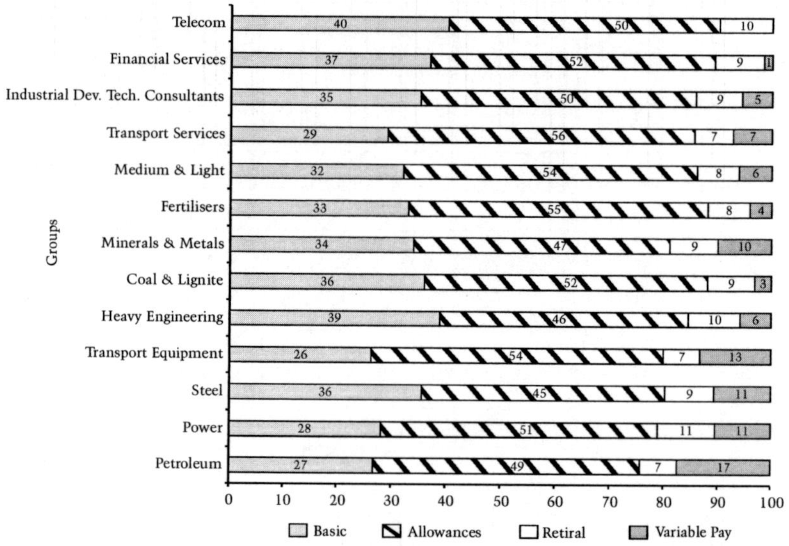

Figure 5.4

Inter-Sector Comparison of Emoluments among CPSEs
Lowest Paid and Highest Paid in Each Group: First Line Executives
(E1 Rs. 8600–14600)

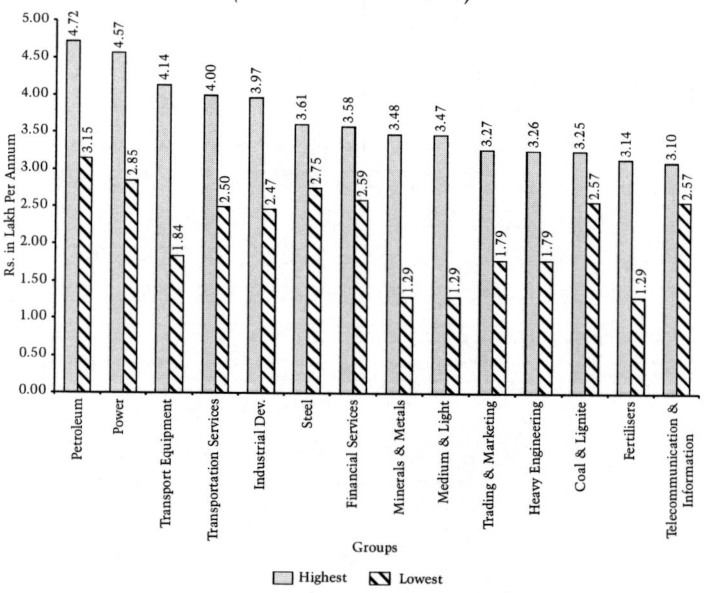

Figure 5.5

Middle Level Managers (E5 Rs. 16000-20800)

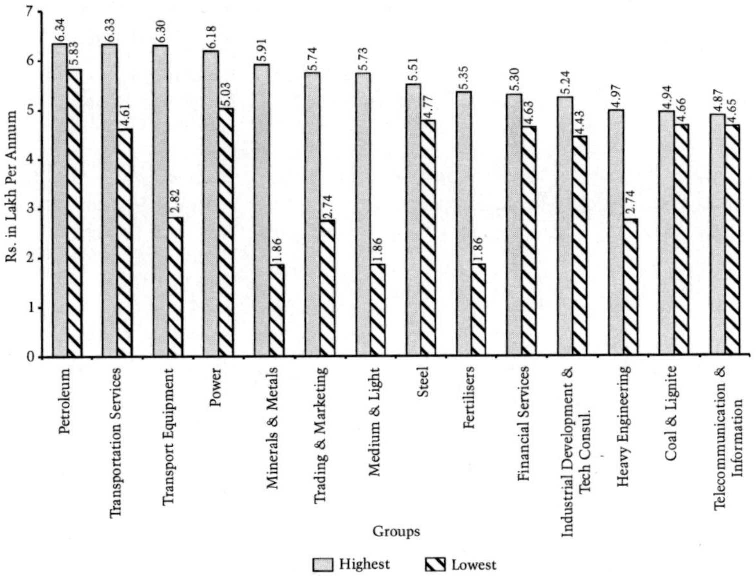

Figure 5.6

Senior Level Managers (E8 Rs. 20500-26500)

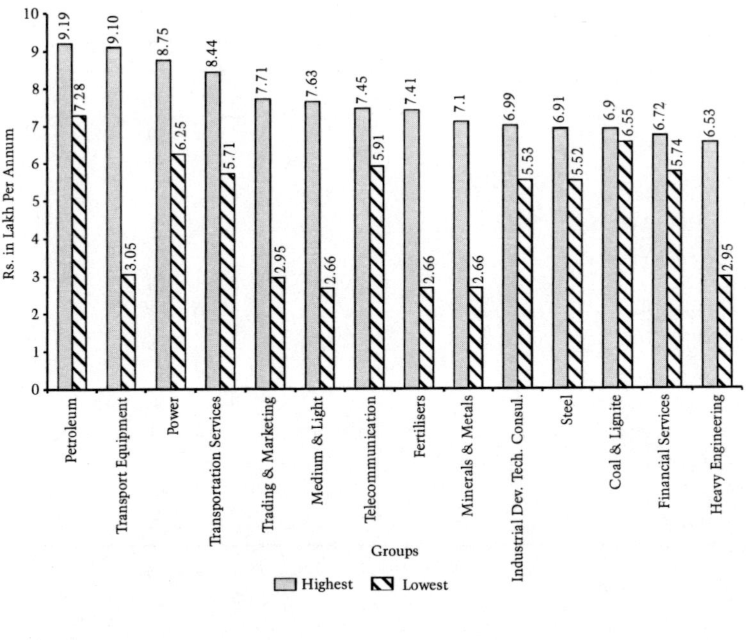

Table 5.25

Highest Paid and Lowest Paid: Group-wise

Group	*Highest Paid*	*Lowest Paid*
Petroleum	Bharat Petroleum Corp. Ltd.	Bongaigaon Refineries
Transport Equipment	Hindustan Aeronautics Ltd.	Hindustan Prefab Ltd.
Power	NTPC	National Hydro Electrical Power Corp.
Transportation Services	Container Corp. Of India Ltd.	Ennore Port Trust Ltd.
Medium & Light	Bharat Electronics Ltd.	National Instruments Ltd.
Trading & Marketing	State Trading Corp. of India Ltd.	Northern Eastern Handicrafts and Handloom Dev. Corp. Ltd.
Telecommunication	BSNL	RailTel
Fertilisers	National Fertilisers Ltd.	Hindustan Fertiliser Corpn. Ltd.
Minerals & Metals	NALCO	J&K Minerals Dev.
Industrial Dev. & Tech. Consul.	Engineers India Ltd.	National Small Industries Corpn. Ltd.
Steel	Rashtriya Ispat Nigam Ltd.	MIDHANI
Coal & Lignite	Neyveli Lignite Corp.	Bharat Coking Coal
Heavy Engineering	Bharat Heavy Electricals Ltd.	Heavy Engineering Corp. Ltd.
Financial Services	HUDCO	IREDA

From the above figures it could be observed that the percentage variation between the highest and the lowest paying CPSE is quite significant as detailed in Table 5.26.

Table 5.26

Percentage Variation between the Highest and the Lowest

Groups	*E1*	*E5*	*E8*
Petroleum	50	9	26
Power	60	23	40
Transport Equipment	125	123	208
Transportation Services	60	37	48
Industrial Dev. & Tech. Consul. Serv.	61	18	26
Steel	31	16	25
Financial Services	38	14	17
Minerals & Metals	170	218	167
Medium & Light Engg.	169	208	187
Trading & Marketing	83	109	161
Heavy Engineering	82	81	141
Coal & Lignite	26	6	5
Fertilisers	143	188	179
Telecommunication & Information	21	5	26

Further, it is seen that although the difference in the total emoluments between the best and the lowest paying CPSEs in each of these groups is wide, the trend of the ratios between E5 to E1 and E8 to E1 is not much different as can be seen from Table 5.27.

Public Enterprises Selection Board (PESB) is responsible for making selection to all the full-time board level positions in CPSEs (referred to as Presidential Appointments). Further, all the appointments at the board level are contractual in nature for a maximum tenure of 5 years at a time or normal age of superannuation which ever is earlier. If the left-over service as per the normal superannuation is more than 1 year after completion of the first term of 5 years, it is necessary for such incumbents to go through the PESB route *de novo* for reappointment. There were a few cases where such reappointments were not made. Consequently, such candidates unselected for reappointment were forced to leave the CPSEs, excepting those who maintained a lien in a below board level post in the same organisation or on a post in the earlier/parent organisation. Despite these special circumstances, no uniform scales are offered for these positions across the CPSEs and the scales of pay are linked to the schedule in which the concerned enterprises are categorised and the pay scales in operation in the concerned CPSEs.

Table 5.27

Highest Payers Comparison of Emoluments Including 'Valued Perks' for the Executives at Board Level

Group	*E1 (Rs. in Lakhs)*	*E5 (Rs. in Lakhs)*	*E8 (Rs. in Lakhs)*	*Ratio of E5:E1*	*Ratio of E8:E1*
Petroleum	4.72	6.34	9.19	1.34:1	1.95:1
Power	4.57	6.18	8.75	1.35:1	1.91:1
Transport Equipment	4.14	6.3	9.10	1.52:1	2.20:1
Transportation Services	4.00	6.33	8.44	1.58:1	2.11:1
Industrial Dev.	3.97	5.27	6.99	1.33:1	1.76:1
Steel	3.61	5.51	6.91	1.53:1	1.91:1
Financial Services	3.58	5.82	6.72	1.63:1	1.88:1
Minerals & Metals	3.48	5.91	7.10	1.70:1	2.04:1
Medium & Light	3.47	5.37	7.63	1.55:1	2.20:1
Trading & Marketing	3.27	5.74	7.71	1.76:1	2.36:1
Heavy Engineering	3.26	4.97	6.53	1.52:1	2.00:1
Coal & Lignite	3.25	4.94	6.90	1.52:1	2.12:1
Fertilisers	3.14	5.35	7.41	1.70:1	2.36:1
Telecommunication & Information	3.10	4.87	7.45	1.57:1	2.40:1

The ratio of pay and emoluments of CEOs in the loss-making CPSEs are even less than half of the emoluments of their counterparts in profit-making CPSEs, even compared at the minimum of the scales as detailed in Table 5.28.

It is generally observed that the difference of total emoluments between the maximum and minimum of the scale with 1997 pay revision is around one lakh as the number of increments in these scales is 6-8 only.

Table 5.28

Ratio of the Highest Paid CEOs: Lowest Paid CEOs at Minimum of Scale

(Rs. in lakhs)

Name of the CPSE	*Schedule*	*Highest Paid CEO*	*Name of the CPSE*	*Lowest Paid CEO*	*% of the Lowest Paid CEO to Highest Paid CEO*
Bharat Petroleum Corp. Ltd. (Highest)	A	13.55	HMT Ltd.(A)	6.09	
GAIL (India) Ltd.	A	13.01	Heavy Engineering Corporation Limited (A)	6.09	
NTPC Ltd.	A	12.97			
Average		13.18	Average	6.09	46.21
Chennai Petroleum Corp. Ltd.	B	11.75	Bharat Pumps and Compressors Limited (Estimated) (B)	5.66	
IRCON International Ltd.	B	11.46	Hindustan Steelworks Construction Ltd. (Estimated) (B)	5.66	
Satluj Jal Vidyut Nigam Limited	B	11.35	HMT (International) Ltd. (Estimated) (B)	5.66	
Average		11.52	Average	5.66	49.13
Indian Renewable Energy Dev. Agency Ltd.	C	9.84	HMT Bearings Ltd. (Estimated)	5.06	
Hindustan Latex Ltd.	C	9.90	Hindustan Salts Ltd. (Estimated)	5.06	
Water and Power Consultancy Ltd.	C	9.78	Northern Eastern Handicrafts and Handloom Dev. Corp. Ltd. (Estimated)	5.06	
Average		9.84	Average	5.06	51.42

It is understandable that the executives in the profit-making CPSEs are enthusiastically waiting with big expectations for a hefty hike in their emoluments after 10 years since the last pay revision was in the year 1997. While it is likely that the existing dearness allowance will be merged with basic pay (i.e., 100 per cent neutralisation of DA), it is obvious that a reasonable hike in the basic pay shall also be allowed as in the past, while formulating the revised scale effective from 1/1/2007. In such a case, the gap between the pay scales of these financially weak CPSEs and profit-making CPSEs would further increase. The number of executives and NUS working in the pre-revised scales is 3 per cent of the total number of such executives and NUS in the CPSEs as a whole.

Figure 5.7

Highest and Lowest Pay of CEOs in Schedule A, B and C CPSEs

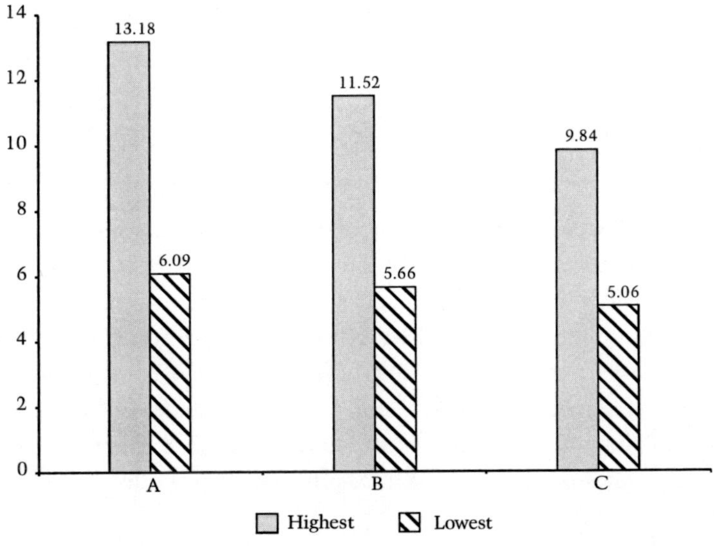

As per the Annual Report 2006-07 of the Ministry of Heavy Industries and Public Enterprise, "Normally the Chief Executive of the enterprise is given the scale of pay attached to the schedule of the company, while the functional Directors are allowed the scale of pay attached to the next below schedule. At times, the posts of Chief Executives or functional Directors are upgraded on personal basis so that exceptionally capable executives are retained in the CPSEs, where they have rendered meritorious service. Such arrangement also helps in attracting talent to sick/high tech enterprises." But in reality such upgradation is granted only in rare cases. It could be observed from a recent PESB notification for filling up of 69 vacancies in various CPSEs that even the scales of the CMDs/MDs/Directors in some of the CPSEs, which are still operating under 1992 or 1987 scales, are even less than the scale of E1 in the revised scales of 1997 as detailed in Table 5.29.

Table 5.29

Position-wise Schedule Offered in CPSEs

Name of CPSE	*Position*	*Schedule of CPSE*	*Scale Offered*
IDPL	Director (Marketing)	C	7500-200-8500
Tyre Corp. of India	CMD	B	8500-200-9500
Hindustan Fluro Carbons	MD	D	9000-300-10500
HMT Chinar Watches Ltd.	MD	C	10000-400-12000
Instrumentation Ltd.	Director	C	10000-400-12000
Burn Standard	Director (Eng.)	C	10000-400-12000
HMT Machine Tools	Director (Tech.)	C	10000-400-12000
Brathwate	Director (PPC.)	C	10000-400-12000
HEC	Director (Mkt.)	B	12000-400-14000
HMT International	MD	B	12000-400-14000
HMT Watches	MD	B	12000-400-14000

It would appear that the government has realised these problems and remedial measures are initiated. In the DPE OM No. 18(II)/2005-GM-GL-88 dated 24th July 2007, it has been stated that the tenure of board level executives who have contributed well in the turnaround of sick CPSEs, may be extended up to the age of 65 years. It has also been decided by the government that chief executive and functional directors of these CPSEs would be considered for a lumpsum incentive up to a maximum of Rs. 10 lakh of the profits out of the CPSE, besides usual pay allowances and perks attached to the post.

It is important to note that the number of board level positions is too small (i.e., around 700 as shown in Table 5.30), compared to the total number of executives in various CPSEs which is more than 3 lakh.

Table 5.30

Schedule-wise Number of Board Level Position

Schedule	*CEOs*	*Functional Directors*
'A'	52	-
'B'	87	194
'C'	54	209
'D'	7	68
Total	200	471

Source: DPE's Annual Survey 2005-06.

In the present era of corporate transparency and collective responsibility at the board level, the board level executives are liable to punitive actions under various provisions of the Companies Act in specific, apart from many other laws relating to the corporate world. Also, it is well known that the senior executives/board level appointees in sick/incipient sick companies have to face more odds and hardships.

The common privilege extended to board level appointees is their eligibility for two valued perks *viz.*: (a) provision of leased accommodation in case the company does not have its own accommodation or facility of self-lease in case of owning house by the incumbent, and (b) provision of staff car along with the facility of use of the same for private purposes also, up to certain specified distances at a specified rate of recovery. Further as per the existing practices in the concerned CPSE, these board level executives are generally allowed for reimbursement of certain out of pocket expenses incurred which are inherently related to the position they hold. Also, they are allowed to become members of two clubs. Considering these special privileges, it is considered prudent to add an appropriate amount towards these "valued perks" to work out a reasonable but uniform estimate of "cost to company". In the case of CEO of schedule 'A', the maximum permissible amount for self-leased accommodation is Rs. 19500 and it is Rs. 18500 in the case of schedule 'B' appointees. Based on this assumption, and the estimated value of Rs. 10,000 towards staff car facility (for private use) and a few special reimbursements which are related to the position including club memberships, a uniform amount of Rs. 35,000 for CEO and Rs. 30,000 for other directors per month in the case of schedule 'A' companies have been taken in to account as the valued perquisites in these workings. Similarly in the case of schedule 'B' enterprises, the valued perks were considered at Rs. 30,000 for CEO and Rs. 25,000 for other directors.

The sum and substance of all the responses and representations by the officers' associations is for granting sizeable increase in the pay and allowances, primarily to the top, senior and middle level executives, to exterminate migration and losing of talent. In the responses received against DPE questionnaire and during the presentations made by the officers' associations, a parity of 1:5 between the first line executive and the CEO, and 15/20:1 in the case of CEO to lowest workmen have been suggested. The Justice Mohan Committee had suggested a ratio of 4:1 between the highest paid officer and the lowest paid officer and 10:1 ratio between the CEO and the lowest workmen. Table 5.31 clearly reflects the gap between the expectations and the existing ground reality.

Table 5.31

CPSE-wise Annual Compensation

Group	*Highest CEO Salary*	*Highest Paid First Line Executive*	*Ratio of Pay of CEOs: First Line Executives*	*Per Capita Emoluments*	*Ratio of CEO: Per Capita Emoluments*
Petroleum	13.55	4.72	2.87:1	5.18	2.62:1
Power	12.97	4.57	2.84:1	2.95	4.40:1
Coal & Lignite	11.12	3.25	3.42:1	2.23	4.99:1
Telecom. & IT Services	10.62	3.10	3.43:1	2.46	4.32:1
Steel	11.78	3.61	3.26:1	3.05	3.86:1
Transport Equipment	12.16	4.00	3.04:1	2.75	4.42:1
Trading & Marketing Service	11.70	3.27	3.58:1	2.85	4.11:1
Medium & Light Engineering	11.29	3.47	3.25:1	2.38	4.74:1
Heavy Engineering	11.71	3.26	3.59:1	3.93	2.98:1

Note: Per capita emoluments are considered in the absence of data of the lowest paid work man.

6 Compensation Packages of CPSE Executives and Central Government Officers

Introduction

For historical reasons, there has been some linkage between the pay scales of employees of the Central government and CPSEs. Even in the matter of dearness allowance (DA) and other allowances and perks, some sort of similarity existed between these two sectors.

The CPSEs are under the administrative control of the concerned ministry/department of the Government of India and the chief executive of the CPSE administratively reports to the secretary of the concerned department. Considering the mechanics of decision-making and the business environment in which the chief executives are to operate, Justice Mohan Committee (First Pay Revision Committee for CPSEs) recommended a relativity of 1.12:1 between the CEOs of Schedule 'A' CPSEs and the secretary to the Government of India. The pay structure and other allowances for other employees of CPSEs were structured almost similar to the government scales at the entry level and calibrated upwards suitably to provide for career progression. Depending on the financial strengths of the CPSEs and also based on the need to attract talent, some CPSEs like NTPC, BPCL, IOC, ONGC and BHEL, are offering higher starts to entry level officers. Of late, some CPSEs have started offering advance increments at the start up stage itself.

The total manpower in CPSEs as at end 2005-06 stood at 16.48 lakh (with around 3 lakh of executives and NUS) as compared to 34.34 lakh Central government employees (excluding defence personnel).

Pay Scales in Government

In the Central government, there are 34 pay scales (S1 to S34) as recommended by the Fifth Central Pay Commission. Out of them, 23 scales (S12 to S34) relate to officer grades. In the central secretariat, the officers' cadre starts at section officer (S12-Rs. 6500-200-10500). The other grades include assistant director (S15-Rs. 8000-275-13500), under secretary (S19-Rs. 10000-325-15200), deputy secretary (S21-Rs. 12000-375-16500), director (S24-Rs. 14300-400-18300), joint secretary (S29-Rs. 18400-500-22400), additional secretary (S30-Rs. 22400-525-24500), secretary (S33-Rs. 26000 fixed) and cabinet secretary (S34-Rs. 30000 fixed).

The pay scales of CPSEs are outlined in Chapter 4 titled 'Compensation in CPSEs'.

Allowances

Dearness Allowance (DA) and Dearness Pay (DP): In the case of Central government employees, DA as announced by the government from time to time is applicable. The government had converted 50 per cent of DA as DP with effect from 1-4-2004. The said DP is treated as a part of basic pay for all purposes including for accrual of DA. The leftover DA (i.e., after conversion of 50 per cent of basic pay as DP) is 35 per cent as on 1-1-2007.

The DA under the IDA scheme stands at 68.8 per cent (without any DA conversion) as on 1.1.2007. The DA to the executives of CPSEs, covered by the CDA scheme will be same as that of Central government. DA is revised once in six months for Central government employees whereas it is revised once in three months for CPSE employees. The AICPI for industrial workers is the basis for revision of DA for both. However, for government, the averaging is done for preceding 12 months while for CPSEs it is done once in three months.

House Rent Allowance (HRA): The HRA rates vary from 5 per cent to 30 per cent depending upon the place of posting. In the case of joint secretary, additional secretary and secretary, HRA has been considered as 30 per cent, since most of them are located in A1 cities like Delhi and Mumbai. However, as the posting of the other officers of the Central government is scattered all over the country, it is felt appropriate to adopt HRA at the rate of 15 per cent of pay including DP. The housing accommodation facilities for employees of both CPSEs and government are to a large extent similar in terms of company/government quarters. In those cases where quarters are not available, the employees of government are paid HRA, as a percentage of basic pay + DP in varying amounts depending on the place of work.

In respect of CPSEs, the rules pertaining to HRA are similar in terms of percentages excepting HRA is worked out on the actual basic pay only. Further, the senior executives of CPSEs at the board level have the options of staying in company leased accommodation or if they so choose, self-leasing their own houses where available. These facilities are also extended to some more levels of executives by some select CPSEs—depending on their financial strengths.

City Compensatory Allowance (CCA): The rates notified by Central government and DPE towards CCA are same. It varies from Rs. 25 to Rs. 300. However, a uniform rate of Rs. 180 per month is adopted, as in the case of CPSEs, and for officers below the rank of joint secretary, for ease of calculations.

Leave Travel Concession (LTC): As per the existing rules, the government employees as well as the employees of CPSEs are entitled to LTC facilities under which they can visit their hometown along with family once in a block of two years and to anywhere in India once in a block of four years. In the case of government, the LTC facility has to be utilised and reimbursement obtained and no encashment of LTC is permitted.

In the case of CPSE employees, depending on the financial health of the CPSEs, the LTC facility is enhanced in varying modes from CPSE to CPSE in respect of type of travel and payment of special allowances. Further, encashment of LTC is permitted in CPSEs. Some CPSEs have, however, suspended this facility because of financial constraints.

Medical Facilities: The Central government employees along with members of their family are covered under the Central Government Health Scheme (CGHS) under which they are provided with medical treatment and medicines in the CGHS dispensaries for which a prescribed amount is deducted as contribution from their pay every month.

In most of the CPSEs, where townships exist, hospital facilities also are created for the employees. In other cases, reimbursements are permitted for treatment as in-patients in select hospitals. In respect of treatments as out-patients and for diagnostics, varying practices are being adopted that range from 100 per cent reimbursement in designated hospitals to prescribed payments in other hospitals.

Conveyance Reimbursement/Transport Allowance: Central government employees (gazetted) are paid an amount ranging from Rs. 400 to Rs. 800 per month towards transport allowance. However, officers of the rank of joint secretary and additional secretary has an option to avail of the facility of using staff car for pickup from residence to office and drop back, in lieu of the transport allowance. In the case of secretary, staff car is provided. Usage of staff car for personal use is also possible subject to payments on a kilometre basis for additional secretary and joint secretary and per month basis to secretary for prescribed limits of usage.

In CPSEs, various amounts are paid to the executives as conveyance reimbursement. In respect of senior officials (board level executives in all cases and other senior executives in some cases), company transport is provided with the facility of using the transport for personal purposes to a limited degree.

Children Educational Assistance: Central government employees get a reimbursement for the education of their children subject to a maximum of Rs. 50 per child per month limited to 2 children.

The children education expenditure is reimbursable in CPSEs. The rate of reimbursement varies from Rs. 50 to Rs. 250 per child per month.

Newspapers/Periodicals: Central government employees are permitted reimbursement of expenses incurred for purchase of newspapers subject to ceilings.

The CPSEs pay varying amounts for purchase of newspapers and magazines by their executives.

Other Allowances

Risk Allowance: Central government employees engaged in duties involving significant occupational hazards or whose health is liable to be adversely affected progressively over a long period of time are allowed a risk allowance. The amount is Rs. 300 per month for gazetted officers and Rs. 180 per month for non-gazetted officers engaged in hazardous operations.

Similar allowance is paid to employees of CPSEs also. The amounts vary from case to case depending on the nature of work and location of work.

Special Allowance: Government officers, posted at project sites and specially designated places like northeastern region, Sikkim, etc., are paid project/special allowances.

Executives of CPSEs posted at project sites, etc., are also paid project allowances as prescribed by the respective CPSEs.

As these allowances are paid to only those persons who are engaged in hazardous operations or posted in project/difficult areas, these are not included for the purpose of working out total compensation.

Retirement Benefits

While in the case of government employees retiral benefits are in the nature of pension and gratuity, in the case of CPSE employees it is in the nature of contributory provident fund (CPF) and gratuity.

Pension: The government employees who joined service before 1.1.2004 are covered under the old pension scheme under which they get a monthly pension equivalent to 50 per cent of basic pay plus DP with admissible dearness relief (DR), provided they have put in a qualifying service of 33 years in Central government. If the qualifying service is less than 33 years but more than 10 years, pension is calculated on *pro rata* basis. In case an employee dies, the spouse gets half the pension as family pension. Pension element of government employees is worked out on the basis of government instructions according to which monthly pension contribution varies from 7 per cent to 23 per cent of the maximum of the pay scale depending upon the years of service a government employee renders. Keeping the above in mind, for the purpose of this study 10 per cent of the basic pay has been considered in the cases of section officer to under secretary level, 15 per cent in the cases of deputy secretary and director, 20 per cent in the case of joint secretary, 22 per cent in the case of additional secretary and 23 per cent in the case of secretary.

The old pension scheme has since been modified and it has been made mandatory for all new recruits to the Central government from 1-1-2004 to join new pension scheme known as 'Defined Contribution Pension Scheme (DCPS)'. According to this scheme, the government servant has to make a contribution of 10 per cent of his basic pay plus DA which will be deducted from the salary of the concerned employee, every month. The government will make an equal matching contribution. The pension scheme will be managed by pension fund managers.

Employees in CPSEs are covered under the employees' pension scheme of 1995. The contributions to the employee pension scheme by the company are from CPF. No additional contribution is made by the enterprise. This pension, however, is a small amount, the maximum of which is Rs. 1800 per month only. However, some CPSEs have taken special steps to provide higher levels of pension amounts through bilateral contributions managed by designated actuaries.

Provident Fund: Central government employees are covered under the General Provident Fund (GPF) rules. While the employees contribute 6 per cent or more of emoluments to GPF, there is no contribution by the government.

However, in the case of CPSEs, the enterprises contribute 12 per cent of the basic pay plus DA, as a matching contribution to the CPF.

Gratuity: Gratuity is paid at the time of retirement/separation at the rate of one-fourth of emoluments for each completed six monthly period of qualifying service subject to a maximum of 16 ½ times of emoluments or Rs. 3.50 lakh, whichever is less. The system of payment is same for CPSEs and government.

Medical Facilities: The employees along with their families can continue to avail the CGHS facilities for lifetime after retirement by paying 10 years contribution in one lumpsum at the time of retirement. This benefit is available to those retired employees who continue to reside in state capitals or a few other important cities like Allahabad, Kanpur, Nagpur and Pune where CGHS dispensaries exist. For others, an amount of Rs. 100 per month is paid along with pension.

Barring few exceptions—limited to financially strong CPSEs—post-retiral medical benefits are not available to CPSE employees/executives.

Salaries of Government Employees

Based on the elements of pay and allowances of government officers detailed above, typical salary levels for some select grades are computed and tabulated at the minimum of the scales (Table 6.1).

The salary levels, if computed at the maximum of the pay scale will be higher by around 43 per cent at S12 grade and 8.5 per cent at S30 grade. The differentials will lie in between for other grades. Similar information in respect of CPSE executives is given in Chapter 5.

Comparative Analysis

Based on the above data and the compensation details of CPSEs elaborated in Chapter 4, the similarities and differences between Central government and CPSEs can be summarised as under:

Similarities

Both the officers of Central government and the executives of CPSEs have structured pay scales.

The pay scales of both CPSE employees and government employees are revised periodically.

Aspects Favourable to Government Employees

Pay Revision: When a pay revision takes place in the Central government, it is applicable to all the employees across the country and the revision comes into effect immediately from the prescribed date.

In respect of CPSEs, only those CPSEs which can absorb the extra expenditure on account of pay revision without depending on budgetary support from the government, can implement pay revisions. On account of non-affordability, 42 CPSEs have not yet implemented the pay revision of 1997, 28 are continuing with 1992 pay scales and 14 with 1987 pay scales.

Table 6.1

Estimated Salaries of Government Officers

Particulars	*S12 Section Officer 6500-10500*	*S15 Asst. Dir. 8000-13500*	*S19 Under Sec. 10000-15200*	*S21 Dy. Sec. 12000-16500*	*S24 Director 14300-18300*	*S29 Jt. Sec. 18400-22400*	*S30 Add. Sec. 22400-24500*	*S33 Secretary 26000 Fixed*
Basic Pay (BP)	6500	8000	10000	12000	14300	18400	22400	26000
Dearness Pay 50% (DP)	3250	4000	5000	6000	7150	9200	11200	13000
Dearness Allowance (DA) = 35% of (BP+DP)	3413	4200	5250	6300	7508	9660	11760	13650
BP+DP+DA	13163	16200	20250	24300	28958	37260	45360	52650
HRA**	1463	1800	2250	2700	3218	4140	10080	11700
CCA	180	180	180	180	180	300	300	300
LTC	500	500	500	500	500	1000	1000	1000
Transport Allowance	400	800	800	800	800	800	800	*
Newspaper	75	75	75	75	75	150	150	225
Children Education Allowance	100	100	100	100	100	100	*	*
Pension Contribution	975	1200	1500	2700	3145	4140	6720	8970
Gratuity	500	500	500	500	500	500	500	500
Total for Month	17356	21355	26155	31855	37476	48390	64910	75345
Total Annual (Rs. Lakhs)	2.08	2.56	3.13	3.82	4.49	5.81	7.78	9.04

Note: Pension is estimated at 10% of the basic pay in the cases of section officer to under secretary, 15% in the cases of deputy secretary and director, 20% in the cases of joint secretary, 22% in the case of additional secretary and 23% in the case of secretary.

** HRA is taken as 15% for officers up to director and 30% for joint secretary and above.

* For joint secretary and additional secretary; an option is given for availing staff car for drop from residence to office and back in the staff car, in lieu of the transport allowance.

[The Supreme Court has ruled on 25th April 2003 that "the employees of the Government Companies are not civil servants and therefore, they have no legal right to claim that Government should pay their salary". It also further observed that economic viability or financial capability of the employer company should be taken in to consideration in the matter of revision of pay scales of the employees.]

Pension: The government employees who joined service before 1-1-2004 are covered under the pension schemes under which they get a pension equivalent to 50 per cent of basic pay and DP with admissible dearness relief (DR). Under the family pension scheme, 50 per cent of the pension is paid to the spouse in the event of the demise of the pensioner.

The employees of CPSEs are covered under the CPF and they do not get pension like government employees. However, this difference is not applicable in respect of Government employees who have joined service after 1.1.2004. The conditions for both CPSEs and officers have become similar.

Medical Benefits after Retirement: The Central government employees along with members of their family are covered under the Central Government Health Scheme (CGHS) under which they are provided with medical treatment and medicines in the CGHS dispensaries even after retirement, by paying 10 years contribution in one lumpsum at the time of retirement. This benefit is available to only those pensioners who continue to stay in major cities where CGHS dispensaries exist.

In most of the CPSEs, medical benefits after retirement is not available.

Guaranteed Payments: Government employees get their pay regularly without fail.

Loss-making and sick CPSEs are not able to ensure similar prompt payments every month to their employees.

Other issues that have a bearing on the emoluments of the government officers and CPSE executives, slated in favour of the government officers are:

a. Differentiation in the taxation of perks for the housing accommodation provided.

b. Interest subsidy on loans taken by CPSE executives for housing and vehicles.

   (where such facilities are extended by a limited number of CPSEs in lieu of house building advances and car loans by the enterprise attracts income tax while the loans given by the government for houses and vehicles do not attract any tax)

c. Retirement age in respect of Central government and most of the CPSEs is 60 while it is 58 in some sick and financially unviable CPSEs.

Aspects Favourable to the Executives of CPSEs

Flexibility in Payment of Various Allowances: CPSEs have flexibility in regard to payment of various types of perquisites and allowances to their executives, subject to the condition that the total of all such allowances, excluding DA, CCA and HRA, should not exceed 50 per cent of the basic pay.

Variable Pay: CPSEs can pay various performance incentives and sharing of profit is also allowed up to 5 per cent of the distributable profits of the concerned enterprise. In respect of industrial/commercial activities managed departmentally, like railways, postal services, defence production activities of ordnance factories, employees are eligible for productivity linked bonus.

Operation of Higher Grades: Some of the CPSEs are offering higher scales to their junior executives than those notified by DPE or granting additional increments across the board as an incentive to attract/ retain talent.

a. Release of DA instalments on quarterly basis.
b. Interest subsidy on loans taken for housing and vehicles.
c. Increments as a percentage of basic pay in a few CPSEs.
d. LTC encashment.
e. Encashment of earned leave every year.

Facilities like club memberships, liberal entertainment allowance, etc., to board level executives.

Comparison between Executives of CPSEs and Government Employees

As the number of pay scales for officers in government is almost double the number of pay scales for executives in the CPSEs, grade to grade comparison is not possible. Nevertheless, notionally the executives in the CPSEs are compared on the premise that the pay scales of CEO of Schedule 'A' CPSE is comparable with that of a secretary to the Government of India. Table 6.2 attempts to draw comparison between select government pay scales and equivalent scales in IDA governed CPSEs.

Table 6.2

Comparison of Pay Scales of Government Officers with CPSE Executives

Government	*Scales*	*CPSE Pay Scale under IDA*	*Grade*
6500-200-10500 Section Officer	S12	6500-200-11350	E0
8000-275-13500 Assistant Director	S15	8600-250-14600	E1
10000-325-15200 Under Secretary	S19	10750-300-16750	E2
12000-375-16500 Dy. Secretary	S21	13000-350-18250 14500-350-18700	E3 E4
14300-400-18300 Director	S24	16000-400-20800 17500-400-22300 18500-450-23900 20500-500-26500	E5 E6 E7 E8
18400-500-22400 Jt. Secretary	S29	22500-600-27300 23750-600-28550	Sch. 'C' E9
22400-525-24500 Additional Secretary	S30	25750-650-30950	Sch. 'B'
26000 (Fixed) Secretary	S33	27750-750-31500	Sch. 'A'

Table 6.3 attempts to compare the salary levels (at minimum scale) of government officers and CPSE executives belonging to: (a) financially strong CPSE, (b) average but profit-making CPSE, and (c) below average (loss-making CPSE).

Table 6.3

Comparison between Government Officers and Executives of CPSEs

(Rs. in lakhs)

Central Government		*CPSEs—Annual Compensation*			
Scale & Designation	*Annual Compensation*	*Grade*	*BPCL*	*NMDC*	*ITI*
6500-200-10500 (S12) Section Officer	2.08	E0	-	-	2.00
8000-275-13500 (S15) Assistant Director	2.56	E1	4.72	3.16	2.55
10000-325-15200 (S19) Under Secretary	3.13	E2	5.35	3.83	3.12
12000-375-16500 (S21) Dy. Secretary	3.82	E3 E4	6.34 7.03	4.59 5.39	3.89 4.30
14300-400-18300 (S24) Director	4.49	E5 E6 E7 E8	7.43 7.69 7.96 9.19	5.78 6.06 6.23 6.42	4.70 5.10 5.37 5.90
18400-500-22400 (S29) Jt. Secretary	5.81	E9	10.31	6.73	6.78
22400-525-24500 (S30) Addl. Secretary	7.78	Sch. B	12.33	10.24	8.60
26000 Fixed (S33) Secretary	9.04	Sch. A	13.55	11.30	9.67

Note: 1. In the case of CPSE scales of Rs. 27750-750-31500 and Rs. 25750-650-30950, valued perks of Rs. 35000 and 30000 respectively per month have been included towards leased accommodation/ self-lease, staff car and other special perks attached to the position held.

2. Entry level (after one year training) in respect of BPCL executive starts at Rs. 12000 as against Rs. 8600 in NMDC and ITI.

7 Compensation in Private Sector

Sources of Data

By tradition and practice, the issue of compensation is treated as a very confidential subject in the private sector. IPE had to depend on multiple sources for collecting and compiling authentic and dependable information needed to compare compensation levels of CPSEs executives with those of comparable private sector companies.

The popular business magazines *Business Today* and *Business World* have carried articles on compensation details of executives from entry level/ junior management cadres to senior management cadres in various industrial sectors. The BT surveys were published on December 31, 2006 for junior management, February 11, 2007 for middle management and April 8, 2007 for senior management. The *Business World* survey appeared in the issue of 5th February 2007.

IPE had on-to-one meetings with HR and recruitment consultants, HR chiefs and directors of private companies, present and past employees of private companies; collected information available from public domains like business press and websites and compiled information from annual reports to the extent possible for remuneration details of board level executives. Attempt was made to correlate and compare the data obtained from these sources to check the dependability and veracity for using the same for comparison with salaries of CPSE executives.

In brief, the basic data included in this study is based on the following:

- Salary survey conducted by Omam Consultants published by *Business Today.*
- Salary survey conducted by Gallup Team published by *Business World.*

- Salary information put on website by *paycheck.in.*
- CEO/director's remuneration details based on study conducted by *Business India.*
- Information collected by IPE through personal interactions.

Compensation in Private Sector

While uniformity has been, by and large, the guiding principle for pay fixation of CPSE executives, differentiation is the driving force for compensation in private sector. This differentiation is generated through the nature of business, the size of the business and the profitability of the business.

Another and more important differentiating factor is the performance of the individual and his or her contribution to wealth generation of the enterprise—as assessed by the organisation's systems.

The third factor that is influencing the compensation levels of the private sector executives is the demand-supply situation in talent. Apart from the fierce competition amongst the private sector players, there is the competition to be reckoned with the MNCs operating in the country where salary levels are decidedly more than the private sector companies. Further, it is also to be noted that India has become a hub for recruitment for postings abroad—especially for the intellectually intensive jobs.

The differentiation in the private sector compensation is also reflected in pronounced terms with the functional responsibilities of the executive.

The data gathered through the sources outlined above corroborates the differentiation structures mentioned above.

Business Today (BT) Survey

The BT reports, based on the work carried out by Rajeev Kumar, Anil Kaul and Ashutosh Kumar of Omam Consultants provide extensive coverage of compensation details based on survey of 102 private companies encompassing 14 sectors. The sectors covered include IT, ITE/BPO, telecom, engineering, automotive, core (power, metals, etc.), pharmaceuticals, chemicals/petrochemicals/fertilisers, textiles, FMCG, consumer goods, banking, retail and real estate. The minimum sample size in each sector is 5 and the maximum 10.

The companies covered are stated to be 'good', 'average' and 'below average' insofar as compensation is concerned and therefore, the average salary levels can be taken as median figures of the respective sectors for the purpose of comparison and analysis. The samples chosen for the study also cover all the zones of the country and comprise a good mix in terms of size and profitability. For obvious reasons, the names of the companies are not revealed but personal discussions revealed that the information can be taken as very representative and authentic.

The cadres covered are segregated into six groups namely junior management 2 and 1 (JM_2 & JM_1), middle management 2 and 1 (MM_2 & MM_1), senior management 2 and 1 (SM_2 & SM_1)—covering the employees from the entry level to senior management positions (below board level).

Executives at the JM_2 level are stated to be frontline executives who have put in 1-1½ years of service after joining the organisation. Typically, the designations of those executives will be assistant manager/senior executives/executives. Junior management executives at the JM_1 level can be considered as heads of small sections—typically designated as manager/deputy manager. Middle management cadres at MM_2 and MM_1 levels can be mapped as sub-functional heads and departmental heads. Typically, designations of MM_2 category of executives will read as senior manager or manager and they will be heading medium sized departments and sections. Executives in the MM_1 category are those who head large departments carrying typical designations like dy. general manager/assistant general manager and senior manager in some cases. Senior management positions are those of executives holding charge of functions and units below board level. Executives in the category of SM_2 hold the number two position in a major function or head relatively smaller functions. Typical designations read as senior general manager/general manager. The SM_1 cadre represents executives one level below managing directors/CEOs and who carry responsibilities for overall operational planning and execution of a functional division. Typically, designations will read as senior vice-president/vice-president.

The elements of compensation packages covered in the survey, break-up into: (i) Basic pay, (ii) Benefits and reimbursements like special allowance, HRA, educational allowance, utility allowance, leave travel allowance, medical reimbursement, conveyance allowances, etc., (iii) Variable pay linked to performance, (iv) Retirals, and (v) Valued perks.

The data contained in this survey is summarised in the following tables:

Table 7.1 indicates the average salaries of executives across the 14 sectors and the 6 grades to highlight the salary differentials among various sectors.

Tables 7.1(a) and 7.1(b) indicate the minimum and maximum salaries of executives in different cadres of management within the sample companies chosen, across the sectors covered in the survey, both in terms of absolute ranges and their percentages. Substantial variations exist in the salary structures in each grade not only across the sectors but also within each sector.

Sectoral Differentials

The stupendous growth in the services sector, the BT report observes, is creating problems for the manufacturing and engineering sectors. An executive working in the IT and telecom company is certainly making twice as much as his counterpart working in the textile or engineering sector. These differentials cause definite gravitation towards the more lucrative and attractive services sector jobs. The locational advantages of the IT/ITE sectors also add to the attraction. The need to attract and retain talent is forcing the managements to continuously hike the compensation packages. The ranges—even at the average values—indicate the desperate efforts of the industry to attract talent at the junior levels and retain the same at the middle and senior levels. A scrutiny of Table 7.1 reveals the following:

Entry and Front Level Managers:

- At the entry and frontline levels (JM_2), the salary levels range from Rs. 2.63 lakh per annum to Rs. 5.59 lakh per annum.

- The textile sector appears to be paying the least, followed closely by the engineering industry and the retail sector.
- The best paymasters appear to be the fast moving consumer goods (FMCG), automotive and IT sectors in that order.
- The trend in the next grade (JM_1) also almost follows the same pattern—with telecom sector occupying position 2 in place of automotive sector.

Middle Level Managers:

- In respect of middle management cadres (MM_2 & MM_1), there is a considerable shift in the rankings.
- The three top positions in MM_2 grade are occupied by ITES/BPO, banking and FMCG respectively.
- The last three positions go to engineering, textiles and core sectors.
- In respect of MM_1 grades, the first three positions are held by FMCG, banking and automotive sectors while the last three positions are similar to MM_2—barring the fact that textile and engineering sectors swap positions.

Senior Level Managers:

- In respect to senior management cadres (SM_2 & SM_1), the profiles appear to be almost similar to the JM_1 profile with few exceptions.
- In SM_2 cadre, FMCG, automotive and banking sectors occupy the first three positions while the last three positions are held by engineering, textile and core sectors—in that order.
- In the case of SM_1 cadre, the first position is held again by FMCG, the second by consumer durables and the third by automotive sector.
- Engineering sector again stands last, followed by textile and real estate sector in SM_1 cadre.

To sum up, by and large, across the grades, it can be stated that:

- FMCG and automotive sectors are seen as the top paymasters.
- IT, telecom and banking sectors form the next higher layer.
- Engineering and textile sectors form the lowest rung, with other sectors falling in between.

Table 7.1

Average Salary Levels of Executives across the Sectors (Inter-Sectoral)

(Annual CTC Rs. in lakhs)

S.No.	Sector	Sample Size	Junior Management		Middle Management		Senior Management	
			JM_2 Asst.Mgr/Sr. Executive/Exe.	JM_1 Manager/Dy. Manager	MM_2 Sr.Mgr/ Manager	MM_1 DGM/Asst. GM/Sr.Mgr.	SM_2 Sr.GM/ GM	SM_1 Sr. VP/ VP
1	FMCG	6	5.59_{1}	8.52_{1}	14.54_{3}	23.07_{1}	39.90_{1}	66.67_{1}
2	Automotive	9	5.41_{2}	8.12_{3}	13.44_{4}	21.93_{3}	33.25_{2}	48.45_{3}
3	IT	9	4.58_{3}	7.82_{4}	12.31_{7}	17.93_{8}	24.37_{9}	35.13_{9}
4	Telecom	5	4.52_{4}	8.14_{2}	13.02_{5}	19.82_{6}	28.00_{5}	38.40_{6}
5	Banking	5	4.49_{5}	6.32_{8}	15.07_{2}	22.66_{2}	31.54_{3}	44.47_{5}
6	Petrochemicals etc.	7	4.12_{6}	6.60_{7}	11.03_{8}	16.24_{10}	24.00_{10}	34.83_{10}
7	Pharmaceuticals	8	4.00_{7}	7.19_{5}	12.39_{6}	20.48_{4}	31.09_{4}	47.06_{4}
8	Consumer durables	10	3.93_{8}	6.77_{6}	10.65_{10}	17.91_{9}	27.13_{7}	48.93_{2}
9	Core	9	3.50_{9}	5.42_{9}	7.49_{12}	11.48_{12}	19.30_{12}	30.51_{11}
10	ITES/BPO	5	3.33_{10}	5.20_{12}	15.29_{1}	20.00_{5}	27.80_{6}	38.40_{7}
11	Real Estate	8	3.13_{11}	5.22_{11}	8.32_{11}	13.26_{11}	21.66_{11}	29.63_{12}
12	Retail	5	2.96_{12}	5.27_{10}	11.02_{9}	19.55_{7}	25.76_{8}	36.55_{8}
13	Engineering	9	2.95_{13}	4.23_{13}	6.95_{14}	11.07_{13}	17.39_{14}	25.47_{14}
14	Textile		2.63_{14}	3.97_{14}	7.25_{13}	12.51_{14}	18.62_{13}	27.92_{13}

Note: The subscripts indicate the relative positions of different sectors as paymasters.

Source: Based on Omam Survey reports carried by *Business Today*.

Table 7.1(a)

Differentials between Minimum and Maximum Salaries across Sectors (Intra-Sectoral)

(In Terms of Absolute Range)

(Annual CTC in Rs. lakhs)

Sectors	JM_2			JM_1			MM_2		
	Min.	*Max.*	*Range*	*Min.*	*Max.*	*Range*	*Min.*	*Max.*	*Range*
FMCG	5	6.73	1.73	6.88	9.75	2.87	12.99	15.7	2.71
Automotive	4.63	6.61	1.98	6.6	10.37	3.77	8.78	19.84	11.06
IT	3.43	5.44	2.01	6.57	9.32	2.75	9.28	14.15	4.87
Telecom	3.28	5.6	2.32	5.5	10.89	5.39	10.61	15.63	5.02
Banking	2.9	5.55	2.65	4.85	8.2	3.35	12.4	18.32	5.92
Petrochemicals etc.	2.65	6.12	3.47	5.02	8.85	3.83	7.62	15.65	8.03
Pharmaceuticals	3	7.86	4.86	4.98	13.89	8.91	7.04	23.34	16.3
Consumer Durables	2.73	4.94	2.21	5.02	10.01	4.99	7.48	17.52	10.04
Core	2.58	5.4	2.82	3.52	10.69	7.17	5.3	10.69	5.39
ITES	2.55	4.31	1.76	3.28	6.34	3.06	12.09	17.8	5.71
Real Estate	2.12	3.95	1.83	3.52	6.47	2.95	7	10.26	3.26
Retail	2.56	3.88	1.32	4.6	6.12	1.52	5.89	16.09	10.2
Engineering	2.25	4.15	1.9	3.24	6.04	2.8	4.73	9.7	4.97
Textile	2.21	2.75	0.54	3.02	4.26	1.24	5.69	9.71	4.02

contd...

...contd...

Sectors	MM_1 Min.	MM_1 Max.	MM_1 Range	SM_2 Min.	SM_2 Max.	SM_2 Range	SM_1 Min.	SM_1 Max.	SM_1 Range	Ratio SM_1 to JM_2
FMCG	18.33	26.25	7.92	34.08	57.23	23.15	44.97	91.65	46.68	12:1
Automotive	5.16	30.29	25.13	27.33	46.7	19.37	38.88	58.91	20.03	9 :1
IT	12.83	23.1	10.27	13.58	31.4	17.82	21.66	46.52	24.86	8 :1
Telecom	16.36	22.74	6.38	25	32	7	34	44	10	8 :1
Banking	18.78	25.6	6.82	26	36.79	10.79	33.01	56.6	23.59	10 :1
Petrochemicals etc.	10.58	22.77	12.19	19.63	27.33	7.7	21.91	57.06	35.15	8 : 1
Pharmaceuticals	10.13	27.11	16.98	18.54	43.77	25.23	34	65.1	31.1	12 :1
Consumer Durables	11.22	25.49	14.27	19.89	35.03	15.14	36.84	68.39	31.55	12:1
Core	7.11	16.49	9.38	14.43	24.23	9.8	19.14	43.58	24.44	9:1
ITES	16.74	23.57	6.83	22	34	12	30	45	15	12:1
Real Estate	9.12	15.48	6.36	17	27.51	10.51	23.18	37.5	14.32	9:1
Retail	12.14	23.61	11.47	20.6	28.05	7.45	28.24	43.04	14.8	12:1
Engineering	7.11	19.33	12.22	12.25	34.13	21.88	19.75	40.36	20.61	9:1
Textile	9.42	17.67	8.25	11.6	28.6	17	22.02	32.45	10.43	11:1

Source: Based on the Omam Survey reports carried by *Business Today*.

Table 7.1(b)

Differentials between Minimum and Maximum Salaries across Sectors (Intra-Sectoral)
(In Terms of Percentage of Ranges)

(Annual CTC in Rs. lakhs)

	JM_2			JM_1			MM_2		
Sectors	*Min.*	*Max.*	*Range as %*	*Min.*	*Max.*	*Range as %*	*Min.*	*Max.*	*Range as %*
FMCG	5	6.73	35	6.88	9.75	42	12.99	15.7	21
Automotive	4.63	6.61	43	6.6	10.37	57	8.78	19.84	126
IT	3.43	5.44	59	6.57	9.32	42	9.28	14.15	52
Telecom	3.28	5.6	71	5.5	10.89	98	10.61	15.63	47
Banking	2.9	5.55	91	4.85	8.2	69	12.4	18.32	48
Petrochemicals etc.	2.65	6.12	131	5.02	8.85	76	7.62	15.65	105
Pharmaceuticals	3	7.86	162	4.98	13.89	179	7.04	23.34	232
Consumer Durables	2.73	4.94	81	5.02	10.01	99	7.48	17.52	134
Core	2.58	5.4	109	3.52	10.69	204	5.30	10.69	102
ITES	2.55	4.31	69	3.28	6.34	93	12.09	17.8	47
Real Estate	2.12	3.95	86	3.52	6.47	84	7.00	10.26	47
Retail	2.56	3.88	52	4.6	6.12	33	5.89	16.09	173
Engineering	2.25	4.15	84	3.24	6.04	86	4.73	9.70	105
Textile	2.21	2.75	24	3.02	4.26	41	5.69	9.71	71

contd...

...contd...

Sectors	MM_1			SM_2			SM_1		
	Min.	*Max.*	*Range as %*	*Min.*	*Max.*	*Range as %*	*Min.*	*Max.*	*Range as %*
FMCG	18.33	26.25	43	34.08	57.23	68	44.97	91.65	104
Automotive	5.16	30.29	487	27.33	46.7	71	38.88	58.91	52
IT	12.83	23.1	80	13.58	31.4	131	21.66	46.52	115
Telecom	16.36	22.74	39	25	32.00	28	34	44	29
Banking	18.78	25.6	36	26	36.79	42	33.01	56.6	71
Petrochemicals etc.	10.58	22.77	115	19.63	27.33	39	21.91	57.06	160
Pharmaceuticals	10.13	27.11	168	18.54	43.77	136	34	65.1	91
Consumer Durables	11.22	25.49	127	19.89	35.03	76	36.84	68.39	86
Core	7.11	16.49	132	14.43	24.23	68	19.14	43.58	128
ITES	2.55	4.31	69	3.28	6.34	93	12.09	17.8	47
Real Estate	2.12	3.95	86	3.52	6.47	84	7.00	10.26	47
Retail	12.14	23.61	94	20.6	28.05	36	28.24	43.04	52
Engineering	7.11	19.33	172	12.25	34.13	179	19.75	40.36	104
Textile	9.42	17.67	88	11.6	28.6	147	22.02	32.45	47

Salary Differentials within and across the Sectors (Intra-Sectoral)

Tables 7.1(a) and 7.1(b) indicate the minima, maxima and the ranges of salaries within and across the sectors pertaining to various grades in absolute values and percentage terms. For instance, in the case of FMCG sector, the maximum of the SM_1 category is Rs. 91.65 lakh per annum, whereas the minimum of the sample is Rs. 44.97 lakh per annum, a range of almost Rs. 50 lakh representing 104 per cent differential. At JM_2 level, ranges span from 24 per cent to 162 per cent (Rs. 0.54 lakh to Rs. 4.86 lakh) within the sectors. At SM_1 level, corresponding figures are 47 per cent to 160 per cent (Rs. 10.43 lakh to Rs. 35.15 lakh). The differentials are very pronounced in the intermediate categories also.

Across the sectors, the differentials in salaries for different grades are far more pronounced as can be seen from Table 7.1(c).

Table 7.1(c)

Differentials in Salaries for Different Grades

(Rs. in lakhs)

	Minimum	*Maximum*
JM_2	2.12	7.86
JM_1	3.02	10.89
MM_2	4.73	23.34
MM_1	7.11	30.29
SM_2	11.60	51.23
SM_1	19.14	91.65

Within total sample sizes of 102 companies, differentials appear to be very significant in the cadres across the sectors as highlighted hereunder:

- Ranging from a minimum of Rs. 2.12 lakh p.a. to a maximum of Rs. 7.86 lakh p.a. in the JM_2 cadre (270%). In respect of JM_1, the figures are Rs. 3.02 lakh p.a. minimum and Rs. 10.89 lakh p.a. maximum (260%).
- The figures in the case of middle management (MM_2) are Rs. 4.73 lakh p.a. minimum and Rs. 23.34 lakh p.a. maximum. The contrast in respect of MM_1 category is Rs. 7.11 lakh p.a. minimum as against Rs. 30.29 lakh p.a. maximum.

- The ranges in respect of senior management are Rs. 11.60 lakh p.a. in respect of SM_2 category and Rs. 51.23 lakh p.a. maximum in respect of SM_1 category, the minimum is reported to be Rs. 19.14 lakh and the maximum of Rs. 91.65 lakh (379%).

It was pointed by the Omam Study team leader that this data pertains to median categories of companies and not to the 'excellent' category of companies. If the best payments are also included, the differentials will be far more pronounced. The data furnished above, highlights the fact that there is no parity whatsoever, in compensation packages for the private sector executives within an industrial sector and more so across the sectors. The salary structures and compensations packages naturally depend on: (a) the magnitude of profitability, (b) the growth of business, (c) the conditions of economy in the country etc., and (d) the geographical domains in the country.

Components of Salaries (Compensation-Mix)

The distribution of the components of the salaries, across the grades for various sectors is summarised in Table 7.2(b). Barring a few exceptions, the compensation mix in the data appears to be in tune with the established HRD practices; the 'fixed part' of the pay is maintained at higher percentage levels at junior levels to attract talent, and more 'variable pay' at senior levels to retain proven talent and to demonstrate that merit and contribution are recognised in the company and serve as differentiators. Table 7.2(a) substantiates this practice.

In summary, this survey, which covers a large number of sectors and sample companies, is considered to provide good representative data. For the purpose of comparison with the CPSEs salary structures, it is proposed to use the average values of the study as the main base, after establishing the veracity in comparison with information obtained from other sources.

It is also to be noted that while the relevance of some of the 14 sectors covered in the BT study on first look may appear limited for comparison purposes with CPSEs, the actual activities of these sectoral companies match with the functions being handled by comparable CPSEs. CPSEs like Rural Electrification Corporation and Power Finance Corporation are handling financial services. A CPSE like NBCC deals with procurement of land for construction purposes. Hindustan Latex deals with items which

Table 7.2(a)

Compensation Mix

Sector	*JM_2 Lowest Level* Basic + Allowances	Others %	*SM_1 Highest Level—Below Board Level* Basic + Allowances	Others %
FMCG	84	16	63	37
Automotive	77	23	66	24
IT	74	27	69	31
Telecom	80	20	75	25
Banking	80	20	74	26
Petrochemicals etc.	72	28	64	36
Pharmaceuticals	83	17	67	33
Consumer Durables	74	26	70	30
Core	77	23	66	34
ITES	78	22	74	26
Real Estate	71	39	76	24
Retail	59	41	74	26
Engineering	76.	24	68	32
Textiles	81	19	68	32

fall into the FMCG category. The activities of HMT Watches Company include manufacturing and retailing. The 'core' sector covered by the BT study includes domains like power, minerals & metals and infrastructure creation—covered by comparable CPSE.

Data from Study Report Carried Out by *Business World*

A study similar to that published in *Business Today,* was carried out by the Gallup Team led by Shri Arish Pande in association with by Shri Shwetabh Jha and Ms. Shilpi Tandon. An article based on this study, authored by Shri M. Anand was published by the *Business World* (BW) magazine in its issue of 5th February 2007. This survey covered four grades of executives in 9 sectors and 55 companies (Table 7.3) which are a subset of the sectors covered in *Business Today* survey. However, the data cannot be straight away compared with the survey results of BT, since the BW study excluded certain items like: (a) Medical benefits which are paid on actuals (b) Spot payments, (c) Deferred payments, (d) ESOPs, (e) Benefits like insurance reimbursements etc. The enterprises that participated in the survey are included in Table 7.3.

Table 7.2(b)

Component-Mix (in %) of Salaries across Various Sectors and Grades

	Average Basic Pay						*Average Benefits & Reimbursements*						*Average Performance Pay*					
Sector	JM_2	JM_1	MM_2	MM_1	SM_2	SM_1	JM_2	JM_1	MM_2	MM	SM_2	SM_1	JM_2	JM_1	MM_2	MM_1	SM_2	SM_1
FMCG	52	54	39	40	38	39	32	30	26	24	24	24	2	2	8	10	11	11
Automotive	40	40	35	29	32	32	38	33	36	41	36	35	8	10	10	10	12	13
IT	42	41	37	35	34	34	32	32	40	39	35	35	7	9	11	13	15	16
Telecom	37	37	32	32	29	29	43	28	44	44	46	46	9	11	14	14	15	15
Banking	36	36	32	33	42	42	44	40	34	36	32	32	9	10	15	13	7	7
Petrochemicals etc.	39	40	35	34	33	35	33	37	32	32	32	29	10	9	10	9	9	9
Pharmaceuticals etc.	39	37	33	33	33	33	44	43	36	34	35	34	8	10	14	15	13	15
Consumer Durables	36	36	34	29	31	31	38	39	45	50	41	39	9	12	9	10	14	17
Core	36	36	38	34	30	33	41	47	33	33	35	33	12	7	11	11	10	10
ITES	34	36	22	23	29	29	44	43	55	55	45	45	11	10	15	14	14	15
Real Estate	33	33	36	36	34	37	28	30	46	42	42	39	13	8	6	6	8	8
Retail	34	33	35	33	33	34	25	45	39	39	38	40	7	9	11	11	11	10
Engineering	33	31	34	33	31	30	43	44	39	38	38	38	15	15	8	7	8	7
Textile	36	36	46	48	45	45	45	43	24	19	23	23	11	11	3	3	5	5
Average	38	38	35	34	34	35	38	38	38	38	38	35	9	10	10	10	11	11

contd...

...contd...

Sector	Average Retirals						Average Valued Perks					
	JM_2	JM_1	MM_2	MM_1	SM_2	SM_1	JM_2	JM_1	MM_2	MM	SM_2	SM_1
FMCG	9	10	12	12	12	13	4	5	13	14	15	13
Automotive	10	12	10	9	9	9	4	6	9	11	11	11
IT	12	11	8	8	8	8	8	8	4	5	8	7
Telecom	8	10	8	8	8	8	3	15	2	2	2	2
Banking	8	10	8	8	13	13	3	4	11	10	6	6
Petrochemicals etc.	12	10	10	10	9	10	6	5	13	15	17	17
Pharmaceuticals etc.	7	8	10	10	10	10	2	2	7	8	9	8
Consumer Durables	11	10	8	7	8	8	6	3	4	4	6	5
Core	10	7	12	10	9	10	1	4	6	12	16	14
ITES	8	9	6	6	8	8	2	3	2	2	4	3
Real Estate	9	9	6	7	6	7	17	20	6	9	10	9
Retail	10	8	6	6	6	6	24	4	9	11	12	10
Engineering	6	8	11	10	9	10	2	1	8	12	14	15
Textile	6	6	10	11	11	11	1	4	17	19	16	16
Average	9	9	9	9	9	9	6	6	8	10	10	10

Note: (i) Benefits and Reimbursements include: special allowance, HRA, educational allowance, utility allowance, LTA, medical and conveyance allowance.

(ii) Retirals include: provident fund, superannuation fund and gratuity.

(iii) Valued Perks include: items like company car/Car-lease, value/subsidy; white goods, lunch subsidy, telephone etc.

Table 7.3

Enterprises Participating in the Business World (BW) Survey

Sector	*Name of the Company*
Manufacturing (#7 Companies)	Jindal Stainless, Tata Motors, Ashok Leyland, Apollo Tyres, Kirloskar Oil Engines, Mahindra and Mahindra and Tata Steels
Pharmaceuticals (# 6 Companies)	Panacea Biotech, Dabur Pharma, Bausch & Lomb, Life Cell, Ranbaxy and Wokhardt
Telecom (# 4 Companies)	VSNL, Ericsson, Avaya Global Connect and Idea Cellular
Financial Sector (# 6 Companies)	UTI Bank, Max New York, Franklin Templeton Asset Mgt., Bajaj Allianz, Kotak Life Insurance and Citibank
Information Technology (# 7 Companies)	Sasken Communication Technology, HCL Technologies, EMC Data Storage Systems, Tech Mahindra, Flextronics, TCS and Wipro
BPO/IT (# 5 Companies)	HCL, EXL Services Com, Wipro BPO, HTMT and Genpact
FMCG (# 5 Companies)	Emami, Pepsi Co, Marico, CavinKare, Dabur
Retail (# 7 Companies)	Barista Coffee, Sports Solution, Raymonds, Pizza Hut, Pantaloons, Adidas and Café Coffee Day India
Consumer Durables (# 8 Companies)	Daikin, Electrolux, Philips, Whirlpool, Godrej, Infotech, Onida and Voltas

The entry level executives as defined in this survey are those with less than two years post-qualification experience perhaps with no financial stake. The junior management executives are those at the operational levels designated as assistant managers with responsibilities for implementation of plans. The middle management executives are those at the tactical levels usually designated as senior manager/deputy general manager. The senior management executives are at the strategic decision-making level, commonly designated as general manager. This cadre of senior managers also does not include directors or board level members—like in the case of BT study. The survey results are summarised in Table 7.4.

As observed from this survey (Table 7.4), the entry level salaries which are considerably low possibly denote the remunerations for the executives during the trainee periods. Nevertheless, a very good correlation exists between the salaries of JM_2, MM_2 and SM_2 levels reported by the BT survey and the junior management, middle management and senior management cadres reported by the *Business World*. The non-inclusion of certain allowances and perks in this survey as explained earlier might be a cause for differentials between the two studies, which probably would narrow down if the same are added back. Yet the divergence in the figures relating to retail sector and BPO/ITES sectors is a bit pronounced, perhaps due to the sample selection.

Table 7.4

Summary of Survey Report of Business World

(Annual figures Rs. in lakhs)

Sector	*Entry Level*	*Junior Mgt.*	*Middle Mgt.*	*Senior Mgt.*
Retail	1.49	2.31	4.68	8.68
BPO/ITES	1.48	3.39	6.96	13.86
Consumer Durables	2.28	4.54	8.52	20.04
Manufacturing	2.61	3.95	6.00	24.00
Information Technology	3.46	7.22	14.16	25.77
Pharma.	1.53	5.22	10.34	26.40
Telecom.	2.70	6.14	12.09	30.93
FMCG	2.40	6.02	15.00	34.80
Financial Sector	3.00	8.04	18.00	50.40

Note: Based on data contained in BW, Feb. 5th 2007, CTC include 1. Guaranteed cash including basic, HRA, commuting allowance, LTA, special allowance and flexible benefit plan; 2. Variable pay: performance incentive—team based, individual and company performance based (does not include ex-gratia payments based on company's performance) 3. Retirals, PF, gratuity, etc.

They do not include: 1. Medical benefits where it is paid on actuals, 2. Spot payments and deferred payments, 3. ESOPs, 4. Benefits like medi-claim, insurance reimbursement, perks or any other head not covered above.

Survey Data of *paycheck.in*

Paycheck is an internet-based labour market research tool and is part of the international wage indicator.

Paycheck in India is managed by IT Professionals Forum (ITPF), Bangalore, IIM, Ahmedabad and Indian Institute of Science (IIS), Bangalore.

Prof. Biju Varkkey and Khushi Mehta of IIM, Ahmedabad and Prof. Anjula Gurtoo and Neha Khombhadia of IISc, Bangalore provide the *Paycheck* research support. The technical support is provided by the ITPF Team, Apex Media and International Wage Indicator Team, Amsterdam.

Paycheck.in has covered the compensation packages in three sectors, namely IT, finance and manufacturing—at various levels of designations and cadres that constitute junior management, middle management and senior management levels.

The survey covers 19 companies in manufacturing sector, 21 companies in the IT sector and 10 companies in the finance sector. In respect of each designation, the data furnished is projected under the heads, maximum, minimum and weighted average. It is reported that companies included in the study are a mix of some private companies and some multi-national companies. It is likely that the 'maximum' category of sales may pertain to the MNCs. The table of CTC packages, Tables 7.5(a), (b) and (c) included here, outlines the 'minimum, maximum, weighted average' figures encompassing junior management, middle management and senior management cadres for the manufacturing, IT and finance sectors. The components are clustered as: (i) Basic salary and allowances like special allowance, house rent allowance, conveyance allowance, medical reimbursement, etc., (ii) Variable pay like performance-related bonuses, etc., and (iii) Retirals like provident fund, gratuity and superannuation fund, etc.

The *paycheck* data clearly shows a functional premium for the finance and IT sector compared to the manufacturing sector. The grade to grade differentiation is very distinct. The compensation packages of the executives at various grades quantitatively compare well with the data reflected in other surveys.

Basic salary and allowances/reimbursements constitute the 'Fixed part of the salary' while performance-related pay, and retiral benefits are linked to the performance and experience levels of the executives.

Data Gathered by IPE

To validate the data obtained from different sources, IPE made concerted efforts to collect first hand information from select sectors by having one-to-one contacts with heads of HR functions, company directors, present and former senior employees of private sector companies. The sectors and areas covered include: (i) Power sector (ii) Steel sector (iii) Telecom equipment manufacturers (iv) Telecom services (v) Aviation sector (vi) IT sector (vii) Paper sector (viii) Fertiliser sector (ix) Manufacturing sector (x) Automobile sector, and (xi) EPC (engineering, procurement and construction) contractors.

Table 7.5(a)

Paycheck.in: Details of Compensation in Manufacturing Sector

(Rs. in lakhs)

Cadre	Minimum				Maximum				Weighted Average			
	Basic & Alw.	Variable Pay	Rtrmnt.	Total	Basic & Alw.	Variable Pay	Rtrmnt.	Total	Basic & Alw.	Variable Pay	Rtrmnt.	Total
Junior Management												
Production Officer	2.04	0.05	0.35	2.44	6	0.78	0.99	7.77	3.65	0.39	0.5	4.54
Corporate Finance	2.52	0.24	0.24	3	5.7	0.45	0.85	7	3.94	1.1	0.31	5.35
Corporate HR	2.58	0.07	0.29	2.94	7.2	1.32	1.06	9.58	3.91	0.55	0.64	5.1
Purchase	2.05	0.31	0.24	2.6	4.77	0.6	0.76	6.13	2.91	0.5	0.44	3.85
Quality Assurance	2.47	0.14	0.32	2.93	5.58	0.7	0.9	7.18	4.06	0.25	0.42	4.73
Research & Dev.	2.62	0.23	0.29	3.14	5.21	1.78	1.02	8.01	2.89	0.62	0.52	4.03
Sales	2.46	0	0.3	2.76	5.68	0.67	0.87	7.22	3.79	0.49	0.46	4.74
IT	2.12	0.04	0.24	2.4	4.84	0.21	0.77	5.82	3.64	0.28	0.58	4.5
Average	2.36	0.14	0.28	2.78	5.62	0.81	0.90	7.33	3.60	0.52	0.48	4.61
Middle Management												
Corporate Finance	4.68	0.48	0.75	5.91	17.68	1.04	2.25	20.97	10.27	1.58	1.53	13.38
Corporate HR	3.94	0.35	0.69	4.98	13.64	0.95	1.98	16.57	10.88	1	1.42	13.3
Purchase	4.16	0.66	0.63	5.45	10.95	1.7	1.38	14.03	9.1	0.65	0.94	10.69
Quality Assurance	3.95	0.63	0.66	5.24	17.64	0.48	1.46	19.58	8.93	1.43	1	11.36
Research & Dev.	3.51	0	0.49	4	16.26	1.08	1.56	18.9	9.61	0.84	1.13	11.58
Sales	8.51	0	1.11	9.62	22.66	2.5	3.03	28.19	15.37	2.93	1.91	20.21
IT	6.95	0.76	0.88	8.59	12.74	1.5	1.91	16.15	9.94	0.9	1.18	12.02

contd...

...contd...

Cadre	*Basic & Alw.*	*Variable Pay*	*Rtrmnt.*	*Total*	*Basic & Alw.*	*Variable Pay*	*Rtrmnt.*	*Total*	*Basic & Alw.*	*Variable Pay*	*Rtrmnt.*	*Total*
Production	5.77	0	0.89	6.66	24.33	2.86	3.64	30.83	13.3	2.11	1.53	16.94
Average	5.18	0.36	0.76	6.31	16.99	1.51	2.15	20.65	10.93	1.43	1.33	13.69
Senior Management												
Plant Head	11.36	1.35	1.79	14.5	32.49	4.99	5.29	42.77	19.63	2.83	2.41	24.87
Sales Head	18.1	5.65	2.8	26.55	57.38	7.68	8.14	73.2	35.8	5.82	4.04	45.66
GM Finance	12.59	0.6	1.23	14.42	42.26	2.96	4.3	49.52	20.4	2.45	2.5	25.35
GM Materials	12.21	3.25	1.87	17.33	33.22	5.7	4.32	43.24	21.22	3.27	2.55	27.04
Average	13.57	2.71	1.92	18.20	41.34	5.33	5.51	52.18	24.26	3.59	2.88	30.73
CFO	11.97	2.82	7.27	22.06	55.85	6.86	2.77	65.48	35.08	3.36	4.37	42.81
COO	22.18	3.32	3.45	28.95	93.49	12.33	13.06	118.88	51.52	13.74	7.04	72.3

Table 7.5(b)

Paycheck.in: Details of Compensation in IT Sector

(Rs. in lakhs)

Cadre	*Minimum*				*Maximum*				*Weighted Average*			
	Basic & Alw.	*Variable Pay*	*Rtrmnt.*	*Total*	*Basic & Alw.*	*Variable Pay*	*Rtrmnt.*	*Total*	*Basic & Alw.*	*Variable Pay*	*Rtrmnt.*	*Total*
Junior Management												
Executive HR (IT)	1.71	0.14	0.27	2.12	6.23	0.25	0.93	7.41	3.19	1.17	0.56	4.92
Sales Executive (IT)	2.71	0.03	0.35	3.09	5.01	0.44	0.79	6.24	3.46	0.51	0.6	4.57
Manager Facilities (IT)	3.72	0.3	0.41	4.43	12.8	1.2	1.64	15.64	5.38	0.65	0.82	6.85

contd...

...contd...

Cadre	*Basic & Alw.*	*Variable Pay*	*Rtrmnt.*	*Total*	*Basic & Alw.*	*Variable Pay*	*Rtrmnt.*	*Total*	*Basic & Alw.*	*Variable Pay*	*Rtrmnt.*	*Total*
Manager HR (IT)	0.91	3.25	0.43	4.59	13.74	4.24	2.84	20.82	10.48	0	1.24	11.72
Software Engineer	3.95	0.3	0.37	4.62	8.86	1.57	1.14	11.57	5.66	0.16	0.78	6.6
Manager IT Support	3.85	0.32	0.57	4.74	10.01	0.5	1.48	11.99	5.46	0.49	0.83	6.78
Average	2.81	0.72	0.4	3.93	9.44	1.37	1.47	12.28	5.61	0.5	0.81	6.91
Middle Management												
Project Leader (IT)	5.41	0.97	0.71	7.09	16.38	1.79	2.34	20.51	12.18	1.84	1.38	15.4
Sr. Software Engineer	6.34	0.84	0.51	7.69	12.63	1.19	1.5	15.32	8.24	0.5	1.2	9.94
Regional Manager (IT)	8.67	0.6	1.12	8.67	19.63	0	2.73	22.36	11.02	2.9	2.03	15.95
Project Manager (IT)	8.47	1.6	0.7	10.77	24.96	1.98	2.93	29.87	14.19	1.55	1.78	17.52
Project Manager(IT)	8.49	1.59	0.69	10.77	24.96	1.97	2.93	29.86	14.19	1.54	1.78	17.51
Head HR (IT)	10.19	2.15	1.47	13.81	35.05	4.06	4.69	43.8	25.54	4.11	3.33	32.98
Average	7.93	1.29	0.87	9.8	22.27	1.83	2.85	26.95	14.23	2.07	1.92	18.22
Senior Management												
Head HR (IT)	10.19	2.15	1.47	13.81	35.05	4.06	4.69	43.8	25.54	4.11	3.33	32.98
National Sales & Marketing Mgr. (IT)	13.33	3.15	2.25	18.73	49.71	9.38	6.89	65.98	28.16	3.32	4.11	35.59
Vice-President	17.7	3.24	2.01	22.95	53.43	7.27	9.24	69.94	45.73	2.79	5.03	53.55
Average	13.74	2.85	1.91	18.5	46.06	6.9	6.94	59.91	33.14	3.41	4.16	40.71

Table 7.5(c)

Paycheck.in: Details of Compensation in Finance Sector

(Rs. in lakhs)

Cadre	Minimum				Maximum				Weighted Average			
	Basic & Alw.	Variable Pay	Rtrmnt.	Total	Basic & Alw.	Variable Pay	Rtrmnt.	Total	Basic & Alw.	Variable Pay	Rtrmnt.	Total
Junior Management												
Executive Corporate Finance	2.20	0.65	0.25	3.10	5.34	0.08	0.83	6.25	4.39	0.58	0.67	5.64
Executive Infotech	2.19	0.64	0.25	3.08	4.93	0.33	0.77	6.03	3.78	0.46	0.67	4.91
Executive Corporate HR	2.48	0.76	0.29	3.53	5.18	0.11	0.83	6.12	4.21	0.20	0.65	5.06
Sales Executive	2.75	0.64	0.36	3.75	5.39	0.97	1.02	7.38	4.17	0.34	0.75	5.26
Area Sales Manager	3.61	0.30	0.67	4.58	7.57	1.87	1.34	10.78	6.42	1.05	1.04	8.51
Average	2.65	0.60	0.36	3.61	5.68	0.67	0.96	7.31	4.59	0.53	0.76	5.88
Middle Management												
Manager Corporate Finance	5.01	0.51	0.80	6.32	16.96	3.87	2.23	23.06	9.67	1.82	1.34	12.83
Manager Corporate HR	4.20	0.44	0.75	5.39	14.96	1.26	1.74	17.96	10.82	1.44	1.38	13.64
Manager IT	6.23	0.00	0.95	7.18	11.93	1.86	1.47	15.26	9.15	0.59	1.19	10.93
Regional Sales Manager	9.15	2.33	1.56	13.04	21.74	4.49	2.91	29.14	15.02	0.86	2.15	18.03
GM Sales and Marketing	13.15	3.15	2.10	18.40	34.33	8.14	6.36	48.83	24.08	2.67	3.07	29.82
GM Corporate HR	13.59	0.66	1.32	15.57	42.68	8.39	5.40	56.47	22.96	3.58	3.41	29.95
Average	8.56	1.18	1.25	10.98	23.77	4.67	3.35	31.79	15.28	1.83	2.09	19.20

contd...

...contd...

Cadre	*Basic & Alw.*	*Variable Pay*	*Rtrmnt.*	*Total*	*Basic & Alw.*	*Variable Pay*	*Rtrmnt.*	*Total*	*Basic & Alw.*	*Variable Pay*	*Rtrmnt.*	*Total*
Senior Management												
Head (HR)	15.38	1.82	1.92	19.12	45.89	7.12	7.55	60.56	37.70	1.30	5.00	44.00
Head (Sales & Mkt.)	19.13	6.05	3.00	28.18	51.43	4.55	8.00	63.98	42.18	6.45	6.13	54.76
Average	17.26	3.94	2.46	23.65	48.66	5.84	7.78	62.27	39.94	3.88	5.57	49.38
Chief Financial Officer	17.57	3.03	2.99	23.59	49.31	7.20	7.63	64.14	42.52	6.37	5.82	54.71
Chief Operating Officer	37.29	3.58	6.58	47.45	88.12	7.50	12.96	108.58	61.18	10.55	9.36	81.09

The data collected is formatted in a manner which facilitates easy one-to-one comparison with information collected from other sources as well as with the remuneration structures of CPSEs.

While the information collected is first hand and authentic, IPE is honour bound not to reveal the names of the sources and the companies for which the information is relevant. For ease of comparison, the equivalence with the BT study is indicated in brackets for various cadres of executives.

All figures indicated are CTC per annum figures in rupees lakhs. In most of the cases, the total remuneration packages offered to the executives include basic salary, allowance and reimbursement, performance based pays/variable pays, retiral benefits and valued perks. In respect of few companies, however, in addition to these packages they have special schemes like holiday plans and other gestures for newly married couples etc., which cannot be quantified in monetary terms easily.

The allowances and reimbursement usually include house rent allowance, conveyance allowance, medical reimbursement/allowance, premia for medical insurance, leave travel plans, children education allowance, remote locality allowance and some special allowance.

The variable pay or performance related pay includes compensation for the performance (*vis-à-vis* the agreed targets) at the individual, team level, division level and the company level. Usually for junior cadres, performance based pay relates mostly to individual level excellence while at senior level, it will be a combination of individual level achievement and also unit/company level achievement. The retiral benefits include provident fund, gratuity and superannuation fund which is usually pegged at 15 per cent of the basic salary. In some special cases, retiral benefits also include medical coverage for the employee and his spouse with caps on levels of medical insurance.

The valued perks, usually reserved for the senior cadre people, include housing loans, vehicle loans, furniture allowance for the soft and hard kind and holidays abroad, etc.

While ESOPs are extended to executives below board level also, commissions and profits are strictly for board level executives only. The compensation figures indicated in Tables 7.6(a)-7.6(k) are for executives below board level, but do not include ESOPs.

Table 7.6(a)

Power Sector

S. No.	*Cadre*	*CTC/P.A. (Rs. lakhs)*
1.	Junior Management (JM_2)	3.5–4.5
2.	Junior Management (JM_1)	7.0–8.0
3.	Middle Management (MM_2)	10.0–15.0
4.	Middle Management (MM_1)	15.0–24.0
5.	Senior Management (SM_2)	25.0–30.0
6.	Senior Management (SM_1)	36.0–45.0

Table 7.6(b)

Steel Sector

S. No.	*Cadre*	*CTC/P.A. (Rs. lakhs)*
1.	Junior Management (JM_2)	5.0
2.	Junior Management (JM_1)	8.0–12.0
3.	Middle Management (MM_2)	12.0–15.0
4.	Middle Management (MM_1)	15.0–18.0
5.	Senior Management (SM_2)	20.0–25.0
6.	Senior Management (SM_1)	25.0–30.0

Table 7.6(c)

Telecommunication Sector (Telecom Equipment)

S. No.	*Cadre*	*CTC /P.A. (Rs. lakhs)*
1.	Junior Management (JM_2)	5.0–6.0
2.	Junior Management (JM_1)	10.0–15.0
3.	Middle Management (MM_2)	15.0–20.0
4.	Middle Management (MM_1)	20.0–30.0
5.	Senior Management (SM_2)	30.0–40.0
6.	Senior Management (SM_1)	40.0–60.0

Table 7.6(d)

Telecommunication Services

S. No.	*Cadre*	*CTC/P.A. (Rs. lakhs)*
1.	Junior Management (JM_2)	4.9–6.0
2.	Junior Management (JM_1)	10.0–11.0
3.	Middle Management (MM_2)	15.0–16.0
4.	Middle Management (MM_1)	17.0–22.0
5.	Senior Management (SM_2)	22.0–30.0
6.	Senior Management (SM_1)	41.0–43.0

Aviation Sector

In respect of aviation sector, historically specific cadres—especially the flying staff have been getting paid industry standard salaries even in the PSUs. The data furnished in Table 7.6(e) relevant to a leading private sector airline is limited to pilots, aircraft maintenance engineers, other engineers and cabin crew. Remuneration packages for other cadres of management, not revealed to us, are expected to be at levels indicated for other sectors.

Table 7.6(e)

Aviation Sector

S. No.	*Cadre*	*Grade*	*CTC/P.A. (Rs. lakhs)*
1.	Pilots		24.0
2.	Senior Commander		48.0
3.	Maintenance Engineers	Entry Level	7.0
4.	Full Scope Licensed Engineer	Entry + 3 Yrs	17.0
5.	Maintenance Manager	Entry + 5-7 Yrs	24.0
6.	Senior Maintenance Manager	Entry + 3 Yrs	36.0
7.	Other Engineers		
	i) Entry Level		3.0
	ii) Junior Management Level	Entry + 2 Yrs	4.0–5.0
	iii) Middle Management Level	Entry + 5 Yrs	7.0–8.0
	iv) Senior Management Level	Entry + 7-9 Yrs	10.0–11.0
8.	Cabin Crew		
	i) Air Hostess/Stewards		3.0–4.0
	ii) Inflight Engineers		5.0–6.0
	iii) Asst. Base Manager		6.0–7.0
	iv) Base Manager		8.0–9.0

Table 7.6(f)

IT Sector

S. No.	Level	Typical Deregulators	CTC (Indicature) (Rs. lakhs/Per Annum)
1.	Junior Management (JM_2)	IT Analyst Trainee, Assistant Systems Analyst etc.	3.5–4.0
2.	Junior Management (JM_1)	Consultant, Sr. Consultant	7.0
3.	Middle Management (MM_2)	Principal Consultant, Systems Manager	12.0
4.	Middle Management (MM_1)	Assistant Vice-President	15.0–20.0
5.	Senior Management (SM_2)	Vice-President, Senior Vice-President	20.0–35.0
6.	Senior Management (SM_1)	Executive Vice-President	35.0–60.0

In contrast to other sectors, it is reported that in IT sector the assured pay and allowances amount to 56 per cent, retiral benefits about 10 per cent and performance based salary about 30 per cent especially in the senior cadres.

The component of the basic pay forms approximately 26-27 per cent of gross or CTC. The variable allowance can be as much as 35 per cent of the gross which is linked to individual's performance and/or the company's performance. The total of benefits can constitute around 22-23 per cent of the gross and the retirals 8-9 per cent of CTC. Conveyance allowance and health insurance constitute around 8-9 per cent of CTC. Thus, the assured pay and allowances amount to about 56 per cent, retirals about 9 per cent and performance based salary of about 35 per cent.

This is a representative break-up of CTCs of cadres 2,3 and 4 (junior management, middle management and senior management) indicated above.

Table 7.6(g)

Paper Sector

S. No.	Cadre	CTC/P.A. (Rs. lakhs)
1.	Junior Management (JM_2)	3.0–4.0
2.	Junior Management (JM_1)	5.0–6.0
3.	Middle Management (MM_2)	8.0–10.0
4.	Middle Management (MM_1)	10.0–15.0
5.	Senior Management (SM_2)	18.0–22.0
6.	Senior Management (SM_1)	22.0–26.0

Table 7.6(h)

Fertiliser Sector

S. No.	*Cadre*	*CTC/P.A. (Rs. lakhs)*
1.	Junior Management (JM_2)	3.5
2.	Junior Management (JM_1)	4.5
3.	Middle Management (MM_2)	6.0
4.	Middle Management (MM_1)	8.0–12.0
5.	Senior Management (SM_2)	18.0–24.0
6.	Senior Management (SM_1)	30.0–35.0

Table 7.6(i)

Manufacturing Sector

S. No.	*Cadre*	*CTC/P.A. (Rs. lakhs)*
1.	Junior Management (JM_2)	3.0–4.0
2.	Junior Management (JM_1)	5.5–6.5
3.	Middle Management (MM_2)	7.5–8.5
4.	Middle Management (MM_1)	12.0–15.0
5.	Senior Management (SM_2)	20.0–25.0
6.	Senior Management (SM_1)	25.0–30.0

The elements of the CTC are: Basic pay, cost of living allowance, HRA, conveyance allowance, education allowance, special allowance, grade allowance etc.

The CTC figures include LTC, outdoor medical expenses, annual performance based recognition pay etc.

The retirals include 15 per cent of basic towards superannuation fund, 4.81 per cent of basic and cost of living allowance towards gratuity and 12 per cent of basic + cost of living allowance towards provident fund.

The valued perks include appliance allowances ranging from Rs. 75,000 to Rs. 350,000 (over a period of five years) for junior to senior Management cadres. Hospitalisation charges are covered by medical insurance taken by the company ranging from Rs. 80,000 to 220,000 per annum per person for a maximum of six persons.

The conveyance allowance/perks covering car+petrol+maintenance can range from Rs. 5.5 lakh for executives of the rank of an AGM, Rs. 8.5 lakh for executives of the rank of a GM and Rs. 12.5 lakh for the executives holding the rank of a vice-president. This perk is extended on a very selective basis and is valid for a period of five years.

Table 7.6(j)

Automobile Sector

S. No.	*Cadre*	*CTC/P.A. (Rs. lakhs)*
1.	Junior Management (JM_2)	3.5–4.0
2.	Junior Management (JM_1)	4.5–5.5
3.	Middle Management (MM_2)	8.0–10.0
4.	Middle Management (MM_1)	13.0–20.0
5.	Senior Management (SM_2)	24.0–33.0
6.	Senior Management (SM_1)	60.0–65.0

Table 7.6(k)

EPC Contractors

S. No.	*'Cadre*	*CTC/P.A. (Rs. lakhs)*
1.	Junior Management (JM_2)	2.5–4.0
2.	Junior Management (JM_1)	5.0–9.0
3.	Middle Management (MM_2)	10.0–15.0
4.	Middle Management (MM_1)	15.0–25.0
5.	Senior Management (SM_2)	25.0–35.0
6.	Senior Management (SM_1)	40.0–55.0

Compensation

The confidentiality of salary related information is maintained with far more seriousness and sanctity in MNCs when compared to even the private sector companies. IPE, through discreet enquiries, could obtain indicatory information highlighting differentials between private sector companies and MNCs in respect of compensation packages.

It is reported that the differentials between median private sector companies and MNCs ranges from 1.5 times to even 2 times at the junior and middle management cadres. At the very entry level, the differential can be around 1.3 times of the comparable figure in the private sector companies. The data obtained from reliable sources substantiates these factors. Quantitative data, furnished in a diffused way, by some consultants also strengthens this premise. In the companies that formed part of the survey carried out by *paycheck.in* (Tables 7.5(a), (b) and (c), it was clarified that there is a fair sprinkling of MNCs. The 'Maximum' category of compensations, essentially relate to MNCs. It can also be noted that in the companies that have participated in the study conducted by the Gallup Team (*Business World*), there is a good mix of MNCs (Table 7.3). In respect of manufacturing sector, the average compensation, across the functions, for an executive belonging to the junior management cadre in MNC companies works out to around Rs. 7.34 lakh compared to a median value of around Rs. 4.5 lakh in private sector companies. In the middle management category in manufacturing sector, the average compensation works out to around Rs. 20 lakh compared to Rs. 11-12 lakh in the private sector companies. In the senior management category even below board level, the compensation levels are observed to increase steeply. As mentioned earlier in the report, the contract payments are determined by one-to-one negotiations and are governed more by the stature of the individuals. Similar situations are reported in respect of automobile, IT, financial and fertiliser sectors from where indicatory data could be obtained.

It is also reported that spot payments and short-term incentives for performance excellence are part of the compensation schemes of the multinational corporations. It is understood that a junior executive can be paid higher emoluments than his superior based on the individual performance rankings. On the same token, it is also reported that a person who fails to meet his agreed targets in two consecutive quarters can be asked to leave the organisation. The reward and punishment schemes are very stringent and are said to be directly linked to the contributions made by the executives for the wealth generation of the enterprise.

Compensation for Board Level Executives

The compensation levels are found to increase steeply as the executives occupy more senior positions in the private sector companies. The compensation situations will be governed by the proven competence of the individuals concerned, the need of the company and the prevailing industry standards. No uniformity can be expected at this level and even if one considers non-promoter directors and CEOs belonging to professional cadres, there will be substantial variation across companies and across sectors. The remuneration packages will be fixed based on one-to-one negotiations and allowances, privileges, perks, commissions and ESOPs will result in CTC levels far far above the levels of other management/ executive cadres.

The CTC details of the CEOs and board level executives of some leading Indian private sector companies are indicated in Table 7.7. The data includes compensation details of some MNC CEOs also—but all belonging to professional management cadres and not part of promoter groups. The data provided is as per information furnished in the *Business India* issue of November 2006 and covers data as of 2005-06. An increase of 15-20 per cent can easily be assumed for current compensation levels.

CEO and board level compensation levels, pertaining to non-promoter category of executives as gathered from press and annual reports are indicated in the table in respect of some companies and sectors.

Table 7.7

CTC Details of Leading Private Sector Companies

Name of the Company & Executives/Shri	*Designation*	*Compensation p.a.*
Tata Steel		
B. Muthuraman	MD	220.14
T. Mukhee	DMD (Steel)	174.9
A.N. Singh	DMD	134.1
TCS		
S. Ramadoai	CEO & MD	214.43
Tata Motors		
Ravi Kant	MD	169.83
Tata Power		
P.K. Kukde	ED (Operations)	68.89
F.A. Vandrevala	MD	65.72
Tata Teleservices		
Charles Antony	MD	110.22
Vivek Selt	CFO	85.08
Tata Chemicals		
Prasad R. Menon	MD	133.67

contd...

...contd...

Name of the Company & Executives/Shri	*Designation*	*Compensation p.a.*
Horni R. Khusrokhan	ED	98.21
P.K. Ghosh	CFO	53.99
Sanjiv Lal	VP	52.65
ACC		
M.L. Narula	MD	79.04
Ashok Leyland		
R. Seshasayee	MD	126.47
Bharti Airtel		
Norman Price	Director	459.54
Akhil Gupta	JMD	321.26
Badri Agarwal	Corporate Director	302.96
J.C. van de Vreede	Alliance Director	192.16
Jagdeep Khandpur	Corporate Director	179.92
HDFC		
Deepak S. Parekh	Chairman	248.93
K.M. Mistry	MD	165.75
R.S. Kamad	ED	158.67
Hindalco		
D. Bhattacharya	MD	378.09
Kim Freeman	COO (Mining)	168.89
Hindustan Lever Limited		
M.K. Sharma	VC	169.59
D. Sundaram	Director (Finance & IT)	140.03
S. Ravindranath	MD (Foods)	127.74
Arun Adhikari	MD (Home & Personal Care)	117.29
ICICI Bank		
K.V. Kamath	MD & CEO	247.8
Lalita Gupte	JMD	188.06
Kalpana Morparia	JMD	136.92
Chanda Kochar	DMD	113.89
Nachiket Mor	DMD	97.74
Infosys		
S.D. Shibulal	Director	101.74
Mohandas Pai TV	Director	75.82
Srinath Batni	Director	68.05
ITC		
Y.C. Deveshwar	Chairman	287.25
S.S.H. Rehman	ED	138.3
A. Singh	ED	132.48
K. Vaidyanath	ED	106.63

contd...

...contd...

Name of the Company & Executives/Shri	*Designation*	*Compensation p.a.*
Larsen & Toubro		
A.M. Naik	CMD	398.92
Y.M. Deosthalee	WTD & CFO	222.7
K. Venkataraman	WTD	220.2
R.N. Mukhija	WTD	216.14
J.P. Nayak	WTD	206.96
K.V. Rangaswami	WTD	176.08
V.K. Magapu	WTD	175.51
Merck		
H. Mauer	MD	97.64
S.M. Gupta	Director	55.88
G.V.S. Rayudu	Director	55.53
Moser Baer		
Deepak Puri	MD	208.22
Ratul Puri	ED	125.02
Nestle		
Martial G. Rolland	CMD	357.7
Shobinder Duggal	Director (Finance)	63.98
Procter & Gamble		
S. Khosla	MD	134.39
A. Chhabra	ED	122.28
Pfizer		
K. Handa	MD	86.45
K.G. Ananthakrishnan	Director	55.38
Yugesh Goutam	Sr. Director (HR)	50.16
Siemens		
H. Gelis	ED	126.9
A.B. Nadkarni	WTD	121.37
O.P. Narula	WTD	100.09
J. Schubert	MD	72.89
Harminder Singh	WTD	70.56
SKF		
Rakesh Makhija	MD	152.79
Carl Johan	Finance Director	52.39

Note: Compensation packages indicated above do not include stock options.

Independent Directors

Another noteworthy point in respect of board level compensation is the sizeable quantums of commissions being paid to independent directors. To give an idea of the amounts being paid to these experienced luminaries, details of the payments made in some leading companies as per the 2006-2007 annual reports are summarised in Table 7.8.

Table 7.8

Payment Details of Independent Directors

Name	*Category*	*Salary & Other Perks*	*Commission*	*Sitting Fees*
WIPRO (2006-07)				
Ashok Ganguly	Independent Non-Executive Director	-	12.00	0.80
B.C. Prabhakar	Independent Non-Executive Director	-	6.00	1.50
N. Vaghul	Independent Non-Executive Director	-	14.00	1.40
Jagdish Seth	Independent Non-Executive Director	-	21.15	0.40
P.M. Sinha	Independent Non-Executive Director	-	10.00	1.40
Bill Owens	Independent Non-Executive Director		25.68	0.30
Infosys (2006-07)				
Deepak Satwalekar	Lead Independent Director	-	22.16	-
M.G. Subrahmanyam	Independent Director	-	20.01	-
Omkar Goswami	Independent Director	-	20.01	-
Rama Bijapurkar	Independent Director	-	20.01	-
Claude Smadja	Independent Director	-	20.01	-
Sridar Iyengar	Independent Director	-	20.01	-
David Boyles	Independent Director	-	20.01	-
Jeffrey Lehman	Independent Director	-	19.24	-
Dr. Reddy's Laboratories Limited (2006-07)				
Anupam Puri	Independent Director	-	26.08	0.60
Krishna Palepu	Independent Director	-	26.08	0.40
Omkar Goswami	Independent Director	-	26.08	0.80
Devarajan	Independent Director	-	26.08	1.00
Ravi Bhoothalingam	Independent Director	-	26.08	0.65
V. Mohan	Independent Director	-	26.08	0.05
Bajaj (2006-07)				
K.R. Potdar	Non-Executive, Independent	-	3.00	1.20
Shekhar Bajaj	Non-Executive	-	2.00	0.80
D.J. Balaji Rao	Non-Executive, Independent	-	5.50	2.20
J.N. Godrej	Non-Executive, Independent	-	3.00	1.20
S.H. Khan	Non-Executive, Independent	-	5.50	2.20
Suman Kirloskar	Non-Executive, Independent	-	2.50	1.00
Naresh Chandra	Non-Executive, Independent	-	5.50	2.20
Nanoo Pamnani	Non-Executive, Independent	-	4.00	1.60
P. Murari	Non-Executive, Independent	-	2.00	0.80

contd...

contd...

Name	*Category*	*Salary & Other Perks*	*Commission*	*Sitting Fees*
Bharti Airtel Limited (2006-07)				
Bashir Currimjee	Independent Director	-	8.72	0.80
Donald Cameron	Independent Director	-	-	0.80
Kurt Hellstrom	Independent Director	-	-	0.40
N. Kumar	Independent Director	-	8.72	0.80
P.C. Prasad	Independent Director	-	-	0.60
V.S. Raju	Independent Director	-	8.72	0.80
Ajay Lal	Independent Director	-	8.72	0.60
S.B. Imam	Independent Director	-	8.72	0.60
A.B. Ram	Independent Director	-	8.72	0.60
Larsen & Toubro Limited (2006-07)				
S. Rajgopal	Non-Executive Director	-	4.50	4.00
B.P. Deshmukh	Non-Executive Director	-	4.00	3.20
Kranti Sinha	Non-Executive Director	-	4.50	3.40
S.N. Talwar	Non-Executive Director	-	4.00	3.60
M.M. Chitale	Non-Executive Director	-	4.00	3.40
Lt. Gen. Surinder Nath (Retd.)	Non-Executive Director	-	4.00	4.00
U. Sundarrajan	Non-Executive Director	-	4.00	2.60
A.K. Shukla	Non-Executive Director	-	2.25	1.60

Other Relevant Issues

In addition to the quantitative data regarding the compensation details of executives, in various sectors and at different grades, there are several other issues which have a critical bearing on the attraction and retention of talent. These are typically, year-on-year increases, career growth opportunities, cadre to cadre jumps, linkage between performance and performance based pays etc. These are touched upon briefly in the following paragraphs:

Year-on-Year Increases:

- In view of the intense demand-supply situation prevailing, driven furiously by the impressive strides being made by the economy in the country, the flight of talent is proving to be extremely difficult to control even within private sector. The year-on-year salary hikes are reported to be ranging from 15-20 per cent in the middle management cadres. The hikes are reported to be as much as 40 per cent in respect of performers with specific skills sets. Similar hikes (15-18 per cent) are reported in the senior management cadres also.

- For intellectually intensive jobs, India is proving to be a fertile recruitment centre not only for MNCs operating in the country but also for MNC postings outside the country.
- At the end of the day, the ability of the companies to pay is inextricably linked to their profitability levels which in turn are linked to the upturn and downturn phenomenon in the economy. Even in the recent past, there was an upturn in the period 1993-1998, a downturn from 1998-2003 and fresh upturn from 2003 till date. It is however to be emphasised that the increases in salary levels cannot exceed the increases in the profitability levels of the companies. The specific percentage increases in wages, in select sectors, reported by *Business World* are indicated in Table 7.9.

Table 7.9

Year-on-Year Pay Hikes

Levels	*Manufacturing*	*IT*	*ITES/BPO*	*Pharma.*	*Telecom*	*Finance*
Entry	13	20	18	15	13	15
Junior Mgt.	17	17	15	15	13	15
Middle Mgt.	17	18	15	20	20	12
Senior Mgt.	15	15	12	20	18	12

Source: Business World, 5th February 2007.

Cadre to Cadre/Grade to Grade Jumps:

- The elevation from one cadre to the next higher cadre in the private sector implies substantial changes to the employee not only in respect of remuneration packages but also in terms of responsibility, accountability and productivity.
- Table 7.12, based on the average sectoral salaries reported by *Business Today*, indicates the following:

Table 7.10

Year-on-Year Pay Hikes

Cadre Jumps	*% Increase in Salaries*		
	Minimum	*Maximum*	*Average*
JM_2-JM_1	41	80	60.5
JM_1-JM_2	57	194	125.5
MM_2-MM_1	31	77	54
MM_1-MM_2	122	163	142.5
SM_2–SM_1	37	80	58.5

- It can be observed that the salary increase is very steep when the executives enter the senior management cadres.
- The average jumps, even in respect of other cadres also range from 50 per cent upwards.
- The last column of Table 7.12 indicates the ratios of salaries of executives of the junior-most level to the senior-most levels (below board level). The ratios range from a minimum of 8 to a maximum of 12.
- Table 7.11 summarises the impact of cadre to cadre jumps as reported by the Gallup Team study published by *Business World*.

Table 7.11

Cadre to Cadre Jumps in Various Sectors (BW Study)

(Annual CTC in Rs. lakhs)

Sector	*EL*	*JM*	*%JM/ EL*	*MM*	*%MM/ JM*	*SM*	*%SM/ MM*	*Ratio (higher to lower)*
Retail	1.49	2.31	55	4.7	103	8.68	85	5.83:1
BPO/ITES	1.48	3.39	129	7.0	105	13.9	99	9.35:1
Consumer Durables	2.28	4.54	99	8.5	88	20.0	135	8.79:1
Manufacturing	2.61	3.95	51	6.0	52	24.0	300	9.20:1
Information Technology	3.46	7.22	109	14.0	96	25.8	82	7.45:1
Pharmacy	1.53	5.22	241	10.0	98	26.4	155	17.25:1
Telecom	2.7	6.14	127	12.0	97	30.9	156	11.46:1
FMCG	2.4	6.02	151	15.0	149	34.8	132	14.50:1
Financial Sector	3.0	8.04	168	18.0	124	50.4	180	17.00:1

Table 7.12

Cadre to Cadre Salary Jumps in Various Sectors (With Respect to Average Salaries) (BT Study)

S. No.	Sector	JM_2 Asst.Mgr./ Sr.Executive/ Exe.	JM_1 Manager/ Dy.Manager	% of JM_1/ JM_2	MM_2 Sr.Mgr./ Manager	% MM_2/ JM_1	MM_1 DGM/ Asst.GM/ Sr.Mgr.	% of MM_1/ MM_2	SM_2 Sr.GM/ GM	% SM_2/ MM_1	SM_1 Sr.VP/ VP	% SM_1/ SM_2	Ratio SM_1 To JM_2
1.	FMCG	5.59	8.52	52	14.54	71	23.07	59	39.9	163	66.67	67	12:1
2.	Automotive	5.41	8.12	50	13.44	66	21.93	63	33.25	142	48.45	46	9:1
3.	IT	4.58	7.82	71	12.31	57	17.93	46	24.37	126	35.13	44	8:1
4.	Telecom	4.52	8.14	80	13.02	60	19.82	52	28.00	131	38.40	37	8:1
5.	Banking	4.49	6.32	41	15.07	138	22.66	50	31.54	129	44.47	41	10:1
6.	Petrochemicals etc.	4.12	6.60	60	11.03	67	16.24	47	24.00	138	34.83	45	8:1
7.	Pharmaceuticals	4.00	7.19	80	12.39	72	20.48	65	31.09	142	47.06	51	12:1
8.	Consumer Durables	3.93	6.77	72	10.65	57	17.91	68	27.13	141	48.93	80	12:1
9.	Core	3.50	5.42	55	7.49	38	11.48	53	19.30	158	30.51	58	9:1
10.	ITES/BPO	3.33	5.2	56	15.29	194	20.00	31	27.80	129	38.4	38	12:1
11.	Real Estate	3.13	5.22	67	8.32	59	13.26	59	21.66	153	29.63	37	9:1
12.	Retail	2.96	5.27	78	11.02	109	19.55	77	25.76	122	36.55	42	12:1
13.	Engineering	2.95	4.23	43	6.95	64	11.07	59	17.39	147	25.47	46	9:1
14.	Textile	2.63	3.97	51	7.25	83	12.51	73	18.62	139	27.92	50	11:1
	Average			61		81		57		140		49	

Attrition in Private Sector

Business Today reported attrition rates between 5-7 per cent of the senior management employees either to nascent or new economy industries like retail, real estate and telecom or to competition within their respective industries. The attrition rates reported in the middle management cadres are in the range of 15 per cent in automotive sector and as high as 22 per cent in the manufacturing sector. It is stated that across most sectors, both new and old, a similar trend prevails. The attrition rates reported in junior management cadres are stated to be as high as 33 per cent in respect of new recruits. The attrition rates reported in the FMCG and consumer durables range from 12-15 per cent.

The percentage figures reported by *Business World* for the year 2006 (grades not specified) are as under:

Manufacturing	*IT*	*ITES/ BPO*	*Pharma.*	*Telecom*	*Finance Sector*	*Consumer Durables*	*FMCG*	*Retail*
13	18	43	18	18	27	16	19	25

The most compelling factors that induce attrition are reported to be: (i) career growth opportunities, (ii) compensation, (iii) learning opportunity, and (iv) job content in that order. Career growth opportunities are taken more seriously than compensation by a factor of two, while factors (iii) and (iv) together are reported to weigh only about 50 per cent in importance with respect to compensation. Other factors such as work-life balance, immediate supervision, talent fit, and lack of recognition and family tasks are also indicative factors for attrition but their sensitivity is reported to be much lower.

8 Comparative Compensation Packages between CPSEs and Private Sector/MNCs in India

Detailed analysis of inter as well as intra-group comparisons on compensation packages have been made in the earlier chapters both in respect of the CPSEs and the private sector. However, for a quick recapitulation of observations made therein a summarised position is given hereunder.

Summary on CPSEs

The public sector enterprises are included in the definition of 'State' under the Article 12 of the Constitution. As a result, apart from statutory audit and internal audit, the CPSEs are subject to continuous and comprehensive transaction audit and supplementary audit of the accounts by the commercial wing of the CAG, whose representatives are posted as 'resident audit parity' in the offices of the CPSEs. The annual accounts of the CPSEs are placed before both the Houses of Parliament. Various Parliamentary Committees visit the CPSEs to check the compliance of Presidential directives and other government guidelines communicated from time to time. All the CPSEs are also under the purview of the Central Vigilance Commission (CVC) liaised through a full time senior executive of the concerned CPSE or an officer of the central services, designated as 'Chief Vigilance Officer', who directly reports to the CEO and works under the guidance of CVC. These are the major differences between the CPSEs, which are required to act on commercial lines while complying with the stringent governmental regulatory mechanisms, as against the working of private sector companies which are free from such extra statutory controls, over and above the normal corporate laws and regulations. Further, the provisions in the 'Right to information Act' also set apart CPSEs from private sector companies.

In terms of financial strength and the paying capacities of various CPSEs, the following are the broad observations:

- The 66 CPSEs which have attained the status of navratna/ miniratna are financially sound, consistently making profits and their net worth is positive. Most of these CPSEs are sharing a part of their net profits to their employees (around 5 per cent as per DPE guidelines) apart from payment of performance incentives which forms part of 'variable pay'. The number of executives and NUS in theses CPSEs constitutes 74 per cent of the total of such employees in the CPSEs.
- There are 46 'other profit-making' CPSEs which have been making profit continuously and have positive net worth but do not qualify to be miniratnas. (This does not include nine Section 25 Companies). The number of executives and NUS in this category is 36,555 accounting for 12 per cent of the total.
- There are 54 CPSEs, which are incurring continuous losses resulting in negative net worth. While most of these CPSEs are yet to implement the 1997 pay revision, they cannot afford to pay any incentives/variable pay to their employees. The number of executives and NUS in such PSEs is 18,006 which constitute 6 per cent of the total.
- The rest 47 CPSEs are marginally profit-making or loss-incurring. Only a few of these CPSEs are sharing their net profit to their employees which forms part of the 'variable pay'.
- While 171 CPSEs have implemented 1997 pay revision, 28 enterprises are still operating 1992 pay scales and 14 are still on 1987 pay scales (i.e., as on 1/1/2007 Annexure A-8.4). The number of executives and NUS in the pre-revised scales is 9829, which is 3 per cent of total executives and NUS in the CPSEs as a whole.
- Consequent on non-implementation of the last pay revision by all the 213 CPSEs under the study, the intra-CPSEs comparison of compensation replicates wide gaps between the highest and the lowest payers.

- On the other hand, inter-group differentials in respect of pay and allowances among the CPSEs are not marked with distinctive demarcation, excepting that the per capita emoluments in certain groups are high. In brief, the nature of the CPSE based on which the classification has been made by DPE did not bring out any significant differences in the pay and allowances as a distinct block/group.
- The scale to scale or cadre to cadre differentials are quite narrow in all the groups. Similarly, the ratio of the total emoluments of managerial cadre (E5) compared to firstline executive cadre (E1), as well as the ratio of pay and allowances of senior managers compared to firstline executives is quite minimal. In fact, these paltry differences do not give an appropriate explanation for the long years of journey of the senior executives who reached these higher levels that entail higher responsibilities.

Summary on Private Sector

- Inter-sectoral/group differentials in pay and allowances are seen in the case of private sector, e.g., FMCG and automotives are the best payers, whose compensation packages are quite higher when compared to the pay packages in textile and engineering groups. Also, the intra-group differentials in pay and allowances among the private sector enterprises are also very distinct and marked.
- The scale to scale or cadre to cadre, differentials in pay and allowances are quite sizeable among all the groups.

Methodology

As explained in Chapter 7, among various surveys covered in the study on private sector, it is observed that the survey conducted by Omam Consultants (published by *Business Today*), is more representative for comparative purposes primarily as it covers: (a) the highest number of groups (i.e., 14 as against 20 in the case of CPSEs) and (b) the highest number of enterprises (i.e., 102) with complete enterprise-wise details, that are presented in numerical numbers for maintaining confidentiality instead of revealing the actual names.

As mentioned earlier, the "Core sector" in BT survey, includes some groups in the manufacturing line, (i.e., steel, power, petroleum etc.) and a few enterprises in mining sector. Further as explained in Chapter 7, the veracity of the data in this survey has been fairly established, in comparison with other information sourced for this study, which is depicted graphically in the concluding part of this chapter. Hence, this survey is reckoned as a representative base for making ultimate comparisons with the executives of CPSEs and executives of private sector/MNCs in India.

The following method is adopted for fair comparisons:

- Only three grades in the case of CPSEs as well as private sector have been selected for this study. The three grades identified from CPSEs' side are: E1 (entry level executives), E5 (middle level managers), and E8 (senior managers). From the descriptions contained in the survey, the grades of JMII (junior management), MMII (middle management) and SMII (senior management) are considered close to E1, E5 and E8 of CPSEs respectively. In other words, the eight scales of executives (below the board level) in the case of CPSEs are considered equal to the six scales covered in the survey.
- Average emoluments within each group are taken into account, in both the cases. As BT survey included mining, steel, power and petroleum groups, under a major classification 'Core sector', the average of all the relevant groups are considered together for a like to like comparison.

On the above lines, a comparison of the pay and allowances of the private sector covered in BT survey is made with CPSEs in Table 8.1. The table clearly brings out the following:

Relating to CPSEs:

- The chemical and pharmaceuticals, textiles and consumer goods groups among the CPSEs list are the least payers in all the three grades.
- The core sectors in CPSEs list (*viz.*: coal, mineral & metals, power, petroleum and steel) are the highest payers.
- Grade to grade comparisons within CPSEs based on the averages reveal that the ratios among them are too minor i.e., (a) E1 to E5 is 1:1.68, (b) E5 to E8 is 1:1.29, and (c) E1 to E8 is 1:2.18.

Table 8.1

Comparative Compensation Packages between CPSEs and Private Sector (BT Survey), Group Averages both in CPSEs and Private Sector

(Rs. in lakh)

Groups As Per DPE	*No. of CPSEs*	*E1*	*E5*	*E8*	*Sectors BT Surveys*	*No. of Co.s*	*JMII*	*MMII*	*SMII*
Average of Coal, Minerals & Metals, Steel, Power, Petroleum Sectors—'Core'	44	3.31	5.32	6.93	Core	9	3.50	7.49	19.30
Chemicals & Pharmaceuticals Fertiliser	22	2.24	3.69	4.35	Chem. & Fertiliser Pharma.	15	4.06	11.71	31.09
Heavy & Light Engg.	35	3.26	4.97	6.53	Engineering	9	2.95	6.95	17.39
Textiles	15	2.69	4.56	5.60	Textiles	7	2.63	7.25	18.62
Consumer Goods	11	2.73	4.87	6.44	FMCG	6	5.59	14.54	39.90
					Consumer Durables	10	3.93	19.65	27.13
Trading & Marketing	13	2.65	4.61	5.82	Retail	5	2.96	11.02	26.76
Contract & Construction	11	2.51	4.71	5.85	Real Estate	8	3.13	8.32	21.66
Industrial Dev. & Tech. Consultancy	15	2.90	4.92	6.17	ITES and BPO	5	3.13	15.29	27.80
Telecommunications & IT	4	3.10	4.87	7.45	Telecom	5	4.52	13.02	28.00
					IT	9	4.58	12.31	24.37
Financial Services	9	3.04	5.23	6.33	Banking	5	4.49	15.07	31.54
Transport Equip.	10	3.01	5.27	7.12	Automotives	9	5.41	13.44	33.25
Transportation Services	11	3.12	5.46	6.74					
Average		2.88	4.85	6.28	Average		3.93	11.11	26.48

Relating to Private Sector:

- FMCG, banking, and automotives are the highest payers in private sector.
- Textiles, engineering and the real estate sectors are the least payers in private sector.
- Grade to grade comparisons within private sector based on the averages reveal that the ratios among them are prominent compared to similar ratios in the case of CPSEs i.e., (a) JMII to MMII is 1:2.82, (b) MMII to SMII is 1:2.38, and (c) JMII to SMII is 1:6.74.

Relating to Comparative Ratios:

- The grade to grade comparisons based on the overall averages between private sector *versus* CPSEs reveal that the ratio of: (a) E1 to JMII is 1:3.6 (b) E5 to MMII is 1:2.29, (c) E8 to SMII is 1:4.22, and (d) E1 to SMII 1:9.19.
- Cadre to cadre distinction is quite pronounced in the case of private sector, unlike in the CPSEs whose grades and cadres are knit very closely.

In Chapters 5 and 7 the intra-group variations in the total emoluments both in the case of CPSEs and private sector were well defined. The reasons for the wide variations in the emoluments are on account of: (a) non-implementation of 1997 pay revision uniformly by all the CPSEs (b) variable pay, though marginal, also contributed for these variations as all the CPSEs are not paying the same. However, as only the averages have been considered in Table 8.1, certain wide variations might have been evened out. To remove any doubts due to limitations in the process of adopting averages, two more alternative means of comparisons have been chosen i.e., comparison with: (a) highest payers in both CPSEs and private sector and (b) highest of CPSEs compared with averages in private sector. The comparative position under these two alternatives is detailed in Tables 8.2-8.4.

As seen from Table 8.2, the gap between the CPSEs and private sector has further widened when the comparison is made by considering the highest payers in both these cases.

Table 8.2

Comparative Compensation Packages between CPSEs and Private Sector (BT Survey)
Highest Payers in both CPSEs and Private Sector

(Rs. in lakh)

Sectors As Per DPE	*E1*	*E5*	*E8*	*Sectors BT Surveys*	*JMII*	*MMII*	*SMII*
Coal, Minerals & Metals, Steel, Power, Petroleum—'Core'	4.72	6.34	9.19	Core	5.40	10.69	24.20
Chemicals & Pharmaceuticals Fertiliser	3.14	5.35	7.41	Chemicals & Pharmaceuticals Fertiliser	2.49	4.09	5.23
Heavy, Medium & Light Engineering	3.26	4.97	6.53	Engineering	4.15	9.70	34.15
Textiles	2.91	3.95	4.93	Textiles	2.75	9.71	28.00
Consumer Goods	2.72	5.06	6.44	FMCG	6.73	15.70	57.23
				Consumer Durables	4.94	17.52	35.00
Trading & Marketing	3.27	5.74	7.71	Retail	3.88	16.09	28.00
Contract & Construction	2.71	5.40	6.62	Real Estate	3.95	7.00	27.50
Industrial Dev. & Tech. Consultancy	3.97	5.24	6.99	ITES and BPO	4.31	17.80	34.00
Telecommunications & IT	3.10	4.87	7.45	Telecom	5.60	10.61	30.00
				IT	5.44	9.28	31.30
Financial Services	3.58	5.30	6.72	Banking	5.55	18.32	36.75
Transport Equipment	4.14	6.30	9.10	Automotive	6.61	19.84	46.00
Transportation Services	4.00	6.65	8.44				
Average	3.46	5.43	7.29	Average	4.75	12.80	32.10

Table 8.3

Comparative Compensation Packages between CPSEs and Private Sector (BT Survey)
Highest of CPSEs Compared with Averages in Private Sector

(*Rs. in lakh*)

Sectors As Per DPE	*E1*	*E5*	*E8*	*Sectors BT Surveys*	*JMII*	*MMII*	*SMII*
Coal, Minerals & Metals, Steel, Power, Petroleum—'Core'	4.72	6.34	9.19	Core	3.50	7.49	19.30
Chemicals & Pharmaceuticals, Fertiliser	3.14	5.35	7.41	Chem. & Pharma. Fertiliser	4.06	11.71	31.09
Heavy, Medium & Light Engg.	3.26	4.97	6.53	Engineering	2.95	6.95	17.39
Textiles	2.91	3.95	4.93	Textiles	2.63	7.25	18.62
Consumer Goods	2.72	5.06	6.44	FMCG	5.59	14.54	39.90
Trading & Marketing	3.27	5.74	7.71	Consumer Durables	3.93	19.65	27.13
				Retail	2.96	11.02	26.76
Contract & Construction	2.71	5.40	6.62	Real Estate	3.13	8.32	21.66
Industrial Dev. & Tech. Consultancy	3.97	5.24	6.99	ITES and BPO	3.13	15.29	27.80
Telecommunications & IT	3.10	4.87	7.45	Telecom	4.52	13.02	28.00
Financial Services	3.58	5.30	6.72	IT	4.58	12.31	24.37
				Banking	4.49	15.07	31.54
Transport Equipment	4.14	6.30	9.10	Automotives	5.41	13.44	33.25
Transportation Services	4.00	6.65	8.44				
Average	3.46	5.43	7.29	Average	3.93	11.11	26.48

Table 8.4

Comparative Compensation Packages between CPSEs and Private Sector (BW Survey) Averages of CPSEs Compared with Averages in Private Sector

(Rs. in lakh)

Sectors As Per DPE	*No. of CPSEs*	*E1*	*E5*	*E8*	*Sectors BT Surveys*	*No. of Co.s*	*JMII*	*MMII*	*SMII*
Average of Coal, Minerals & Metals, Steel, Power, Petroleum Sectors— 'Core'	44	3.31	5.32	6.93	Manufacturing	9	3.50	7.49	19.30
Fertiliser	22	2.38	4.08	5.31	Pharmaceuticals	15	4.06	11.71	31.09
Consumer Goods	11	2.73	4.87	6.12	FMCG	5	6.02	15.00	34.80
					Consumer Durables	8	4.54	8.32	20.04
Trading & Marketing	13	2.65	4.61	5.82	Retail	7	2.31	4.68	8.68
Industrial Dev. & Tech. Consultancy	15	2.90	4.92	6.17	ITES and BPO	5	3.39	6.96	13.86
					Telecom	4	6.14	12.09	30.93
Telecommunications & IT	4	3.10	4.87	7.45	IT	7	7.72	14.16	25.77
Financial Services	9	3.04	5.23	6.33	Financial Services	6	8.04	18.00	50.40
Average		2.87	4.84	6.30	Average		5.20	10.62	26.10

As may be seen from Table 8.3, the comparative position of the highest of CPSEs compared with averages in private sector has not shown any significant change from the conclusions drawn earlier, since the gap between CPSEs *versus* private sector is very visible and pronounced.

To establish the veracity of the above conclusions, a comparison is made with reference to the survey of *Business World* in Table 8.4.

Table 8.4 reaffirms and validates the conclusions drawn earlier; especially figures contained in both the surveys of BT and BW are very close.

Data directly collected by IPE: The average figures of the 10 sectors for which data has been collected by IPE (i.e., excluding aviation) is also observed to be close to the findings contained in the surveys conducted by BT and BW detailed above i.e., for the selected grades of JMII (E1) it is Rs. 4.57 lakh, for MMII (E5) it is Rs. 11.50 lakh and for SMII (E8) it is Rs. 25.30 lakh.

paycheck.in Data: The weighted average figures for the manufacturing sector contained in the *paycheck.in* survey, which is more dominated by MNCs also are found to be close with the BT and BW surveys and the data collected by IPE for 10 groups.

The comparative data of the above four independent surveys is depicted in Figures 8.1-8.3 to establish the validity in choosing the BT survey as the representative one for ultimate comparisons with the executives of CPSEs and that of the private sector.

Comparison of Compensation of the Executives of CPSEs, with Officers of the Government, Executives of Private Sector and MNCs

As mentioned above, the average figures relating to BT survey are considered representative among the four alternatives set of figures from private sector. Also for the reasons explained earlier, separate set of figures could not be compiled for MNCs, as they were included as a part of private sector studies. However, for comparative purposes they are assumed to be 50 per cent higher over the private sector compensation packages. With these assumptions the comparative position of the CPSEs (the highest figures) *versus* government officers, private sector and MNCs is depicted in Figure 8.4.

Figure 8.1

Junior Management

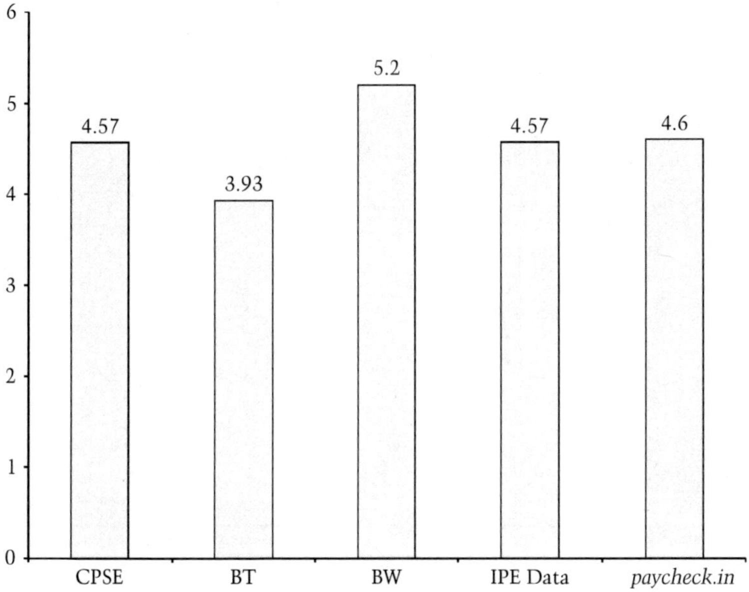

Figure 8.2

Middle Management

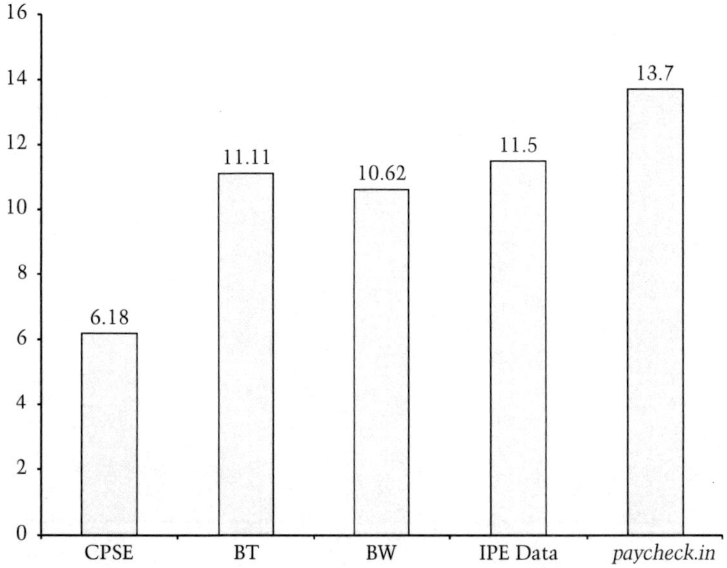

Figure 8.3

Senior Management

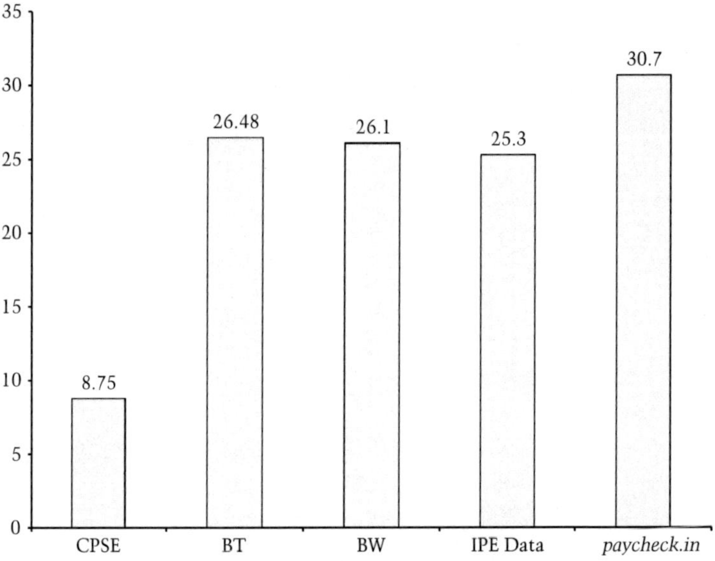

Figure 8.4

Comparison of Compensation of the Executives of CPSEs, with Officers of the Government, Executives of Private Sector and MNCs

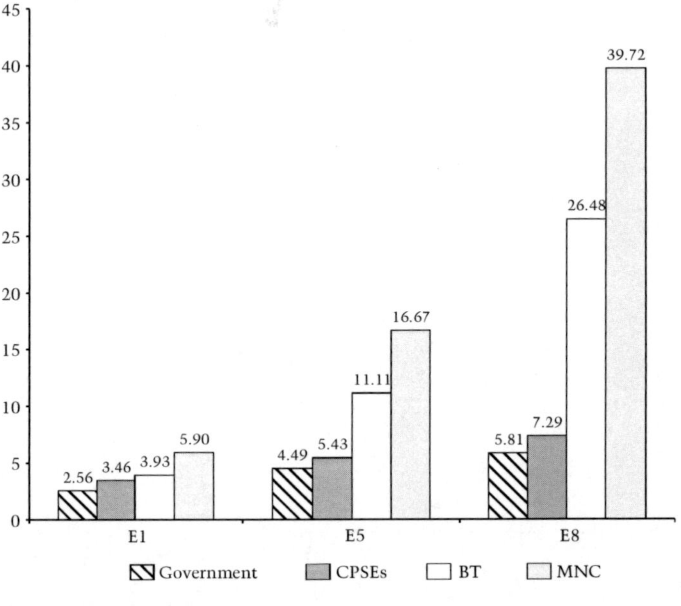

As may be seen from Figure 8.4, at the initial levels JMII (E1), the pay both in public as well as private sectors is almost close. However, the pay at the middle level managers (E5) in CPSEs is demonstrably lower compared to private sector. Similarly in the case of senior managers in CPSEs (E8), the pay is much lesser compared to private sector.

Board-level Executives: As seen from the huge figures of compensation packages of some of the selected companies detailed in Chapter 7, the figures range from Rs. 50 to 400 lakh for the board Level executives in private sector/MNCs. They are far in reach for a possible comparison with the highest paid CEOs in CPSEs, whose pay including valued perks even at the maximum of the scale might not exceed, even say Rs. 15 to 20 lakh. Further, as seen from Chapter 7, even independent directors in private sector receives commissions apart from sitting fees which range between Rs. 4–27 lakh. Therefore, it could safely be concluded that the CEOs in CPSEs are getting a pay even 3 to 15 times lesser than their counterparts in private sector/MNCs.

Career Growth: It is stated that an average time span of 20-22 years is needed to reach the SM_1 level position for an executive starting his career at the entry level of the organisation and that about 20 per cent of the employees succeed in going up the corporate ladder in this way. However, in exceptional cases, very talented people may rise to the top positions in 15-18 years. But such cases will be limited to about five per cent of the sample. Figure 8.5 highlights the contrast between private sector companies and CPSEs in the growth profile of the executives. The rapid growth prospects in the private sector companies naturally attract talent.

Evaluation of Performance

Commensurate with the handsome salaries and attractive rises, the standards of performance evaluation, levels of responsibility, accountability and expectations regarding productivity are very high in the context of private sector companies.

Figure 8.5

Growth Comparisons between CPSEs and Private Sector

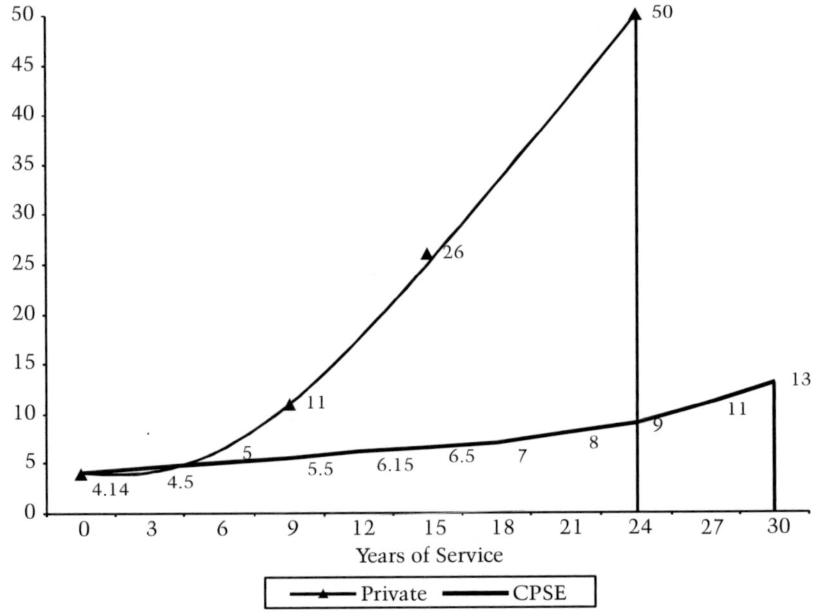

Typically, the performance level of an executive is ranked as: Rank 1 – Excellent; Rank 2 – Very Good; Rank 3 – Good; Rank 4 – Average; and Rank 5 – Poor. The nomenclature used may vary from company to company. The profile of ranking with respect to grading and percentage, executives categorised in the corresponding rank will be as indicated below:

a)	Excellent	:	5%
b)	Very Good	:	15%
c)	Good	:	60%
d)	Average	:	15%
e)	Poor	:	5%

It is understood that those executives who are ranked at levels 4 and 5 receive no rises. The "Good" are reported to get a rise ranging from 8 to 12 per cent. The "Very Good" ranking fetches a rise of 15 to 18 per cent and executives ranked as "Excellent" are given a rise to 20 to 25 per cent.

The promotions are reported to be limited to a maximum of 5 per cent. It is understood that executive getting ranked in the levels of 4 and 5 will be observed keenly for some time and asked to leave if no signs of improvement are visible. The more benign companies provide some observation time whereas in the case of more critical companies, the quitting orders are immediate.

Figure 8.6 highlights the structured profiling of the executives and the associated rewards. It is stated that the 'Excellent' category of executives cannot exceed 5 per cent on one hand and the 'Poor' category of executives have to be a minimum of 5 per cent.

Figure 8.6

Typical Pay Rises in Private Sector Companies

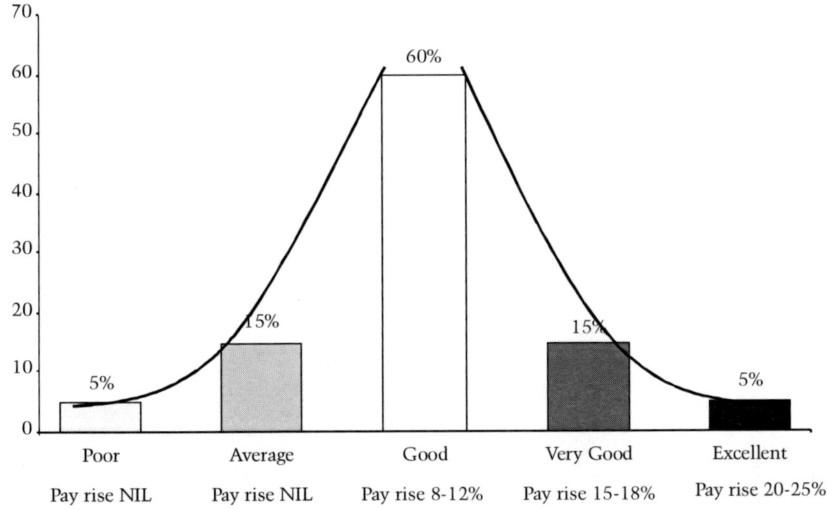

The principle of 'differentiation', as mentioned at the beginning of the chapter is very rigorously practised in the private sector companies. By and large, the philosophy of compensation, the evaluation systems and the linkages between performance and rewards will be based on the practices adopted in USA as most of the leading companies retain the services of reputed US consulting firms to design their HR practices.

9 Public Sector: Situation Abroad

Coverage

While there are industrial undertakings and business establishments functioning under the government control in several countries, the nature of work that gets carried out in these establishments does not appear to have the depth and breadth of CPSEs functioning in India. A limited study could be carried out on Canada, Singapore, Australia and France to provide an overview on areas of operations, parity with private sector companies, methodology of pay fixation, frequency of pay revision, linkages of remuneration to performance etc.

Some points related to compensation of senior government officers are also included in some detail, as they may be informative. The country of Singapore is intensely focusing on efficiency and thoroughness in all its endeavours. The government machinery, be it civil service, statutory bodies or government controlled business houses is laying great emphasis on talent. The remuneration is not taken as a constraint for inducting or retaining talent including in civil services.

Areas of Operations

Canada

The government business enterprises in Canada operate at three levels: (a) at the federal level, (b) at the provincial and territorial level, and (c) at local government level. The businesses conducted at these three levels are distinctly different.

At the federal level, the nature of activities carried out cover: (a) railway operations, (b) broadcasting, (c) mortgage and building construction, (d) air transport security, (e) postal operations, (f) currency trading, (g) bullion trading, (h) nuclear power generation, and (i) mint and banking operations. The business enterprises operating at the federal level are referred to as crown corporations.

At the provincial and territorial level, the businesses handled are reported as: (a) gaming business and lotteries, and (b) sale of alcohol.

At the local government level, the activities carried out are limited to: (a) bus transport, (b) management of utilities like electricity and gas.

The terms government, government run business houses and other activities handled by the government like education in schools, colleges, vocational training etc., have the umbrella coverage of public sector. In the year 2006, out of 3.1 million employees under the category of public sector, only 0.26 million (about 8.5%) are stated to be employed in government business enterprises. The business enterprises at the federal level enjoy significant autonomy and operate under approved budgets.

Singapore

The span of coverage with respect to industrial activity under government control appears to be very pronounced in Singapore. The government control is reported to be operative under two conditions: (a) government linked companies (GLC), and (b) government statutory boards.

The GLCs are controlled through a wholly owned government holding controlling company called TEMASEK holdings—which holds shares in the business entities like Mapletree Investments (real estate)—100 per cent, Singapore Power (electricity and gas)—100 per cent, Power Seraya (power generation, transmission & distribution)—100 per cent, Senoko (power generation, distribution & retailing)—100 per cent, PSA International (ports)—100 per cent, Neptune Orient Lines (shipping)—67 per cent, Chartered Semiconductor Manufacturing (semiconductor)—60 per cent, Sing Tel (telecommunications)—56 per cent, SMRT (rail, bus and taxi services)—55 per cent, Singapore Technologies Engineering (engineering)—53 per cent, Media Corp. (mass communications)—100 per cent and Singapore Airlines (air transport)—55 per cent.

The government also holds significant stakes in the Sem Corp Industries (engineering)—49 per cent, Sem Corp Marine (ship building)—32 per cent and DBS (largest bank in Singapore)—28 per cent.

Compared to Canada, the span of coverage of government controlled companies in Singapore is much wider. The activities covered include engineering, air transport, broadcasting and mass communications, public transport, telecommunications, power generation, transmission & distribution, electricity & gas retailing, real estate, ship building, shipping and port management etc. The situation in Singapore appears closer to India, in terms of government's participating in industrial and business activity.

Australia

Similar to Singapore, Australia also has a holding company concept for promoting and monitoring its government business enterprises (GBEs). Apart from closely monitoring the physical and financial performance of its GBEs, the holding company, working under the guidance of Government Businesses Advice Branch (GBAB), explicitly brings out the Statement of Corporate Intent (SCI) of its enterprises, in consultation with its share holder ministries.

The GBEs include: (a) ASC Pty Ltd., (b) Australian Government Solicitor, (c) Australian Postal Corporation, (d) Australian Rail track Corporation, (e) Defence Housing Australia, (f) Health Services Australia Limited, and (g) Medibank Pvt. Ltd.

Comparatively, the degree of coverage in the government controlled business in Australia appears to be much less in scope. The accent is on public utilities and welfare activities like rail transport, postal services, health services, banking and housing.

France

The public sector was massive in France in the mid-80s in all areas of economy, including banks and automotive industry. This was the result of nationalisation of several enterprises in different areas in 1936, 1945 and 1981. However, privatisation is carried out since 1986 and a number of these enterprises like France Telecom, Air France, Snecma, Toll Motorway Companies have been privatised. Air France is merged with KLM and Snecma is merged with SAGEM a few years back. Privatisation of a number of public sector enterprises like Airbus, Arianespace and Safran have been carried out wherein the state equity stake dropped below 50 per cent. The number of public enterprises have come down from 3500 in 1996 to 1400 in 2005. The number of employees in these enterprises has come down to 900,000 in 2005 from 2,350,000 in 1996. In spite of this, the public enterprises in France remain substantial in sectors like transport, health, energy etc.

The major public sector enterprises in France include Electricite de France (EDF), Gaz de France (GDF), Aerospatiale, France Telecom, Renault and Airport de France. Public sector enterprises had played a key role in major infrastructure programmes in the areas of energy, transport and telecommunications. Some of these programmes include French Telecommunications Programme launched in 1974, French Nuclear Programme launched also in 1974 (nuclear plants now provide more than 75 per cent of electricity produced in France), Fast Train TGV (covers Paris-Marseilles in three hours). Government Shareholding Agency oversees the affairs of the state-owned enterprises.

The major strengths on which the French PSEs are leveraging on are, ability to cope with long-term objectives, ability to carry high debt with the state guarantees and ability to define a strategy including public service priorities.

Factors which are generally quoted as the weaknesses of Indian CPSE structure are referred to in the same context in France also. Typical of these are political influence in the management, overstaffing with conservative trade unions, Difficulty to cope with a competitive environment and slow to react when facing problems.

Public enterprises in France played a key role in major infrastructure programmes that include areas like energy, transport and telecommunications. The France Telecom is cited as a successful public enterprise in terms of improving the infrastructure in the period 1975-1985, when the need was very acutely felt and when things have substantially improved, the sector was opened up for competition with increased privatisation. In the early 70s, the telephone density in France was the lowest in Europe and the quality of service was poor. An ambitious investment plan was launched and carried on by France Telecom, which was a 100 per cent public company. The enterprise France Telecom was the pioneer of new technologies (digital switching) and data networks (Minitel). Within a decade, the quality of the telephone service became one of the best in Europe. France Telecom was very profitable, which created a lot of envy as it was operating as a monopoly.

In the period 1985-2005, the telecom markets were progressively opened to competition in the areas of mobile services, business services, international and residential connections. Challenged in the home markets, the telephone companies started to look for new markets abroad. The human resources were diversified and the top managements were changed with induction of CEO from private sector. A new competitive spirit was nurtured without forgetting the value of public service. For years, the privatisation of France Telecom has been a very controversial issue; it happened late when the controversy had dissipated. In 1997, a minority stake of FT was listed in the stock markets of Paris and New York. The employees were offered shares at attractive prices. The initial public offerings (IPO) was very successful. The state ownership was progressively reduced from 80 per cent to 51 per cent and in 2003 the ownership dropped below 50 per cent in a seamless way.

The major holdings in state public enterprises are now held by an autonomous agency created in 2003 called 'The French Government Shareholding Agency'. The French policy aims at diversifying the shareholding structure that will team up public and private investors and employees.

The state equity stake dropped below 50 per cent in the major private/public partnerships in the high technology—strategic domains of aerospace, defence and aviation sectors in the cases of EADS/Airbus, Arianespace and Safran. Public enterprises are floated in the stock market while retaining state control, for providing funds to the budget, changing the management/culture of the company, complying with standard accounting rules and promoting employees equity stake.

The basic rules adopted in France for the management of public enterprises are:

- In spite of privatisation programmes, public enterprises remain numerous in several sectors: transport, health, energy.

- The market is always the best judge of performances.
- Control must be done by a professional and independent body.
- Competition is often the best way to put pressure on the management and change corporate culture.
- Developing employee ownership is a great incentive.
- Private investors are most often necessary as an additional source of funds.
- Public authorities to function as good strategic stakeholders and put in position organisations and procedures adopted to this goal including in the choice of CEOs.

Methodology of Fixation of Compensation

Canada

The salaries and performance pay ranges, and the actual pay of crown corporation CEOs are finalised by the governor-in-council. The pay ranges are set each year on the recommendation of the advisory committee known as the Stephenson committee. This committee also makes recommendations on compensation for government executives (categorised under 5 levels as Ex1 to Ex5) and deputy ministers (catergorised under 4 levels as DM1 to DM4) and a few other governor-in-council appointees in agencies, boards and commissions. For the CEOs of crown corporations, Hay Associates compare the remuneration of Group 1 (the lowest level) position with the median (i.e., 50th percentile) compensation for a set of private sector jobs at the same level in order to propose a salary range adjustment. Salaries for higher groups are based on relativities among crown corporations. The risk pay is in the range of 10 to 25 per cent of salary.

The Strong Committee was established in 1997, to mainly address the issue of salaries for CEOs of crown corporations. In their first report, in January 1998, the Committee observed that the general freezing of federal public sector salaries over most of the first half of the decade had a perverse effect on internal relativities within these enterprises and in many cases among the larger corporations, led to retention and recruitment difficulties. A comprehensive review was undertaken of these key jobs with the assistance of Hay Associates who have furnished the needed data after studying 466 large companies.

The results indicated that existing total cash compensation for the 10 groups lagged well behind the Hay medians for analogous jobs with financial/industrial employers. The compensation approach that was adopted on the basis of the Strong Committee recommendations involves benchmarking the Group 1 CEO salary range to the 25th percentile of actual salaries of incumbents of private sector jobs of equivalent scope in the Hay position evaluation database. Higher group job rates are then set at a fixed differential ranging from 12 per cent for the lower to 20 per cent for the upper level groups. A risk pay would be paid in addition, based on performance, to a maximum of 10 per cent of salary for the lower groups, and 25 per cent for the group 10 crown corporations. This relativity was later amended to 50th percentile of the comparable private sector compensation levels in the year 2005.

The relative compensation levels of CEOs from Group 1 to Group 10 for the year 2005 are indicated in the Table 9.1. The salary details of some senior government executives and deputy ministers are given in Table 9.2.

Table 9.1

CEO Compensation Levels of Crown Corporations for Different Groups in 2004-05

(In Canadian Dollars)

Level	*Job Rates 2004*	*Job Rates 2005*	*Maximum At-Risk Pay*
Group 1	$121,700	$125,400	10%
Group 2	$136,300	$140,400	10%
Group 3	$152,700	$157,300	10%
Group 4	$171,000	$176,200	10%
Group 5	$191,500	$197,300	10%
Group 6	$220,200	$226,900	15%
Group 7	$253,200	$260,800	15%
Group 8	$291,200	$300,000	15%
Group 9	$349,400	$359,900	20%
Group 10	$419,300	$431,900	25%

Note: One Canadian dollar is equivalent to about Rs. 38.50.

It can be seen from the Table 9.1 that the risk pay or performance related pay is kept lower at 10 per cent for the CEOs of smaller corporations and raised to 25 per cent for CEOs of large corporations. The relativity of the CEO of the smaller crown corporation to the senior most CEOs of largest crown corporation is 1:3.4.

Table 9.2

Salaries of Senior Government Officers and Deputy Ministers during 2004-05

Level	*Job Rates 2004*	*Job Rates 2005*	*Maximum At-Risk Pay*
EX1	$104,800	$108,000	10%
EX2	$117,400	$121,000	10%
EX3	$131,500	$135,500	10%
EX4	$151,000	$155,600	15%
EX5	$169,200	$174,300	15%
DM1	$189,400	$195,100	15%
DM2	$217,700	$224,300	20%
DM3	$243,800	$251,200	20%
DM4	$273,100	$281,300	25%

Compensation Levels of Other Executives: The largest crown corporation, Canada Post, is about three quarters unionised. Its compensation philosophy is to pay at the market average in order to balance costs with the need to attract and retain the required talent. For example, Canada Post defines its comparator market as a group of about 20 large, profitable employers that operate nationally. Other corporations are essentially non-unionised. Canada Mortgage and Housing Corporation (CMHC), for example, composed largely of professional staff, aims to set total cash compensation at the 75th percentile of the base pay line of the Hay Associates' All Organisations Survey, which covers over 400 public and private employers across Canada. The Bank of Canada generally targets the median of established comparison markets. However, to ensure it can attract and retain the specialised staff it needs to carry out its work, the bank provides special market adjustments on a temporary basis to specified occupational groups who are in high demand in the market and can draw significantly higher salaries externally.

Variable or Performance Pay: Practices in the area of variable or performance pay go much further in some crown corporations than in the rest of the federal public sector. For executives and non-unionised staff, there are several cases of a two-tier incentive pay structure, recognising both overall corporate (or team) and individual performance. At CMHC, the corporate incentive award rewards employees for the achievement of specific objectives as set by the board and publish it at the beginning of each year. For 2002, the payment was up to 3 per cent of salary for employees with a performance rating of at least "succeeds". In addition, a lumpsum individual incentive award can be earned based on an employee's performance rating and position level. Maximum awards for an "outstanding" rating range from 10 per cent at lower levels of the organisation to upto 15 per cent at the vice-president rank. Canada Post's plan for executives and non-unionised staff provide a corporate team incentive based on overall Canada Post performance, as well as individual awards based on performance against pre-set objectives. The corporate performance component is based on an assessment of three factors:

- Profit *versus* financial targets—40%.
- Service levels against standards—30%, and
- Customer satisfaction survey results—30%.

The board of a crown corporation may decide to provide benefits other than remuneration. Remuneration for crown corporation vice-presidents and other executives is the responsibility of the board of directors. Concerns expressed about 'pay inversion' (i.e., vice-presidents earning more than CEOs) led to a review whose results were reported in the May 2003 report of the Stephenson Committee. Inversion occurs in some cases because the variable pay for vice-presidents is not limited as for CEOs, but follows more closely the higher levels found in the private sector. The Committee also concluded that the existence of some pay compression or inversion was not out of line with experience for public sector corporations in other countries.

For senior executives, the combined value of these two awards could be as much as 25 per cent to 40 per cent, and it is for this reason the vice-president may end up getting a higher compensation package than the CEO.

Pensions: Pension arrangements vary among crown corporations, but are broadly similar to that of the core public service. All offer defined benefit plans, with benefits based on years of service and average salary over a specified period. In some cases, the terms are more favourable for executives, for example using the three instead of five consecutive best years as the basis for calculating average salary. The larger crowns manage their own pension plans, which are funded. Accumulated contributions are invested in the market. At a given time, such funds may have an actuarial surplus or deficit. Many smaller crowns, including all the cultural crown corporations, participate in the plan that applies to the core public service.

Annual Salaries of Public Sector Employees—Some samples:

Table 9.3

Ontario Power Generation Corp. (OPGC)

	Canadian Dollars
Nuclear Operator	101904
Senior Technical Engineer/Officer	104594
Sr. Officer Performance Improvement	111308
Section Manager, Procurement Engineering	119660
Senior Technical Expert	121153
Hydroelectric Operating Supervisor	127672
Sr. Technical Engineer/Officer	149604
Business Manager	150162
First Line Manager, Control/Mechanical	161994
Chief Risk Officer	202898
Vice-President, Engineering and Modifications/Chief Nuclear Engineer	269462
Chief Information Officer	352931
Executive Vice-President and Chief Operating Officer	1015540

Table 9.4

Toronto Community Housing Corporation

	Canadian Dollars
Director	103002
Manager	103025
General Manager Access Housing Corp.	121343
Manager	132400
Vice-President	155687
Chief Financial Officer	167650
Vice-President	168150
President and Chief Executive Officer	204000
Chief Executive Officer	209372

Source: Disclosure for 2006 under the Public Sector Salary Disclosure Act, 1996.

Table 9.5

Hydro One (Subsidiary of OPGC)

	Canadian Dollars
Regional Maintainer 2 - Lines	100698
Maintenance Engineer	101000
Senior Network Management Engineer/Officer	106596
Business/Account Manager	107233
Senior Financial Advisor External Financial Reporting and Control	127531
Manager—Work Management	139625
Regional Maintainer I - Lines	139930
Standards Development Manager	142867
Distribution Superintent Provincial Lines	147056
Manager Financial Model and Analysis	153162
Vice-President and Chief Regulatory	270338
Vice-President, Internal Audit and Chief Risk Officer	282868
Chief Financial Officer	474166
Executive Vice-President & Chief Operating Officer	1015540

Singapore

Singapore has only one level of government i.e., national and local government is one and the same in view of the country's small population of about 4 million. As a governing body for both the nation and the city, the Singapore government is responsible for planning, budgeting for and supervising the majority of key services. The actual delivery of some services has been devolved to statutory boards. These are autonomous government agencies set up by special legislation to perform specific functions. Some statutory boards have formed subsidiary companies to add further flexibility to their operations like, charging fees for service provided. Others have been further corporatised and subsequently privatised. These include power and gas provision, telecommunications and broadcasting. There are a little over 114,500 people working in the Singapore public sector, including members of the civil list, political appointments and civil servants who work in 14 ministries and employees of the statutory boards. The public sector accounts for around 5.23 per cent of the total working population. The civil service proper employs close to 63,300 staff, or 55 per cent of the overall public service. The Singapore civil service is generally regarded as efficient, thorough, strategic and pragmatic having facilitated demonstrated improvements in service delivery over recent years. A mixture of privatisation, corporatisation, formation of statutory boards and other managerial initiatives has been used as tools to enhance and maintain efficiency of government organisations. There were no recruitment freezes but hiring policies were limited to replacements for necessary personnel. Pay reform in the Singapore civil service has taken place in the broader context of personnel-related reform. In particular, this included constitutional amendments in 1995 to delegate recruitment and promotion functions, for all grades of staff except the administrative service, from the Public Service Commission to the various ministries, through a system of personnel boards.

Key developments that have characterised the pay reform include:

- Introduction of a flexible wage system in July 1988 driven by the economic recession of 1985. This enabled the award of wage increases, on top of salary increments, as a mid-year or year-end variable bonus. It also provided the government with increased flexibility to adjust wages in response to future economic situations.
- Move towards more competitive salaries for top civil servant talent. There was a substantial salary increase for both administrative service officers (about 20%) and other senior civil servants (from between 21% to 34%) at the end of 1993 in response to low recruitment and high resignation rates. In 1994, salaries for senior staff were pegged to those in the private sector by setting formal benchmarks. Two points are used: Superscale G for senior civil servants and Staff Grade I for ministers. Other salaries are then interpolated or extrapolated from these two points.
- Introduction of performance related pay for all civil servants, linked to individual performance.
- Gradual phasing out of pensions as part of the government's move to reduce liabilities for the future generations.
- Introduction of salary ranges for senior civil servants to increase flexibility in personnel management. Officers can be rewarded with merit increments within their salary range each year depending on their assessed potential and demonstrated performance.

Pay Principles: The civil service operates on the following pay principles:

- Comparability with the private sector. In recent years, there has been an increased emphasis on competitiveness of civil servants' pay *vis-a-vis* the private sector, although the policy is for their pay to be pegged to, but not to lead the market.
- Annual salary reviews. To remain competitive, annual salary reviews are conducted to identify salaries that need revision. The civil service takes into account the annual wage adjustment recommendations of the National Wage Council and follows its principles of wage adjustment in salary revision exercises.
- Flexibility in the wage structure of civil servants. The wage structure for civil servants is made up of a number of components which can be adjusted based on the performance of the economy without affecting take home pay too adversely. An additional flexibility has been added through introduction of performance bonus linked to individual performance.
- "Clean wage" policy. Civil servants are paid "all cash" wages which is indicative of a move away from paying a wide variety of allowances, provision of free housing, and offering free medical benefits. One initiative was a transfer from the Civil Service Pension scheme to a national Central Provident Fund (CPF) scheme.
- Internal relativity. Educational qualifications remain an important factor in determining starting salaries and for entry into the civil service.
- Long-term strategic view. The civil service adopts a long-term strategic view on pay administration matters. This has had some important implications for the design of the pay structure and system.

Approach Taken in Designing Pay Structures: Pay structures are designed using a hybrid of the job-based approach. Job evaluation is used to rank jobs within a certain scheme of service into ascending levels of difficulty and responsibility. The aim is to ensure:

- Equal pay for equal jobs.

- Promotion always involves movement to positions of higher job responsibility.

The internal relativity of the various schemes of service and their salary ranges, however, are not an issue in practice as they are all pegged to their respective market rates according to qualifications and, in most cases, age. Although salaries are benchmarked against the market, promotion and movement up the grades are still perceived to be generally slower than in the private sector except for the administrative service.

The pay structure for most of the civil services is characterised by fixed salary scales with fixed minimum, maximum and increments. The exception is the administrative service' salary scale and salary points which have been replaced by a system of salary ranges in 2000. Under the current arrangements, the variable and semi-variable components can amount to 30 per cent to 40 per cent of the base salary to provide an adequate cushion for adjusting salaries during times of economic recession. Employees are constantly reminded that a significant part of their earnings are 'at risk' and dependent on the health of the economy as a whole. With the exception of senior civil servants, pay administration is the responsibility of the respective ministers.

Actual Pay Levels and Pay Adjustment Mechanisms: For senior civil servants, a formula has been set to peg pay to salaries of top earners from a basket of six professions. These have been chosen based on similarity with the nature of work performed by such civil servants e.g., bankers, accountants, engineers, lawyers, multinational companies and local manufacturers. The point of comparison is the average of the principal earned income of the 15th highest tax payer, aged 32 years old, belonging to each of the six professions.

It is clearly stated that the benchmark figure is an estimated average, not a fixed entitlement and includes basic pay, non-pensionable annual pay (NPAA), annual variable component (AVC), a typical performance bonus, a car allowance and special allowance. Benchmarks are computed annually, based on income tax returns data. Salaries automatically follow the benchmarks up or down, albeit after a lag. The benchmarks are reviewed every five years. For most civil servants (ministers are an exception), the benchmark is not "discounted". This is based on the argument that it would be unrealistic and unfair to expect civil servants to make a financial sacrifice compared to their private sector peers, in order to enter public service.

The first review of the administrative service benchmark in 2000 revealed that salaries in the private sector were anything up to 50 per cent higher. Services suffering from critical staffing level will be given interim market adjustments when the gap with the benchmark widens beyond a certain amount, for example 15 per cent. Government considers that in times of economic downturn, it has a duty to send a clear signal of the gravity of the situation and to set an example by taking the lead in wage restraint. Political appointment holders and senior civil servants, whose salaries are tied to the private sector salary benchmarks, had their monthly salaries cut by 10 per cent from November 2001 for 12 months. No year-end AVC payments were made except to lower level civil servants whose salaries are lower. All other adjustments to their salaries would be frozen during this period. The cuts affected the variable components of the monthly salary but not the basic pay.

Performance Bonus: The civil service performance bonus (was first introduced to superscale officers and the administrative service in 1989 and later extended to all civil servants in 2000) allows the civil service to link pay directly with individual performance on the job. This gives the salary structure added flexibility and provides management a finer tool with which to reward deserving officers. The bonus amounts for all civil servants are set out below:

Officers	*Performance Bonuses*
Majority of Civil Servants	Base Rate of 0.5 Months of Salary
Administrative Officers	Average 5 Months of Salary
Senior Administrative Officers	Average 3 to 4 Months of Salary

Recent Increase in Variable Component for Senior Civil Servants and the GDP Bonus: For the senior civil servants, the variable component of the 13th month—the NPAA, the AVC and the performance bonus together make up 30 per cent of the total annual remuneration. In 2000, the proportion was increased to 40 per cent for senior officers. This increase comprises individual performance bonuses and the GDP-related bonus (i.e., bonus which is linked to the state of the economy).

Economic Growth in the Calendar Year	*Bonus Months Pay*
8% or More	2 Months
5% (mid-point of longer term growth potential of 4 to 6%)	1 Month
2% or Less	0 Month

To retain officers, the government also introduced a 'bonus pool' concept in 2000 but for senior civil servants only. Under this system, an officer would be paid half his/her performance bonus for the year immediately, and the other half will be placed into a bonus pool. The officer will be entitled to receive the amount in the bonus pool in two equal instalments 12 and 24 months later, provided (s)he continues in service. Officers who resign or are dismissed from the service would not be allowed to withdraw any balance in the pool, although officers who retire are able to do so.

Public Enterprises: Statutory bodies are established by special Acts of Parliament. The Acts specify the functions, duties and powers of the bodies so established, and their relationship to the responsible ministers. Government-owned companies are incorporated under the Companies Act. Statutory boards such as Housing Development Board, Economic Development Board, Monetary Authority of Singapore, Post Office Savings Bank, Singapore Broadcasting Corporation, Singapore Institute of Standards and Industrial Research were also established.

Public enterprises statutory boards are empowered to recruit, promote and remove their own staff. Rates of staff remuneration broadly follow the rates applicable to civil servants.

Government-owned Companies: The nature of activities carried out by government-owned business enterprises was outlined earlier.

Boards of government-owned companies have the power to recruit, promote and remove their own staff. In setting rates of pay, they have total flexibility and autonomy in that they are not obliged to adopt pay scales applicable to civil servants. Staffing conditions and remuneration are based solely on market forces—the government exercises no direct control. The wage structures between private and public business enterprises are considered as same.

Australia

The Executive Employment Policy: It appears that each state of Australia has its own distinct executive employment policy that will cover its public services, declared authorities and the public sector companies. For the present study, the practices adopted by the State of Victoria are summarised.

Government: The executives are corporate resources of government who are managed and developed as a group of morale, competent and effective leaders. Remuneration packages are designed to attract, retain and motivate valued executives. The Victoria Public Service do not aim to be a leader in the executive remuneration market.

TRP: With regard to compensation, a total remuneration package (TRP) approach is adopted where the cost of the employer is transparent. This package has three components:

- Salary
- Non-salary benefits
- Superannuation contributions

Not less than 50 per cent of TRP is to be taken as monetary remuneration subject to specially granted exemptions, especially related to superannuation funds. The permissible non-salary benefits, apart from superannuation, include:

- A motor vehicle through executive vehicle scheme,
- Membership of professional associations or professional subscriptions,
- Child care expenses in particular circumstances,
- Financial counseling,
- Home working facilities related to employment,
- Health insurance,
- Mobile telephones,
- Notebook/laptop computers,
- Disability/income protection insurance,
- Self-education expenses.

The minimum employer contribution under the superannuation guarantee charge is 9 per cent from 2002. The TRP is segregated within three broad bands for executive employment, as approved by the public employment ministries (PEM). The remuneration of secretaries is determined by PEM. The PEM determines and adjusts remuneration and conditions of Band 1 executives.

The agency heads can approve employment and set and adjust remuneration for executives at Band 2 and Band 3 level under delegation from the PEM and in accordance with guidelines set out in a handbook. The table below shows the band remuneration ranges.

Band	*Range*	*Coverage*
Band 1	AS$ 199034–290000	Agency head of a substantial public authority and other senior executives classified at this level like most senior programme managers, deputy secretaries in VPS.
Band 2	AS$ 136959-218214	Deputy secretary, first assistant secretary and agency heads of major agencies divisions.
Band 3	AS$ 110000-152771	Programme, policy and service delivery managers, regional and area manager and mostly departments and agency heads of smaller agencies.

Note: One Australian dollar is equivalent to around Rs. 36.

Remuneration Review: The remuneration will be reviewed every 12 months. The reviews used to be once in two years before July 2005.

Public Sector: The government issues guidelines to assist organisations in managing executive remuneration. The Victorian government remuneration levels are based on work value and market relativities with some capacity to account for specific market factors. Remuneration packages are provided to attract, retain and motivate valued executives, without necessarily seeking to match the private sector in every case.

France

Civil Service Pay: Civilian employees in the government are basically divided into three categories A, B and C. The officers are covered under Category A. Within the category 'A', there are 10 scales in the civil services. The initial pay starts at around 1900 euros per month and goes up to around 6300 euros per month (one euro is equivalent to around Rs. 59).

Civil service pay comprises basic pay and supplementary bonuses and allowances. Basic pay consists of the salary, the amount of which is fixed depending on the officer's grade and position on the pay scale.

The following allowances are in addition to salary:

- Family allowance, based on the number of dependent children and the index held;
- Cost of living allowance, depending on the geographical location of service and the index held;
- If applicable, the new indexed premium, commonly known as the NBI, for the exercise of a responsibility or a particular technical specialty.

The various bonuses, allowances and benefits are allocated according to corps, qualifications or as compensation for particular constraints (financial responsibility, etc.). The main allowances are the fixed allowance for additional work, the administrative and technical speciality allowance and the technical duties allowance. Salaries may also be supplemented by a performance bonus or by a special allowance.

Public Sector Companies: It is reported that the compensation levels of the government-controlled industrial and business organisations are driven by market forces and pegged to comparable private sector companies. The pay levels are decided by the managements of the enterprises in a decentralised manner.

10 Private Sector: Situation Abroad

Coverage

An attempt is made in this chapter to provide indicatory information about the compensation levels of executives in different industries in USA, Singapore, France, Australia and Canada. Other issues covered in this chapter include: i) Compensation levels of top level CEOs in USA and Europe, (ii) Year-on-year increases in various countries, (iii) Differentiations practised within flat salary budgets, (iv) Real wages in different countries corrected for inflation and taxes, and (v) Comparative compensation levels between CEOs, government, armed forces and Senate in USA and other related issues.

The data included in this chapter is essentially based on averages and median values pertaining to large sample sizes as reported by the agencies that carried out the surveys. The variances between top level companies and average/below average companies can be very large especially in a country like USA. The variations are characterised by: (a) The country in which the industry is located, (b) The geographical location within the country, (c) The nature of the industry, (d) The size of the industry, (e) The function being handled by the executive, and (f) The responsibility level of the executive.

A Comparative Scenario

The website *www.payscale.com* provides indicative information about the compensation levels of executives pertaining to various industries in five countries: (i) USA (ii) Canada (iii) UK (iv) Australia and (v) India. The data provided includes executive compensation as it existed five years earlier, as it exists today and the projections after five years. The information is based on large sample sizes and national median values. Table 10.1 summarises this information on an aggregate basis for all industries.

Table 10.1

Comparative Scenario of Five Countries

		Country				
S. No.	*Designation*	*USA (US$)*	*Canada (C$)*	*UK (£)*	*Australia (Aus$)*	*India (INR)*
1.	Chief Executive Officer	1,65,926	1,45,325	1,00,534	1,53,886	27,06,424
2.	Chief Operating Officer	1,36,985	1,31,439	1,03,844	1,57,971	18,45,354
3.	Chief Finance Officer	1,20,057	1,31,058	97,521	1,42,672	17,41,475
4.	President	1,52,197	1,50,938	1,55,000	2,00,000	36,00,000
5.	Vice-President	1,22,971	1,28,100	90,181	1,86,696	23,77,963
6.	Project Manager	86,122	78,398	40,826	82,779	10,35,470
7.	Senior Manager Marketing	1,05,763	87,142	51,737	1,10,944	7,43,897
8.	Finance Manager	82,360	65,737	34,629	76,458	6,07,363
9.	Marketing Manager	60,427	56,977	30,740	65,288	4,14,228
10.	HR Manager	56,165	60,074	32,052	74,665	4,36,259
11.	Senior Engineer	83,007	83,200	35,598	90,451	3,92,783
12.	Engineer	65,095	54,695	27,486	52,482	3,05,552

Note: US$: Rs. 39.50; C$: Rs. 38.50; £:Rs. 80.00; Aus$: Rs. 36.00.

Source: www.payscale.com

There appear to be some variation with respect to the designations but the information is fairly representative for average and just below average companies. The data pertaining to USA tallies well with the information provided by the Bureau of US Labour Statistics.

In rupee terms, the ratios of remunerations between USA, Canada, UK, Australia and India are tabulated for three grades below:

	Country				
Grade	*USA*	*Canada*	*UK*	*Australia*	*India*
Engineer	8.4	6.9	7.2	6.1	1
Finance Manager	5.3	4.1	4.5	4.5	1
CEO	2.4	2.0	2.9	2.0	1

Normalised Wage Payments

The Hay Group, after conducting a study in 29 countries, has outlined the real salaries of senior executives at the level of departmental heads—after normalising the salaries to cover taxes and the cost of living in the respective countries. Table 10.2 summarises these findings.

Table 10.2

Normalised Wage Payments

Rank	*Country*	*Average Real Salary: Senior Managers (€)*
1	Turkey	79,021
2	India	77,665
3	Russia	77,355
4	Switzerland	76,913
5	Brazil	76,449
6	Poland	76,269
7	Spain	75,904
8	Germany	75,701
9	Japan	69,634
10	Austria	66,243
11	Portugal	66,191
12	Ireland	62,608
13	USA	61,960
14	Greece	60,785
	Average	59,651
15	Netherlands	58,915
16	Czech Rep.	57,416
17	Australia	55,505
18	Canada	54,032
19	Italy	53,003
20	France	51,396
21	Belgium	51,196
22	Denmark	48,228
23	UK	46,809
24	Slovakia	45,389
25	Norway	42,939
26	China	42,288
27	Hungary	41,406
28	Finland	41,018
29	Sweden	37,652

Note: € is equivalent to around Rs. 59.50.

Hay Group's World Pay Report, on compensation, reveals that senior managers in Turkey take home the highest real pay levels worldwide, earning an average net salary equivalent to €79,000 when bonuses, tax and cost of living are taken into account. Hot on their heels, riding high on the country's outsourcing boom, senior managers in India earn the equivalent of €77,700 in real terms, placing them second in Hay Group's World Pay rankings.

Year-on-Year Increases

It is reported that according to 2007-08 US Compensation Planning Survey from Mercer Human Resource Consulting, US employers plan to award average increases of 3.8 per cent in 2007, just slightly more than the increase granted in 2006 (3.7%). Pay increases are projected to remain flat at 3.8 per cent in 2008. These raises, compared to the pay raises being witnessed in India in the private companies and multinational corporations are significantly low. Table 10.3 indicates the grade-wise, budgeted and projected pay rises in 2007 and 2008 as per the Mercer study in USA.

Table 10.3

Budgeted Pay Raises: 2007-08

	Budgeted 2007	*Projected 2008*
All Employees	3.8%	3.8%
Executives	4.1%	3.9%
Management	3.8%	3.8%
Professional (Sales & Non-Sales)	3.8%	3.7%
Office/Clerical/Technician	3.7%	3.7%
Trades/Production/Services	3.6%	3.6%

Source: Mercer Human Resources Consulting, 2007/08 US. Compensation Planning Survey.

The point that merits taking note of is that pay increases will also depend on the competition in the industries for talent and the general economic growth rates. The competition for talent is as hot as the competition for business. The philosophy of competition and its linkages to environmental situations have evolved well in a country like USA which has encouraged and flourished in market-driven economy. The relatively low percentage increases in pay have to be reckoned against this background and also the fact that the existing levels of compensation are much higher compared to a country like India, even if one considers the differential purchasing capacities of USA and India.

As pay budgets remain flat, employers always strive to pay high performers than low performers and are widening the performance differentials by granting significantly larger salary increases to higher performing employees, compared to those in the lower performing categories. The different pay increases for varying levels of performance are summarised in Table 10.4 based on the Mercer study.

Table 10.4

Base Pay Increases as a Function of Performance

	Percentage of Workforce	*Average Pay Increase*
Higher Rates	12%	5.7%
Next Higher Rates	28%	4.5%
Middle Rates	52%	3.5%
Low Rates	6%	2.0%
Lowest Rates	2%	1.7%

The segregation is similar to the Bell-Curve distribution of performing cadres, made use of in the leading Indian private companies—barring the differences in the percentages (5, 15, 60, 15 and 5) of the performing cadres. The noteworthy point is that top performers are getting salary increases that are about three times that of low performers. Steven. E. Gross, global leader of Mercer's broad-based performance and rewards consulting business, points out that companies are looking for new ways to pay for performance and segmenting their workforce, to help them identify their most valuable contributors. Rewarding top performers is essential for the ongoing success of the company according to Mr. Gross.

In addition to the segmentation of workforce by differential pay increases, organisations are also distinguishing among employees by differential incentives by performance rating. Mercer's survey shows that the ratio for short–term incentive pay-outs by employee performance is consistent with that for base pay increases for most employee groups. Table 10.5 is indicative of the differentiation in the incentives.

Table 10.5

Short-term Incentive Pay-outs by Performance

	Executive	*Management*	*Professional (Sales & Non-Sales)*	*Official/ Clerical/ Technician*	*Trades/ Promotion/ Service*
Highest Rated	64%	27%	20%	15%	13%
Middle Rated	44%	20%	14%	11%	11%
Lowest Rated	30%	10%	7%	6%	4%

Mr. Gross also points out that as companies struggle to afford and sustain compensation levels for employees, they continue to focus on variable pay and that incentives are a useful tool for supporting high levels of performance without increasing the fixed cost of base pay. The increased shares in US companies of short-term incentives are reflected in Table 10.6.

Table 10.6

Average Incentive Pay-out (As a Percentage of Base Pay)

Designation	*2007 (based on 2006 Performance)*	*2006 (based on 2005 Performance)*
Executives	47%	40%
Management	22%	19%
Professional (Non-Sales)	13%	10%
Office/Clerical/Technician	8%	5%
Trades/Production/Services	9%	5%

Source: Mercer Human Resources Consulting, 2007/08 US Compensation Planning Survey.

(This differential incentive payment profile or variable pay based on annual performance, coincides with the situation in India between junior and senior management cadres of private sector companies.)

Pay Increases and Inflation

The following tables provide data regarding the pay rises above inflation for different countries. Table 10.7 covers EU countries, Table 10.8 some select countries and Table 10.9 the top 5 and bottom 5 countries in respect of pay rises.

Table 10.7

EU Countries

Country	*Average Pay Increases*	*Inflation Rates*	*Pay Above Inflation*
Lithuania	8.5	3.0	5.5
Estonia	7.5	2.5	5.0
Slovakia	6.3	2.8	3.5
Latvia	8.3	5.3	3.0
Hungary	6.0	3.4	2.6
Czech. Rep.	5.0	2.5	2.5
Slovenia	4.7	2.3	2.4
Netherlands	2.7	0.5	2.2
Italy	3.8	1.8	2.0
Finland	3.6	1.6	2.0
Greece	4.9	3.0	1.9
Ireland	4.2	2.4	1.8
Belgium	3.5	1.8	1.7
UK	3.5	2.0	1.5
Denmark	3.3	1.8	1.5
France	3.0	1.7	1.3
Sweden	3.1	1.9	1.2
Luxembourg	3.1	2.0	1.1
Germany	2.1	1.0	1.1
Portugal	3.2	2.1	1.1
Austria	2.7	1.7	1.0
Spain	4.0	3.2	0.8
Poland	3.1	2.6	0.5
Malta	1.7	1.9	-0.2

Table 10.8

Select Countries

Country	*Average Pay Increases*	*Inflation Rates*	*Pay Above Inflation*
India	11.3	4.0	7.3
China	7.8	3.0	4.8
Indonesia	11.3	7.0	4.3
Brazil	7.5	4.6	2.9
Japan	2.5	0.1	2.4
Singapore	3.8	1.5	2.3
Hong Kong	3.2	1.1	2.1
Argentina	10.5	8.6	1.9
Costa Rica	11.3	9.5	1.8
Canada	3.6	1.9	1.7
Peru	4.2	2.5	1.7
Australia	4.2	2.8	1.4
Mexico	5.0	3.9	1.1
New Zealand	3.8	2.8	1.0
Switzerland	2.0	1.0	1.0
USA	3.6	2.6	1.0

Table 10.9

Top 5 and *Bottom 5 Ranked Countries*

Country	*Average Pay Increases*	*Inflation Rates*	*Pay Above Inflation*
TOP 5			
India	11.3	4.0	7.3
Egypt	12.0	4.9	7.1
Lithuania	8.5	3.0	5.5
Estonia	7.5	2.5	5.0
Bulgaria	8.4	3.5	4.9
BOTTOM 5			
Malta	1.7	1.9	-0.2
Nicaragua	6.8	6.8	0.0
Turkey	6.3	6.1	0.2
Poland	3.1	2.6	0.5
Israel	2.5	1.8	0.7

Note: The data pertains to the year 2006 and India is ranked as the country with the highest pay rises.

CEO Compensations

The remuneration levels of CEOs vary very widely depending on the type, size, profitability etc., of the industry and the enterprise. The CEO compensations appear to be the highest in USA and even within USA, there are orders of magnitude differences between the leading listed companies and the fund management companies.

Table 10.10 outlines the compensation levels of the highest earning private equity and hedge fund managers. The highest pay packet is an astounding US$ 1.5 billion while the average is US$ 657 million.

Table 10.10

Top 20 Highest Earning Private Equity and Hedge Fund Managers

	Executive	*Company*	*2006 Compensation*
1.	James Simons	Renaissance Technologies	$1,500,000,000
2.	Steven Cohen	SAC Capital	$1,200,000,000
3.	Kenneth Griffin	Citadel Investment Group	$1,200,000,000
4.	T. Boone Pickens	BP Capital	$1,100,000,000
5.	George Soros	Soros Fund Management	$950,000,000
6.	Stephen Schwarzman	Blackstone Group	$940,000,000
7.	Edward Lampert	ESL Investments	$940,000,000
8.	John Arnold	Centaurus Energy	$760,000,000
9.	Bruce Kovner	Caxton Associates	$590,000,000
10.	Henry Kravis	Kohlberg Kravis Roberts & Co.	$450,000,000
11.	George Roberts	Kohlberg Kravis Roberts & Co.	$450,000,000
12.	David Shaw	DE Shaw & Co.	$430,000,000
13.	Paul Tudor Jones II	Tudor Investment	$430,000,000
14.	Carl Icahn	Icahn Partners	$350,000,000
15.	Stephen Feinberg	Cerberus Capital	$330,000,000
16.	Wesley Edens	Fortress Investment Group	$330,000,000
17.	Michael Novogratz	Fortress Investment Group	$320,000,000
18.	Peter Briger Jr.	Fortress Investment Group	$320,000,000
19.	Daniel Och	Och-Ziff Capital Management	$300,000,000
20.	David Rubenstein	Carlyle Group	$260,000,000
		Averages	$657,500,000

Source: Forbes Magazine, May 21, 2007.

The top 20 highest paid CEOs of publicly-held US companies get an average pay of US$ 36 million with the highest getting US$ 71 million. Table 10.11 provides the details. The bonuses and stock options form a significant part of the pay packet of these top notch executives.

Table 10.11

Top 20 Highest Paid CEOs of Publicly-Held US Companies

Company	*CEO*	*Salary*	*Bonus and Other*	*Stock & Other Options*	*2006 Total Comp.*
1. Yahoo	Terry Semel	$250,001	$125	$71,410,090	$71,660,216
2. XTO Energy	Bob Simpson	$1,208,334	$31,229,525	$27,052,065	$59,489,924
3. Occidental Petroleum	Ray Irani	$1,300,000	$5,958,639	$45,563,945	$52,822,584
4. Merrill Lynch	E. Stanley O'Neal	$700,000	$18,875,298	$26,800,049	$46,375,347
5. Danaher	H. Lawrence Culp. Jr.	$1,100,000	$3,949,746	$41,165,925	$46,215,671
6. Countrywide Financial	Angelo Mozilo	$2,866,667	$21,115,639	$19,012,000	$42,994,306
7. Ford	Alan Mulally	$666,667	$18,834,433	$19,627,000	$39,128,100
8. Apollo Group	Todd Nelson	$281,250	$32,345,192	$0	$32,626,442
9. AT&T	Edward Whitacre	$2,100,000	$7,512,964	$22,152,797	$31,765,761
10. Altria Group	Louis Camilleri	$1,750,000	$19,909,987	$10,017,675	$31,677,662
11. Aetna	Ronald Williams	$1,073,077	$7,803,155	$21,983,853	$30,860,085
12. Nabors Industries	Eugene Isenberg	$825,000	$22,122,620	$6,595,000	$29,542,620
13. Comcast	Brian Roberts	$2,501,000	$14,734,210	$10,623,690	$27,858,900
14. JP Morgan Chase	James Dimon	$1,000,000	$13,487,858	$13,000,000	$27,487,858
15. Duke Energy	James Rogers	$0	$322,821	$27,162,928	$27,485,749
16. Wells Fargo	Richard Kovacevich	$995,000	$9,043,521	$16,826,149	$26,864,670
17. Terex	Ronald DeFeo	$875,000	$8,817,155	$17,131,971	$26,824,126
18. American Int'l Group	Martin Sullivan	$1,000,000	$16,667,088	$9,018,512	$26,685,600
19. Citigroup	Charles Prince	$1,000,000	$13,458,338	$10,413,273	$24,871,611
20. Viacom	Philippe Dauman	$653,846	$2,059,744	$22,087,941	$24,801,531
				Average:	$36,401,938

Source: Associated Press survey, released June 11, 2007.

The startling contrast in compensation of the top rung people in USA is brought out in Figure 10.1.

Figure 10.1

Average Pay of the 20 Highest Paid US Leaders, by Sector, 2006

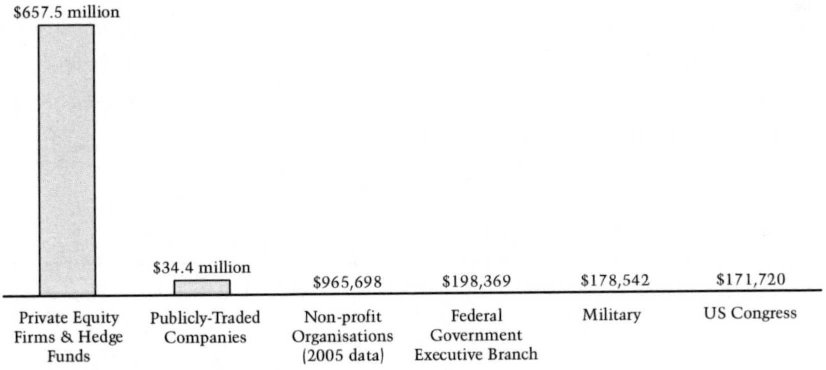

The contrast in compensation levels of USA will be complete with the following data:

- The average worker in USA is reported to get paid about US$ 29,500.
- The President of USA is paid a base salary of US$ 400,000 while the Vice-President gets US$ 208,575. The cabinet secretary of USA is reported to be paid US$ 186,600. The chairman of the joint chiefs of the staff is given a base salary of US$ 187,390.

The CEOs of European enterprises appear to be drawing significantly lower salaries compared to their US counterparts. Table 10.12 outlines the total compensation levels of the top 20 highest paid executives of European companies. The average European salary for these 20 highest paid executive is 1/3rd of the average of the US executives.

Compensation in US Industries

The Economic Research Institute (ERI) of USA (*Source: Abbott-Langer.com*) carried out a salary survey of 250,000 organisations in 2006 covering various industries. For the current study, their findings and data in respect of: (i) engineering, science & technology (ii) manufacturing (iii) utilities (iv) information technology and (v) pharmaceuticals are included. It is to be pointed out that the samples chosen by ERI apparently belong to medium and large corporations which will definitely fall above the national median (as reported by *payscale.com*). The data put out by the US Labour Statistics also covers the entire information and individual states with sample sizes are largely characterised by far more heterogeneous composition. The following tables of ERI covering the executive cadres are expected to provide representative information pertaining to relatively high technology companies wherein technical skills play more critical role than compared to normal industries.

Table 10.12

Top 20 Highest Paid Executives of European Companies

	Company	*Country*	*Name*	*Total 2006 Compensation*
1.	Renault	France	Carlos Ghosn	$45,500,000
2.	L'Oreal	France	Jean-Paul Agon	$19,300,000
3.	Unicredit Group	Italy	Alessandro Profumo	$18,100,000
4.	Vodafone	Great Britain	Arun Sarin	$15,200,000
5.	Assicurazioni Generali	Italy	Antoine Bernheim	$14,200,000
6.	Deutsche Bank	Germany	Josef Ackermann	$12,400,000
7.	AXA	France	Henri de Castries	$12,100,000
8.	Total	France	Thierry Desmarest	$10,800,000
9.	Societe Generale	France	Daniel Bouton	$10,700,000
10.	Banco Santander	Spain	Alfredo Saenz	$10,600,000
11.	UBS	Switzerland	Marcel Ospel	$10,500,000
12.	Vinci	France	Xavier Huillard	$9,100,000
13.	Fiat	Italy	Sergio Marchionne	$8,700,000
14.	Air Liquide	France	Benoit Potier	$8,000,000
15.	Aegon	Netherlands	Donald Shepard	$8,000,000
16.	Royal Bank of Scotland	Great Britain	Frederick Goodwin	$7,800,000
17.	Bouygues	France	Martin Bouygues	$7,800,000
18.	Group Danone	France	Franck Riboud	$7,300,000
19.	Roche Group	Switzerland	Franz Humer	$6,900,000
20.	Alstom	France	Patrick Kron	$6,700,000
			Average:	$12,485,000

Table 10.13

Engineering, Science and Technology Group

Position	*Total Compensation** 2006
Chief Executive Officer	$342,986
Chief Operating Officer	$247,865
Executive Vice-President	$214,398
Top Legal Officer	$209,212
Top Financial Officer	$208,733
Admin. Engineering Supervisor	$166,426
Project Manager	$117,091
Astronomer	$101,126
Engineering Manager	$93,718
Test Engineering Manager	$89,307
Design Engineering Manager	$86,455
Physicist PhD.	$86,135
Admin. Engineering Manager	$84,270
Engineering Supervisor Generic	$80,367
Test Engineering Supervisor	$77,847
Design Engineering Supervisor	$74,930
Systems Analyst Lead	$74,369
Lead Computer Programmer	$73,552
Meteorologist	$68,389
Electrolysis Engineer	$67,865
Seismologist	$67,043
Sales Area Manager	$63,166
Systems Analyst	$56,399
Applications Programmer	$55,615

Note: * includes base annual salary, all cash bonuses.

Table 10.14

Manufacturing Group

Position	*Total Compensation** 2006
Chief Executive Officer	$370,597
Chief Operating Officer	$252,554
Top Legal Officer	$217,183
Top Financial Officer	$211,148
Top Administrative Officer	$203,443
Plant Manager	$108,170
Engineering Manager	$94,374
Research & Development Manager (Technical)	$91,555
Design Engineering Manager	$87,040
Environmental Manager Engineering	$81,627
Applications & Programming Supervisor	$79,056
Project Engineer	$78,404
Research Engineer	$78,326
Sales Product Manager	$77,906
Regional Sales Manager	$77,475
Computer System Hardware Analyst	$69,202
Materials Engineer Generic	$66,953
Safety Engineer	$66,706
Plant Engineer	$65,772
Sales Area Manager	$63,524
Sales Engineer	$63,428
Quality Assurance Programmer	$61,445
Systems Analyst	$56,629
Applications Programmer	$55,851
LAN/WAN Administrator	$52,203

Note: * includes base annual salary, all cash bonuses.

Table 10.15

Utilities Group

Position	*Total Compensation* 2006*
Chief Executive Officer	$297,333
Chief Operating Officer	$206,448
Top Legal Officer	$189,528
Top Administrative Officer	$179,322
Top Financial Officer	$176,539
Engineering Manager	$90,725
Nuclear Fuels Reclamation Engineer	$84,800
Systems & Programming Manager	$81,545
Nuclear Fuels Research Engineer	$80,971
Financial Analysis Manager	$76,021
Marketing Manager	$75,708
Plant Personnel Manager	$74,721
Nuclear Engineer	$74,171
Nuclear Equipment Test Engineer	$73,961
Nuclear Criticality Safety Engineer	$73,447
Systems Analyst Lead	$72,345
Lead Computer Programmer	$71,510
Water Treatment Plant Manager	$67,471
Operator Nuclear Reactor	$64,212
Sales Area Manager	$61,539
Power Plant Operator	$57,947
Systems Analyst	$55,359
Reactor Operator Test and Research	$52,456
Solar Energy Systems Designer	$47,960

Note: * includes base annual salary, all cash bonuses.

Table 10.16

Information Technology Group

Position	*Total Compensation* 2006*
Chief Executive Officer	$371,471
Chief Operating Officer	$262,032
Top Financial Officer	$224,638
Top Legal Officer	$221,997
Top Marketing & Sales Officer	$217,880
Software Design Manager	$95,825
Systems Analysis Manager	$89,392
Systems & Programming Manager	$85,722
Programming Manager	$85,608
Network Control Manager	$84,872
Applications & Programming Supervisor	$79,945
Systems Analysis Supervisor	$79,454
Systems Project Manager	$77,590
Programming Supervisor	$77,068
Computer Software Developer	$71,264
Computer System Hardware Analyst	$69,890
Data Recovery Planner	$69,715
Software Engineer	$69,329
Computer Hardware Engineer	$69,085
Network Control Supervisor	$67,153
Sales Area Manager	$64,178

Note: * includes base annual salary, all cash bonuses.

Table 10.17

Pharmaceuticals Group

Position	*Total Compensation** 2006
Chief Executive Officer	$431,944
Chief Operating Officer	$307,936
Top Financial Officer	$252,662
Top Legal Officer	$246,544
Top Marketing & Sales Officer	$243,165
Engineering Manager	$98,902
Pharmacist	$89,605
Systems & Programming Manager	$88,594
Financial Analysis Manager	$82,403
Marketing Manager	$82,200
Personnel Manager	$79,597
Lead Computer Programmer	$77,100
Biochemist	$68,861
Sales Area Manager	$66,001
Quality Control Engineer	$63,242
Production Engineer	$63,119
Systems Analyst	$58,226
Chemist	$55,728
Market Research Analyst	$51,310

Note: * includes base annual salary, all cash bonuses.

Tables 10.13 to 10.17 outline the relative compensation levels of executives in five sectors of industries for different positions in the executive grades. At the CEO levels, the pharmaceutical sector is the topmost payer, followed by information technology. The variation from utilities to pharmaceuticals is as much as 45 per cent. At the junior most level, namely at the engineer/programmer levels, the IT sector is leading. At the junior level, salaries are ranging from US$ 50,000 to 65,000. In the managerial cadres, the compensation levels range from US$ 85,000 to 100,000. At the CEO level, the salaries are ranging from US$ 297,000 to 431,000.

Industry to Industry Variation

To illustrate the existence of definite functional premium, a sample of compensation levels at the manager level is taken from the data furnished by the US Labour Statistics for aggregate industries. The functions covered in the sample include sales, marketing, public relations, IT, finance, human resources, purchase, construction, engineering, transportation etc. There is a definite premium visible in the high-tech areas like computers and IT, engineering and marketing. Marginal differences are visible in respect of other disciplines. The sample sizes are also included in Table 10.18 and the values indicated pertain to national median levels.

Table 10.18

Management Occupation

S. No.	*Occupation Title*	*Employment Sample*	*Mean Annual Wage (USD)*
1.	Advertisement and Promotion Manager	41710	81250
2.	Marketing Manager	166470	101990
3.	Sales Manager	317970	98510
4.	Public Relations Manager	43770	85820
5.	Administrative Service Manager	239410	69540
6.	Computer and IT Manager	259330	102360
7.	Financial Manager	471950	96620
8.	Compensation and Benefit Manager	51470	76300
9.	Training and Dev. Manager	28720	80180
10.	Human Resource Manager	57830	89950
11.	Industrial Production Manager	153950	81960
12.	Purchasing Manager	69300	81440
13.	Transportation	84870	75130
14.	Construction Manager	192610	81760
15.	Engineering Manager	187410	105470
16.	Managers	340720	83530

Situation in Canada

The salary structure in the private sector in Canada for different hierarchical positions is outlined in Tables 10.19 and 10.20.

Table 10.19

Compensation Levels of Engineering People in Canada

S. No.	*Designation*	*25th Percentile*	*Median*	*75th Percentile*
1.	Top Engineering Executive	123,971	146,515	172,512
2.	Project Manager Engineer	116,070	131,486	147,868
3.	Industrial Engineering Manager	75,753	87,887	105,895
4.	Electrical Engineer I	49,212	55,891	63,172
5.	Electrical Engineer II	66,450	75,908	92,849
6.	Mechanical Engineer I	44,853	48,512	52,575
7.	Mechanical Engineer II	56,862	62,465	68,920
8.	Mechanical Engineer III	67,396	78,493	88,667
9.	Software Engineer I	48,076	57,670	69,123
10.	Software Engineer II	58,017	63,297	69,261
11.	Software Engineer III	69,783	79,736	89,684
12.	Telecommunications Engineer I	41,840	46,617	51,717
13.	Telecommunications Engineer II	55,169	62,696	69,044
14.	Telecommunications Engineer III	70,677	78,519	88,567
15.	Materials Engineer I	50,336	64,060	65,895
16.	Materials Engineer II	62,956	80,396	81,131

Source: Canadian Salary Survey available at *Canadinvisa.com*

Table 10.20

Salary of Senior Executives and Managers (Including Bonuses)

(Canadian Dollars)

S. No.	*Designation*	*25% Percentile*	*Median*	*75% Percentile*
1.	Chief Executive Officer	251,295	391,007	650,394
2.	Chief Financial Officer	145,986	189,480	256,674
3.	Chief Information Technology Officer	125,083	156,713	205,083
4.	Chief Operating Officer	160,816	211,076	423,836
5.	Materials Director	76,029	80,633	98,342
6.	Production Director	77,328	83,231	96,217
7.	Top Business Development Executive	97,992	135,681	201,904
8.	Top Research and Development Executive	163,364	192,384	228,122
9.	Compensation and Benefit Director	100,378	127,839	141,808
10.	Finance Director	90,584	109,975	128,142
11.	Maintenance Director	81,641	90,608	10,7151
12.	Software Development Director	79,807	94,918	79,807
13.	Labour Relations Director	75,203	86,654	102,828
14.	Top Accounting Executive	107,310	122,618	157,746
15.	Top Administrative Executive	150,803	202,523	378,556
16.	Government Affairs Director	72,487	99,286	103,064
17.	Quality Assurance Director	78,272	87,599	105,780
18.	Customer Service Director	86,714	102,468	115,471
19.	Top Audit Executive	106,169	134,465	193,467
20.	Help Desk Manager	63,308	79,312	94,388

At the junior positions, the engineering cadres are segregated into 3 levels, namely, Engineer 1, 2 and 3. Broadly, Engineer 1 cadre has 0-3 years experience, Engineer 2 cadre has 2-5 years experience and Engineer 3 will have 7-10 years of experience. Table 10.19 summarises the compensation levels of engineering professionals. The national median figures along with data pertaining to 25th and 75th percentile positions are included in the table for different engineering disciplines.

Table 10.20 outlines the compensation levels of executives in senior position in Canada upto CEO level.

Considering the fact that the Canadian dollar is almost equivalent to US dollar now, it can be stated that the compensation levels in Canada are almost on par with the compensation levels in USA.

Situation in Singapore

The compensation details for various grades, various functions and various industries in Singapore are outlined below along with coverage of some associated issues like variable pay etc.

The strong economic performance has led to improved compensation for firms in 2006. The total wages comprising basic wages and bonuses in the industry rose by 4.5 per cent in 2006 and the labour productivity rose by 1.2 per cent. The wage increase in 2006 is the fastest in six years, reflecting the tightening in the job market. After adjusting for inflation, the total wages rose by 3.5 per cent. The tightening of the job market for professionals, managers and executives resulted in junior and senior management enjoying a higher wage increase of 5.4 per cent and 5.6 per cent in 2006. The rank and file employees received a total wage increase of 3.9 per cent in 2006 as globalisation held down the wage gains for workers at the lower end. Eighty-one per cent of the private sector enterprises were profitable in 2006. In this year, 66 per cent firms increased their wages by an average of 5.8 per cent whereas 7 per cent of the firms have cut their salaries by an average of about 3.4 per cent. The remaining 27 per cent firms kept their wages unchanged at the 2005 level.

Wage increases were strongly correlated with firm profitability, as more firms restructured their wage system to tie wages more closely with business performance. The highly profitable firms gave a total wage increase of 5.9 per cent. With tighter labour market, even the weak performing firms were under pressure to give wage increases to retain their workers.

Variable Component: On an average, the private sector paid out a variable component which forms about 15 per cent of total wages in 2006. In 11 per cent of the enterprises, the variable pay is more than 25 per cent of their total wages. In 13.3 per cent of enterprises, the variable pay is 17 to 25 per cent, whereas 21 per cent of enterprises, had no variable pay. Typically, variable component would be higher for management staff as a greater share of their pay package is flexible and tied to performance, as the figures in Table 10.21 below would state.

Table 10.21

Variable Component as Per cent of Total Pay Industry-wise in 2006

S.No.	*Industry*	*Total*	*Junior/Senior Management*	*Rank and File*
1.	All Industries	18.17	20.92	16.33
2.	Manufacturing	18.83	21	17.42
3.	Construction	10.17	11.83	9.08
4.	Services	18.58	21.58	16.58
5.	Wholesale & Retail Trade	18.17	20.75	16.33
6.	Transport & Storage	22.75	23.17	22.67
7.	Hotels & Restaurants	9.92	11.75	9.17
8.	Information & Communications	22.58	22.17	23.58
9.	Financial Services	27.42	23.92	29.42
10.	Real Estate & Leasing Services	10.67	17.25	8.83
11.	Professional Services	17.83	21.67	12.92
12.	Administrative & Support Services	8.33	14.92	8.75
13.	Community, Social & Personnel Services	18.83	20.33	18.00

Wage Restructuring: A tripartite taskforce on wages restructuring had issued the following guidelines in January 2004 which are being implemented.

- Implement variable bonus linked to key performance indicators (KPI).
- Introduce the monthly variable component (MVC) in wage structure.
- Narrow the maximum-minimum salary ratio for the majority of their employees to an average of 1.5 or less.

Good progress was made in the implementation and by December 2006, 83 per cent of the workforce in the private sector was under some form of flexible wage system. In large establishments, the vast majority (90 per cent) of the workforce have at least one key wage recommendation in their wage system. As on December 2006, only 17 per cent of the firms had implemented MVC while 1 per cent had decided to or were in the process of implementation. Sixty per cent of the firms had no intention of implementing and 12 per cent were unaware of the MVC. Nearly 95 per cent of employers in the unionised sectors shared information with their employees.

Summary of Actual Pay in 2006: Professionals started at the median gross wage of 2,000 Singapore dollars.

- Wages were commonly observed to rise with age, especially for white-collar occupations, reflecting premium on skills, years of experience and seniority gained over the years.
- Wages of those in lesser skilled blue-collar occupations typically declined with age after peaking in their thirties, as the work involved is largely manual.

The range of median annual gross monthly wages for different occupational groups is given in Tables 10.22 and 10.23. Engineers continue to occupy the top five positions among entry level professionals, namely semi-conductor engineers ($2,850), manufacturing ($2,697), quality control engineers ($2,680), and civil engineers ($2,257). IT programmers started at the least median salary of only $1,742. Accountants, network, systems and database administrators and social work professional had a median commencing wage of $2,000.

Summary: The entry level salary for professionals (executives) is about 2000 Singapore dollars per month and the median salary of top level executive is S$ 12000. The ratio of the median pay between the entry level executive and the top executive is about six. The unskilled workers wage per month at the entry level is S$ 600 per month. The ratio of the median pay of the entry level executive to entry level workmen is 3.33. The ratio of the median pay of the top executive and the lowest paid worker is about 20.

Table 10.22

Median Annual Gross Wages of Employees Aged 35-39 by Industry and Occupational Group

S. No.	Occupational Group	Managers	Professionals	Associate Professionals	Clerical Workers
1.	Total	71400	52300	35400	24000
2.	Manufacturing	66600	49400	36400	23300
3.	Construction	53800	38400	31200	14400
4.	Services	75200	56600	35300	24600
5.	Wholesale & Retail Trade	66100	51000	36000	22500
6.	Transport & Storage	71000	65200	37800	22600
7.	Hotels & Restaurants	40800	36700	30000	17100
8.	Information & Communications	85500	57000	35500	23000
9.	Financial Services	94800	62000	42000	26100
10.	Real Estate & Leasing Services	59700	40400	30700	22000
11.	Professional Services	84400	55200	37700	26000
12.	Administrative & Support Services	53100	40000	28600	21300
13.	Community, Social & Personnel Services	58900	60500	28400	22000

Table 10.23

Median Annual Gross Wages at Different Levels

S. No.	Occupation	Median Annual Gross Wage ($)
1.	Managing Director	1,53,000
2.	General Manager	1,34,400
3.	Operations Manager (Finance)	76,200
4.	Engineering Manager	75,130
5.	Research and Development Manager	74,200
6.	Computer and Information Systems Manager	71,700
7.	Computer Operations and Network Manager	70,4000
8.	Technical Manager	69,600
9.	Training Manager	67,000
10.	Corporate Planning Manager	64,200
11.	Chemical Engineer (Petroleum)	62,500
12.	Manufacturing Plant and Production Manager	62,400
13.	Marketing Manager	62,300
14.	Procurement Manager	61,700
15.	Industrial Health, Safety and Environment Engineer	60,300
16.	Sales Manager	60,000
17.	Aeronautical Engineer	58,800

Situation in Australia

Exhaustive information is available in the public domain regarding compensation levels in Australia for various industries, executive positions and differentials related to 10 geographical centres. For the present study, information pertaining to the resources and mining sector alone is chosen for one state for indicative purposes as it is considered very relevant to our own coal and mining industry.

Resources and Mining Sector: There has been substantial increase in investment in the mining sector in Australia and New Zealand. The Chinese demand for iron ore, the doubling of uranium exploration, significant development of coal mines, and substantial growth in oil & gas exploration has resulted in demand for skills across all levels. As there are a large number of projects in the early stages of development, demand of design engineers remain high particularly with structural or piping experience. Mining engineers with 3 to 5 years experience are in great demand. Geology specialists were the big salary winners across Australia during 2006 with an increase in salaries of about 20 per cent on year to year basis.

It is observed that there is substantial variation in the compensation levels between one state to another state in Australia. Generally compensation levels appear to be very high in the state of Western Australia and relatively low in the state of Victoria. The information furnished in respect of resources and mining sector pertains to state of Victoria. The range between the lowest to highest *vis-à-vis* the geographical locations appears to be 1:1.35 in Australia—for the same positions and for the same disciplines.

The compensation details in the resource and mining sector pertaining to various disciplines and for various designations in the state of Victoria are indicated in Table 10.24.

Table 10.24

Compensation Details in Resource and Mining Sector for Different Disciplines in Different Grades

(Figures in Australian Dollars)

Mineral Processing

Area	*Mill Superintendent*	*Senior Metallurgist*	*Metallurgist*	*Graduate Metallurgist*	*Process Engineer Mid-level 3-7 years*
Mineral Processing	110,000-130,000	90,000-110,000	70,000-85,000	50,000-65,000	75,000-100,000

Maintenance

Area	*Maintenance Superintendent*	*Maintenance Planner*	*Maintenance Supervisor*	*Mechanical Engineer Mid-level 3-7 years*	*Electrical Engineer Mid-level 3-7 years*
Maintenance	100,000-1200,000	80,000-110,000	80,000-100,000	75,000-100,000	75,000-100,000

Mining Engineering

Area	*Mine Manager*	*Underground/ Quarry Manager*	*Project Manager*	*Senior Mining Engineer*	*Project Engineer*	*Mining Engineer*
Mining Engineering	120,000-145,000	100,000-120,000	100,000-130,000	100,000-120,000	85,000-110,000	85,000-105,000

Coal Technical Positions

Area	*Project Manager*	*Technical Services Manager*	*Production Superintendent*	*Project Engineer*	*Senior Engineer*	*Mine Planning Engineer*
Coal Technical Positions	120,000-140,000	90,000-120,000	100,000-120,000	85,000-105,000	100,000-130,000	90,000-120,000

Coal Technical Positions

Area	*Graduate Engineer*	*Project Geologist*	*Graduate Geologist*	*Surveyor*	*OH&S Officer*	*OH&S Manager*
Coal Technical Positions	60,000-80,000	80,000-95,000	65,000-75,000	65,000-80,000	70,000-80,000	85,000-110,000

Industrial Design

Area	*Engineering Manager*	*Principal/Lead Engineer*	*Project Manager*	*Senior Design Engineer*	*Design Engineer*	*Senior Project Engineer (EPCM)*
Industrial Design	140,000-180,000	130,000-160,000	120,000-200,000	100,000-130,000	70,000-95,000	110,000-150,000

contd...

...contd...

Industrial Design					
Area	*Project Engineer (EPCM)*	*Design Manager/Chief Drafter*	*Senior Design Drafter*	*Design Drafter*	*Piping Designer*
Industrial Design	75,000-100,000	90,000-120,000	60,000-90,000	50,000-70,000	80,000-100,000

Industrial Construction						
Area	*Project Manager*	*Construction Manager/ Superintendent*	*Senior Estimator*	*Planning Manager*	*Contracts Manager*	*Project Engineer (Civil/Mech./ Elec.)*
Industrial Construction	140,000-180,000	130,000-170,000	100,000-120,000	120,000-160,000	110,000-130,000	85,000-105,000

Note: One Australian dollar is equivalent to Rs. 36.00.

Perceivable differences in compensation exist for different functions and distinct compensation premium is visible for executives in the mining discipline. While graduate engineers are reported to be paid around 60,000 Australian dollars, the design engineers are in higher compensation bracket at 75,000 Australian dollars. Managers are in the pay bracket of 120-145,000 Australian dollars. The mining sector in Australia definitely appears to be at a higher rung in compensation levels when compared to other sectors and is almost on par with a high technology sector like IT.

Situation in France

Typical remuneration levels in vogue in France pertaining to the executive in the disciplines of IT, Finance and HR management are indicated in Tables 10.25-10.27. The data is based on the survey conducted by M/s Robert Walters for the year 2006.

The compensation levels in private sector companies abroad are characterised by wide variations dictated essentially by the demand-supply situation of talent. While the remuneration levels appear to be fairly comparable across the countries in Europe and North America at junior and middle levels, the variance is very pronounced at the senior levels, especially in a country like USA. Performance is an essential element in the remuneration packages of the executives. When the salary budgets become more and more flat, differentiation in terms of incentives and pay rises between valued contributors and others through rational measures is exercised to ensure commitment of the performing population of executives to the enterprise. Though a small country, Singapore appears to be adopting progressive but pragmatic measures to attract and retain talent in all its organisations.

Table 10.25

Typical Remuneration Level: IT

Role	*Permanent Salary Per Annum (€)*			
	3-5 Yrs' Exp.	*5-7 Yrs' Exp.*	*7-11 Yrs' Exp.*	*11+ Yrs' Exp.*
IT				
Chief Information Officer				150k+
IT Director			75-100k	90-130k
Head of Technical Strategy			65-90k	85-120k
Programme Manager		80-110k	80-110k	120k+
IT Manager	45-60k	60-80k	60-80k	60-80k
Systems/Technical Architect	50-55k	60-65k	60-65k	70k+
ERP Consultant	40-45k	45-55k	50-65k	70k+
ERP/CRM Implementation Manager	40-45k	45-55k	50-65k	70k+
Security Specialist	45-55k	50-60k	55-80k	90k+
Project Manager	45-60k	60-80k	75-100k	80-110k
Network Administrator	38-42k	40-55k	40-55k	40-55k
IS Audit Senior			65-80k	70-90k
IS Audit Junior	45-50k	50-60k		
Oracle/Sybase Developer	45-60k	45-60k	45-60k	45-60k
Oracle/Sybase DBA	45-60K	45-60K	55-80K	55-80K
IT Administrator	30-40k	40-50k	50-60k	
Consulting/Organisation and Management Consulting				
Senior Consultant	45-60k	45-60k		
Managing Consultant		60-85k	60-85k	60-85k
Principal/Senior Manager				90-130k
VP/Partner				150k+
Strategy Consulting				
Senior Consultant	65-100k	65-100k		
Managing Consultant		90-120k	90-120k	
Senior Manager			150-200k	
VP/Partners				250k+

Note: Figures are basic salaries exclusive of benefits/bonuses unless otherwise specified.

Table 10.26

Typical Remuneration Level: Finance

Role	*Permanent Salary Per Annum (€)*			
	3-5 Yrs' Exp.	*5-7 Yrs' Exp.*	*7-11 Yrs' Exp.*	*11+ Yrs' Exp.*
Chief Financial Officer			130-170k	150-250k
VP Finance			110-160k	140-200k
Finance Director			100-150k	130-200k
Group Controller		70-90k	80-130k	110-180k
Controller	55-70k	60-80k	70-90k	80-120k
Business Analyst	45-55k	50-70k	55-80k	75-95k
Internal Audit	45-60k	55-80k	70-120k	90-150k
Consolidation Reporting	45-65k	60-80k	70-90k	85-110k
Accounting Manager		55-75k	65-90k	85-110k
Credit Controller	35-45k	45-65k	65-85k	85-95k
Project Finance	50-65k	65-75k	75-100k	95-125k
Corporate Finance	55-65k	65-80k	75-100k	90-120k
Treasury	40-53k	50-65k	60-85k	80-110k
Strategy	60-70k	70-85k	75-105k	100-185k
Audit	40-60k	60-85k	80-120k	110-150k+

Note: Figures are basic salaries exclusive of benefits/bonuses unless otherwise specified.

Table 10.27

Typical Remuneration Level: Human Resources

Role	*Permanent Salary Per Annum (€)*			
	3-5 Yrs' Exp.	*5-7 Yrs' Exp.*	*7-11 Yrs' Exp.*	*11+ Yrs' Exp.*
HR Director			90-120k	110-180k
HR Manager	40-50k	50-70k	70-90k	85-130k
Compensation and Benefits Manager	40-55k	55-75k	65-90k	90-150k
Recruitment Manager	35-45k	45-65k	60-75k	70-90k
Training and Development Manager	35-45k	45-55k	55-75k	70-90k
Labour Law Director			70-90k	85-130k
Labour Law Manager	40-45k	45-65k	60-75k	70-90k
Head of Personnel and Administration			55-75k	75-90k

Note: Figures are basic salaries exclusive of benefits/bonuses unless otherwise specified.

11 Feedback

The present study report is not meant to be a recommendatory report but IPE would like to summarise some of the inputs it received in the course of interactions with the senior officials of some CPSEs. The competition faced by the CPSEs today, either for business or for talent is from the private sector companies and MNCs. The need of the hour is to approach the industry standards of compensations which vary significantly from group to group and company to company.

There is, however, complete awareness in most of the CPSEs about the need to link compensation with performance and affordability not withstanding the pressing need to attract and retain talent especially in the middle and senior management cadres. The general consensus seems to be that the compensation packages can be broadly divided into four elements.

The first element can be the 'fixed' element which can be bound within some framework or uniformity—again linked appropriately to the paying capacity of the individual CPSEs.

The second element can comprise allowances and reimbursements which could provide for the industry specificity—aimed at approaching the industry standards of compensations.

The third element can be the 'variable' or 'performance linked' element which can be very carefully and judiciously linked to the individual, group and unit performance *vis-à-vis* the desired and agreed targets. The performance-linked payments should form a substantial part of the individual's salary. Further, this element is to be substantially higher for the senior cadres of executives. Individual's performance can have a higher weightage in the variable pay in respect of junior cadres whereas, unit/organisational performance should determine the quantum of variable pay in respect of senior executives.

The fourth element can be linked to the remoteness of location or the hazards linked to the nature of the person's work—at least to partly offset the inconvenience to which the person and the family are subjected to due to the nature of work. This becomes more and more important since the action is moving from the factories to the field in most cases. Installation and commissioning on time, maintenance and performance monitoring on continuous basis as demanded by the customers are becoming mandatory in the context of almost all the industries.

Thus, in addition to the basic fixed pay and allowances, serious thought could be given to design:

- Allowances to make the compensation industry specific *vis-à-vis* profitability and industry standards;
- Incentives to reward excellent performance;
- Compensation for the inconveniences associated with the job and insurance schemes for the risks.

Such a methodology will ensure that salaries will be linked to profitability of the enterprise and not become an inflexible and permanent burden to the company. The surpluses generated by an enterprise will have defined destinations:

a. Taxes to the government,
b. Dividend to the owner—Government of India and other shareholders,
c. IEBR (internal and extra budgetary resource) to the company towards investments for future, and
d. Rewards to the employees who have made the surpluses possible.

The reward schemes which will be the spin-offs from (d) above and can be board-driven, since the company's position regarding affordability to pay present and future is best known to the company's board and these schemes should be company-specific.

The principle of differentiation amongst the employee population becomes a must since the CPSEs are competing with private sector/MNC companies for talent. This calls for transparent, logical and sustainable goal setting and evaluation methods in CPSEs. When there are limits to the overall payment capacity, the available surplus should go to the deserving and contributing population in the CPSEs. This will be the most difficult and challenging task to be accomplished with care and complete transparency. There is a compelling need to do away with the uniformity syndrome. Shift from uniformity to differentiation is not an easy task to accomplish. There will be however, no choice for CPSEs since they have to be competitive, profitable and still in a position to attract and retain the needed talent.

The differentiation schemes have to be on par with the industry standards and have to be top down in structure and content. The CEOs of CPSEs and other senior members on the board are in fact contract employees of the Government and hiring of these senior executives, on contract, can be on lines similar to private sector companies through appropriate search committees or open advertisements—with industry standard remunerations and commissions. Since the shadow of the top man will fall on the entire organisation, the organisation stands to gain if the best is at the helm of affairs. The associations of executives from different product groups of CPSEs have presented to the honourable committee their concerns and expectations. The concerns centre around talent migration to private sector, hazards of occupation, vast differentials in remunerations between CPSEs and leading private companies and MNCs, stagnation problems, anomalies in the pay fixation and the hike.

In respect to the specific questions included in the DPEs questionnaire, in regard to: (a) continuance of the present classification of CPSEs into Schedule A, B, C & D, (b) uniformity of pay scales, (c) separate scales for navratna and miniratna CPSEs, (d) rate of increments etc., the responses from the CPSEs are summarised and reflected below:

a. 41 out of the 70 responses (representing 59%) felt that, the existing classification of CPSEs in to Schedule A, B, C, & D could continue, 26 respondents (37%) proposed revision. However, 3 respondents (4%) did not respond.

b. 26 respondents (representing 37%), mostly the financially healthy CPSEs) desired no uniformity in the pay scales, 41 respondents (59%) proposed for continuance of uniform scales.

c. 23 respondents (33%) proposed for separate pay scales for navratna and miniratna CPSEs, 36 respondents (51%) did not suggest for any separate pay scales for them. Eleven respondents (16%) did not respond.

d. 57 respondents (representing 81%) proposed variable rate of increment, i.e., on a percentage basis, 13 respondents (19%) supported for fixed rate of increment and a majority suggested for 4-5% of basic pay as the rate of increment. A majority expressed that stagnations are at E5 and above.

Further, the following are the major observations drawn made in various representations of the officers associations, and the responses to DPE questionnaires.

- Compensation is an important tool for attracting and retaining talent and the same has to conform to market trends for performing CPSEs.
- The pay scales of the CPSEs within the schedule should be uniform. Separate pay scales may be decided for performing/non-performing CPSEs.
- The number of pay scales may remain the same as at present, but the existing pay scales should be replaced by open-ended pay scales.
- More emphasis be laid on variable components of pay, which will help managements to liberally bring about variations in the pay structure to retain talent at individual or group level.
- The decisions regarding the perquisites should be left to the individual CPSEs to be decided depending upon their capacity to pay, their productivity and the profit.
- The desirable ratio of pay between top level and entry level executive may be kept at 1:6 or more, and the ratio of pay between the lowest workmen and CEO to be 1:10 or more.
- The desirable ratio of the minimum and the maximum of the pay scale is 1:2. However, it depends on the periodicity of pay revision. Sufficient care is to be taken that employees do not stagnate at the maximum of scale.
- A better pay package may not always be the sole factor for migration of talent. The good working environment, work culture, job

satisfaction area of operations, personnel policies are some of the intangible factors which people take into consideration before moving to another organisation.

- The individual CPSEs will have to ensure that the quality of working environment avenues for growth and development and empowerment that facilitate inculcating a sense of ownership amongst the executives are taken care of, to retain the talent in the organisation.
- One of the measures to retain talent could be to revise the pay scales every five years since the economic/industry scenario changes drastically over a long period of 10 years, thus rendering the exercise of pay revision ineffective.

12 Affordability and Sustainability

A brief on the financial situation of CPSEs was mentioned in Chapter 8 *viz.*:

i. 66 CPSEs that are enjoying the status of navratnas and mini-ratnas are financially sound and are consistently making profits backed by positive net worth.

ii. 46 CPSEs (i.e., other than Section 25 companies) which are making profits and are maintaining positive net worth are empowered with special financial powers.

iii. 47 CPSEs are presently making profits, a majority of which have positive net worth.

iv. 54 CPSEs are incurring continuous losses with negative net worth.

The number of executives and NUS engaged in the financially sound CPSEs covered in (i) and (ii) above, amount to 84 per cent of the total number of executives covered in the study. While 8 per cent of the executives and NUS are engaged in the 47 CPSEs covered in (iii) above, 6 per cent are working in CPSEs covered in (iv) above. Nevertheless, most of the CPSEs (i.e., barring around 20-30 CPSEs) cannot afford any substantial pay hikes, while fulfilling the main criteria of not increasing the labour cost per physical unit of output on one hand and on the other, maintaining the same quantum of profitability with improved turnovers.

Under the circumstances, the CPSEs of India face a very tricky but serious problem of having to attract and retain talent which has become a very costly and in-demand commodity on one hand and ensuring that the costs of manpower do not adversely affect the profitability of the organisations both in the near future and years ahead, on the other.

The problem, in fact, is not limited to CPSEs alone. It is a problem for the Indian private sector companies too. India has become a recruitment hub for the MNCs operating not only in India but for their operations abroad too. The countries in the Gulf and the Southeast Asian countries find India as an attractive talent reservoir to draw from.

Traditionally, CPSEs have been the coveted training schools for the Indian private sector companies and MNCs to draw talent at the entry and junior management levels. The attrition of talent in the recent past is being reported at the very senior levels of CPSEs which certainly will be a matter of serious concern to the managements of CPSEs. In the post-liberalisation phase of the country, after the 1990s, the Indian industry has opened up opportunities to the private players within the country and the industrial giants outside the country to benefit from the booming Indian economy and markets. The competition for the CPSEs became very fierce not only for business but also for talent.

The issues of affordability and more importantly, sustainability are enterprise-specific and will be governed by industry trends and characteristics. The future projections of sales and profitability become more and more difficult to judge in an atmosphere of intense competition. In a situation of this kind, it may be more appropriate to take decisions on wage enhancements on a year to year basis at the enterprise level than commit the company for a long-term salary burden which the enterprise may or may not be able to absorb.

The study of a specific case like that of SAIL may be informative in this regard.

This steel giant, after suffering losses continuously for five years, from 1998-99 to 2002-03, staged a tremendous turnaround from 2003-04 and has been recording substantial profits from then on. Table 12.1 summarises the salient data for the last four years.

The admirable turnaround of SAIL can be traced to favourable market conditions and also exemplary corrective actions taken internally. Even in this favourable climate, the enterprise suffered a dip in the profits in the year 2005-06. The increase in manpower costs by Rs. 930 crore (22 per cent) in 2006-07 was, however, more than offset by the increase in value addition of Rs. 5,072 crore and SAIL recorded the second highest PBT of Rs. 9,422 crore in 2006-07.

Table 12.1

Sail: Salient Data for the Last Four Years

S.No.	*Description*	*2003-04*	*2004-05*	*2005-06*	*2006-07*
1.	Turnover (Rs. cr) (% increase over pr. year)	24,410 (26)	32,085 (31)	32,708 (2)	39,188 (20)
2.	Value Added (Rs. cr) (% increase over pr. year)	10,054 (35)	15,279 (52)	11,775 (-23)	16,847 (43)
3.	Value Added/Turnover (%)	41	48	36	43
4.	Manpower Cost (% increase over pr. year)	4,758 (28)	3,811 (-20)	4,157 (9)	5,087 (22)
5.	Manpower Cost to Turnover (%)	19	12	13	13
6.	Manpower Cost to Value Added (%)	45	24	35	30
7.	Profit Before Tax (PBT) (Rs. cr) (% increase over pr. year)	2,663 (from a loss of 293 cr in 2002-03)	9,427 (253)	5,716 (-60)	9,422 (65)

Note: The data for the years 2003-04 to 2005-06 is from DPE survey reports. Data pertaining to 2006-2007 is from annual report of SAIL.

Within the four year period 2003-04 to 2006-07, considerable fluctuations are seen in the profitability levels. Increased competition will mean reduced margins at unit level. The percentage of value addition to sales of 43 per cent in 2006-07 will be severely stressed with increased competition.

The sales volumes have to go up significantly to protect and improve the profitability levels when the manpower costs go up and the value added percentages come down.

The interrelationships of value addition, profitability, desirable levels of sales when the manpower costs go up by: (i) 20 per cent (ii) 30 per cent and (iii) 40 per cent—under varying conditions of value addition and targeted profits, are outlined below:

Condition 1 : % of Value addition intact (43%); Profit at 2006-07 level (PBT: Rs. 9422 crore)

Condition 2 : % of Value addition intact (43%); Targeted profit 20% above 2006-07 level (PBT: Rs. 11,306 crore)

Condition 3 : % of Value addition intact (43%); Targeted profit 30% above 2006-07 level (PBT: Rs. 12,248 crore)

Condition 4 : % of Value addition (43%); Targeted profit 40% above 2006-07 level (PBT: Rs. 13,190 crore)

Condition 5 : % of Value addition (40%); Targeted profit 20% above 2006-07 (Rs. 11,306 crore)

Condition 6 : % of Value addition (40%); Targeted profit 30% above 2006-07 level (Rs. 12,248 crore)

Condition 7 : % of Value addition (35%); Targeted profit 40% above 2006-07 level (Rs. 13,190 crore)

Condition 8 : % of Value addition (35%); Targeted profit 20% above 2006-07 level Rs. 11,306 crore)

Condition 9 : % of Value addition (35%); Targeted profit 30% above 2006-07 (Rs. 12,248 crore)

Condition 10 : % of Value addition (35%); Targeted profit at 20% above 2006-07 (Rs. 13,190 crore)

Table 12.2

Inter-relationships by Value Addition, Profitability, Desirable Level of Sales

		Desired Levels of Sales (& % Increase over 2006-07 Level)		
S.No.	*Conditions*	*Manpower Cost up by 20%*	*Manpower Cost up by 30%*	*Manpower Cost up by 40%*
1.	Profit at 2006-07 level & VA % intact at 43%	41,553 (6%)	42,736 (9%)	43,918 (12%)
2.	Profit up by 20%, Value added % intact at 43%	45,935 (17%)	47,118 (20%)	48,299 (23%)
3.	Profit up by 30%, Value added % intact at 43%	48,125 (22%)	49,308 (25%)	50,490 (28%)
4.	Profit up by 40%, Value added % intact of 43%	50,315 (28%)	51,499 (31%)	52,681 (34%)
5.	Profit up by 20%, Value added % at 40%	46,440 (18%)	47,713 (21%)	48,983 (24%)
6.	Profit up by 30%, Value added % at 40%	48,795 (24%)	50,068 (27%)	51,338 (31%)
7.	Profit up by 40%, Value added % at 40%	51,150 (30%)	52,423 (33%)	53,693 (7%)
8.	Profit up by 30%, Value added % at 35%	47,476 (21%)	48,390 (24%)	50,382 (28%)
9.	Profit up by 30%, Value added % at 35%	50,168 (28%)	51,622 (31%)	53,073 (35%)
10.	Profit up by 40%, Value added % at 35%	52,859 (34%)	54,313 (38%)	55,765 (42%)

Table 12.2 is based on the premise that wage increases will not be at the cost of profitability. The expected sales levels, expected levels of value additions, other increases in fixed costs, competitive situations etc., are best known to the enterprises concerned. The targets related to profits will be set by the enterprises based on the ground realities. The enterprises will be in a position to judge as to how much increase in manpower costs can be absorbed *vis-à-vis* the targeted profits on a year to year basis.

It is stated that, as a policy in the private sector companies, the increase in manpower costs will not be allowed to be more than the increase in profits. Further, the percentages of manpower costs in terms of sales and value addition are expected to be 10 per cent and 25 per cent respectively in respect of financially healthy companies. The enterprises can probably be given the framework of expected profits *vis-à-vis* the existing conditions and the likely scenario of future to determine the quantum of increases in the remuneration levels.

As can be seen from the Tables 12.1 and 12.2, the sensitivity of the reduced margins and increased profits can be very high on the desired levels of sales. The enterprises concerned could critically examine the business possibilities and permissible wage increases. These two have to be looked at simultaneously and cannot be de-linked.

The situations pertaining to enterprises which are in border line positions with respect to profitability will be more critical in relation to the increases in wages.

It is in situations of this kind that the need for differentiation becomes more acute. The discerning and contributing segments of employees and executives—at individual level, section level, unit level—will be required to be identified for monetary rewards as opposed to across the board hikes in salaries.

The issues that will inevitably surface and need critical examination before a view is taken about increases in compensation levels are:

(i) The desirable linkage between profitability and employee/executive compensation.

(ii) The methodologies to be put in position to gradually and yet effectively shift from the uniformity model to differentiation model in respect of compensation packages and career progression.

(iii) Designing rational and transparent methods of performance evaluation of executives (and employees).

(iv) Evolving dependable tools and techniques to be used to assess the affordability and sustainability of wage increases *vis-à-vis* the characteristics of the particular CPSE in terms of future business prospects, the intensity of competition and the demand and cost of talent.

(v) The desirable break-up of the elements of compensation package that will cover: (a) fixed and assured pay, (b) allowances and reimbursements to match the industry standards, (c) performance linked variable pay, and (d) risk and occupation related compensation.

(vi) The periodicity of wage revisions and the systems to be kept in position.

(vii) Compensation packages in respect of currently loss-making CPSEs which have the definite potential to rally back if the needed talent can be mobilised.

The most important issue, which takes precedence over every other issue, is the need for survival and growth of the enterprise. The issues related to wage revisions are inextricably linked with the nurturing and protection of the institution of CPSEs itself. In the present context, the responsibility rests with the CPSEs themselves as budgetary support from the government cannot be expected any longer for any business-related expenditure.

Annexures

Annexure A-1

Comparable Public Sector Enterprises and Private Sector Companies

Public Sector Enterprises	*Private Sector Enterprises*
Steel	
Ferro Scrap Nigam Ltd.	Lloyds Steel Industries Ltd.
Maharashtra Elektrosmelt Ltd.	Ispat Industries Ltd.
Mishra Dhatu Nigam Ltd.	Tata Sponge Iron Ltd.
Rashtriya Ispat Nigam Ltd.	Tata Steel Ltd.
Sponge Iron India Ltd.	JSW Steel Ltd.
Steel Authority of India Ltd.	
Minerals & Metals Trading Corps of India Ltd.	
Bharat Refractories Ltd.	Hindalco Industries Ltd.
FCI Aravali Gypsum & Minerals India Ltd.	Madras Aluminium Company Ltd.
Hindustan Copper Ltd.	Sesa Goa Ltd.
Indian Rare Earths Ltd.	Ashapura Minechem Ltd.
J&K Mineral Development Corpn. Ltd.	
Kudremukh Iron Ore Co. Ltd.	
Manganese Ore(India) Ltd.	
National Aluminium Company Ltd.	
National Mineral Development Corpn. Ltd.	
Uranium Corporation of India Ltd.	
Coal & Lignite	
Bharat Coking Coal Ltd.	
Central Coalfields Ltd.	
Coal India Ltd.	
Eastern Coalfields Ltd.	
Mahanadi Coalfields Ltd.	
Neyveli Lignite Corpn. Ltd.	
Northern Coalfields Ltd.	
South Eastern Coalfields Ltd.	
Western Coalfields Ltd.	
Power	
Narmada Hydroelectric Development Corp. Ltd.	Tata Power Company Ltd.
NHPC Ltd.	Torrent Power Ltd.

contd...

...contd...

Power Grid Corporation of India Ltd.	Reliance Energy Ltd.
North Eastern Electric Power Corporation Ltd.	Jaiprakash Hydro-Power Ltd.
NTPC Ltd.	
Nuclear Power Corp. of India Ltd.	
Satluj Jal Vidyut Nigam Ltd.	
Petroleum	
Oil and Natural Gas Corporation Ltd.	Reliance Natural Resources Ltd.
Indian Oil Corporation Ltd.	Essar Oil Ltd.
Mangalore Refinery and Petrochemicals Ltd.	
Numaligarh Refinery Ltd.	
Bharat Petroleum Corpn. Ltd.	
Bongaigaon Refinery and Petrochemicals Ltd.	
Chennai Petroleum Corporation Ltd.	
GAIL (India) Ltd.	
Hindustan Petroleum Corpn. Ltd.	
Fertilisers	
Brahmaputra Valley Fertilizer Corpn. Ltd.	Coromandel Fertilizers Ltd.
Fertilizer Corpn. of India Ltd.	Deepak Fertilisers and Petrochemicals Corp. Ltd.
Fertilisers & Chemicals Travancore Ltd.	Godavari Fertilizers and Chemicals Ltd.
Hindustan Fertilizer Corpn. Ltd.	Nagarjuna Fertilizers and Chemicals Ltd.
Madras Fertilizers Ltd.	
National Fertilizers Ltd.	
Rashtriya Chemicals and Fertilizers Ltd.	
Chemicals & Pharmaceuticals	
Bengal Chemicals & Pharmaceuticals Ltd.	Dr. Reddy's Laboratories Ltd.
Bharat Immunologicals & Biologicals Corp. Ltd.	Ranbaxy Laboratories Ltd.
Hindustan Antibiotics Ltd.	Pfizer Ltd.
Hindustan Fluorocarbons Limited	Cadila Healthcare Ltd.
Hindustan Insecticides Ltd.	Cipla Ltd.
Hindustan Organic Chemicals Ltd.	
Hindustan Salts Ltd.	
Indian Drugs & Pharmaceuticals Ltd.	
Indian Medicines and Pharmaceutical Corpn. Ltd.	
Karnataka Antibiotics & Pharmaceuticals Ltd.	
Orissa Drugs & Chemicals Ltd.	
Projects & Development India Ltd.	
Rajasthan Drugs & Pharmaceuticals Ltd.	
Sambhar Salts Ltd.	
Heavy Engineering	
Bharat Bhari Udyog Nigam Ltd.	Alfa Laval (India) Ltd.
Bharat Heavy Electricals Ltd.	Walchandnagar Industries Ltd.
Bharat Heavy Plate & Vessels Ltd.	UB Engineering Ltd.
Bharat Wagon & Engg. Co. Ltd.	AIA Engineering Ltd.
Braithwaite & Co. Ltd.	

contd...

...contd...

Burn Standard Company Ltd.	
Heavy Engineering Corpn. Ltd.	
Triveni Structurals Ltd.	
Tungabhadra Steel Products Ltd.	
Medium & Light Engineering	
Andrew Yule & Company Ltd.	Salora International Ltd.
Antrix Corporation Ltd.	MIRC Electronics Ltd.
Balmer Lawrie & Co. Ltd.	Ion Exchange (India) Ltd.
Bel Optronics Devices Ltd.	Thermax Ltd.
Bharat Dynamics Ltd.	Windsor Machines Ltd.
Bharat Electronics Ltd.	Action Construction Equipment Ltd.
Bharat Pumps & Compressors Ltd.	Bharat Forge Ltd.
Biecco Lawrie & Co. Ltd.	
Central Electronics Ltd.	
Electronics Corpn. of India Ltd.	
Hindustan Cables Ltd.	
HMT Bearings Ltd.	
HMT Chinar Watches Ltd.	
HMT Ltd.	
HMT Machine Tools Ltd.	
HMT Watches Ltd.	
ITI Ltd.	
IDPL (Tamil Nadu) Ltd.	
Instrumentation Ltd.	
Rajasthan Electronics & Instruments Ltd.	
Richardson & Cruddas (1972) Ltd.	
Vignyan Industries Ltd.	
Transportation Equipment	
BEML Ltd.	Mahindra and Mahindra Ltd.
Central Inland Water Transport Corpn. Ltd.	Tata Motors Ltd.
Cochin Shipyard Ltd.	Ashok Leyland Ltd.
Garden Reach Shipbuilders & Engineers Ltd.	Eicher Motors Ltd.
Goa Shipyard Ltd.	
Hindustan Aeronautics Ltd.	
Hindustan Shipyard Ltd.	
Hooghly Dock and Port Engineers Ltd.	
Mazagon Dock Ltd.	
Scooters India Ltd.	
Consumer Goods	
Artificial Limbs Mfg. Corpn. of India	Gujarat Ambuja Cements Ltd.
Cement Corpn. of India Ltd.	Andhra Cements Ltd.
Hindustan Latex Ltd.	Paper Products Ltd.
Hindustan Newsprint Ltd.	West Coast Paper Mills Ltd.
Hindustan Paper Corporation Ltd.	

contd...

...contd...

Hindustan Photo Films Manufacturing Co. Ltd.	
Hindustan Vegetable Oils Corpn. Ltd.	
Hooghly Printing Company Ltd.	
Nagaland Pulp & Paper Company Ltd.	
NEPA Ltd.	
Security Printing & Minting Corpn. of India Ltd.	
Tyre Corporation of India Ltd.	
Textiles	
Birds Jute & Exports Ltd.	Suryalakshmi Cotton Mills Ltd.
British India Corporation Ltd.	Vardhman Textiles Ltd.
Brushware Ltd.	Century Enka Ltd.
National Jute Manufactures Corporation Ltd.	Garden Silk Mills Ltd.
National Textile Corpn. Ltd.	
Trading & Marketing	
Central Cottage Industries Corpn. of India Ltd.	
Central Railside Warehouse Co. Ltd.	
Central Warehousing Corpn.	
Cotton Corpn. of India Ltd.	
Food Corpn. of India	
Handicrafts & Handloom Exports Corp. of India Ltd.	
HMT (International) Ltd.	
India Trade Promotion Organisation	
Jute Corpn. of India Ltd.	
Karnataka Trade Promotion Organisation	
MMTC Ltd.	
MSTC Ltd.	
National Handloom Development Corporation Ltd.	
North Eastern Handicrafts & Handloom Dev. Corpn. Ltd.	
NTPC Vidyut Vyapar Nigam Ltd.	
PEC Ltd.	
State Trading Corpn. of India Ltd.	
STCL Ltd.	
Tamil Nadu Trade Promotion Organisation	
Transportation Services	
Air India Air Transport Services Ltd.	Jet Airways
Air India Charters Ltd.	Essar Shipping Ltd.
Airline Allied Services Ltd.	Shreyas Shipping & Logistics Ltd.
Airports Authority of India Ltd.	Varun Shipping Company Ltd.
Container Corporation of India Ltd.	
Dredging Corpn. of India Ltd.	
Ennore Port Ltd.	
Fresh & Healthy Enterprises Ltd.	
National Aviation Co. of India Ltd.	
Pawan Hans Helicopters Ltd.	

contd...

...contd...

Shipping Corporation of India Ltd.	
Contract & Construction Services	
BBJ Construction Company Ltd.	Kalindee Rail Nirman (Engineers) Ltd.
Bridge & Roof Co.(India) Ltd.	Bhagheeratha Engineering Ltd.
Hindustan Prefab Ltd.	Petron Engineering Construction Ltd.
Hindustan Steelworks Construction Co. Ltd.	
IRCON International Ltd.	
Konkan Railway Corporation Ltd.	
Mineral Exploration Corpn. Ltd.	
Mumbai Railway Vikas Corporation Ltd.	
National Buildings Construction Corpn. Ltd.	
National Projects Construction Corpn. Ltd.	
Rail Vikas Nigam Ltd.	
Industrial Deveploment & Tech. Consultancy Services	
Broadcast Engg. Consultants India Ltd.	
Central Mine Planning & Design Institute Ltd.	
Certification Engineers International Ltd.	
Educational Consultants India Ltd.	
Engineering Projects India Ltd.	
Engineers India Ltd.	
HSCC India Ltd.	
IndianOil Technologies Ltd.	
Mecon Ltd.	
National Informatics Centre Services Incorporated	
National Research Development Corpn.	
National Small Industries Corpn. Ltd.	
RITES Ltd.	
Telecommunications Consultants India Ltd.	
WAPCOS Ltd.	
Financial Services	
Balmer Lawrie Investments Ltd.	Infrastructure Development Finance Company Ltd.
Export Credit Guarantee Corpn. of India Ltd.	Bajaj Auto Finance Ltd.
Housing and Urban Dev. Corpn. Ltd.	
India Infrastructure Finance Co. Ltd.	
Indian Railway Finance Corporation Ltd.	
Indian Renewable Energy Devt. Agency Ltd.	
Kumarakrupa Frontier Hotels Ltd.	
National Backward Classes Finance & Devp.Corp.	
National Film Dev. Corpn. Ltd.	
National Handicapped Finance & Devpt. Corpn.	
National Minorities Devp. & Finance Corpn.	
National Safai Karamcharis Finance & Devpt. Corpn.	

contd...

...contd...

National Scheduled Castes Finance & Devp. Corpn.	
National Scheduled Tribes Finance & Devp. Corpn.	
Power Finance Corporation	
Rural Electrification Corpn. Ltd.	
Telecommunication Services	
Bharat Sanchar Nigam Ltd.	Videsh Sanchar Nigam Ltd.
Mahanagar Telephone Nigam Ltd.	Himachal Futuristic Communications Ltd.
Millennium Telecom Ltd.	Bharti Airtel Ltd.
RailTel Corporation India Ltd.	Tata Consultancy Services

Annexure A-2

Executives and Non-Unionised Supervisors of Navratna, Miniratna I and Miniratna II CPSEs

Navratna

	Names of the CPSEs	*Executives*	*NUS*	*Manpower*
1.	Bharat Heavy Electricals Limited	10353	8329	54388
2.	Bharat Petroleum Corporation Limited	3925	0	13876
3.	GAIL India Limited	2276	0	3443
4.	Hindustan Petroleum Corporation Limited	3849	0	10778
5.	Indian Oil Corporation Limited	10745	0	30048
6.	Mahanagar Telephone Nigam Limited	1130	6658	51212
7.	NTPC Limited	10293	1524	24044
8.	Oil and Natural Gas Corporation Limited	18906	4198	35227
9.	Steel Authority of India Limited	10672	4534	138211
10.	Bharat Electronics Ltd.	3808	714	12262
11.	Power Finance Corp. Ltd.	183	27	312
12.	Hindustan Aeronautics Ltd.	1616	2000	29668

Miniratna I

	Names of the CPSEs	*Executives*	*NUS*	*Manpower*
1.	Bharat Dynamics Limited	622	0	2814
2.	Balmer Lawrie & Co. Ltd.	469	76	1437
3.	Bharat Earth Movers Limited	1080	1056	11975
4.	Bharat Sanchar Nigam Limited	61857	0	326948
5.	Bongaigaon Refinery and Petrochemicals Limited	562	0	1726
6.	Coal India Ltd.	413	0	4540
7.	Central Warehousing Corporation	781	640	6413
8.	Chennai Petroleum Corporation Limited	470	41	1672
9.	Container Corporation of India Limited	195	124	1028
10.	Dredging Corporation of India Limited	307	0	869
11.	Engineers India Limited	1222	921	2588
12.	Garden Reach Shipbuilders & Engineers Limited	576	676	5088
13.	Goa Shipyard Ltd.	167	294	1543
14.	Western Coalfields Ltd.	2345	401	67378
15.	Hindustan Aeronautics Limited	9379	0	38754
16.	Hindustan Latex Limited	119	143	1801
17.	Hindustan Newsprint Limited	185	90	1039
18.	India Tourism Development Corporation Limited	347	0	2904
19.	IRCON International Limited	719	571	1723
20.	Kudremukh Iron Ore Company Limited	431	181	1889
21.	Mazagaon Dock Limited	791	230	8090

contd...

...contd...

22.	Mahanadi Coalfields Ltd.	1246	0	20876
23.	Mangalore Refinery and Petrochemicals Ltd.	121	200	967
24.	MMTC Limited	623	0	2031
25.	MSTC Limited	142	0	305
26.	National Aluminium Company Limited	1770	0	7406
27.	National Fertilizers Limited	1326	144	4769
28.	National Mineral Development Corporation Ltd.	973	251	5885
29.	Neyveli Lignite Corporation	3766	389	19023
30.	Northern Coalfields Ltd.	1382	0	16914
31.	Numaligarh Refinery Limited	318	0	702
32.	Oil India Limited	1685	0	12287
33.	Power Grid Corporation of India Limited	2882	1523	7101
34.	Rashtriya Ispat Nigam Limited	3532	0	16574
35.	Rural Electrification Corporation Limited	150	153	707
36.	RITES Limited	1221	897	2655
37.	Shipping Corporation of India Limited	2497	1248	6242
38.	South Eastern Coalfields Ltd.	2745	7964	85871
39.	State Trading Corporation of India Limited	160	200	928
40.	Telecommunications Consultants India Limited	547	0	924
41.	HUDCO Ltd.	510	70	1098

Miniratna II

	Name of the CPSE	*Executives*	*NUS*	*Manpower*
1.	Educational Consultants (I) Limited	30	14	89
2.	Engineering Projects (I) Limited	374	0	473
3.	Ferro Scrap Nigam Limited	148	0	1166
4.	HMT (International) Limited	48	10	68
5.	WAPCOS Ltd.	266	59	483
6.	India Trade Promotion Organisation	190	120	1191
7.	Indian Medicines Pharmaceuticals Corporation Ltd.	12	0	127
8.	Manganese Ore (India) Limited	247	0	6998
9.	Mecon Limited	1284	0	1513
10.	National Film Development Corporation Limited	124	0	217
11.	PEC Limited	101	40	192
12.	Rajasthan Electronics & Instruments Limited	51	49	194
13.	HSCC (India) Ltd.	99	0	133

Annexure A-3

CPSEs Operating 1987 Pay Revision

Name of the CPSEs	Executives	NUS	Manpower
1. Indian Drugs and Pharmaceuticals Ltd.	108	120	375
2. Orissa Drugs and Chemicals Ltd.	3	15	83
3. Bharat Opthalmic Glass Ltd.	4	0	6
4. National Jute Manufacturers Corp. Ltd.	65	54	1333
5. Hindustan Photo Films Manufacturing Co. Ltd.	90	66	1071
6. Fertilizer Corp. of India	47	0	61
7. Hindustan Fertilizer Corp. Ltd.	39	0	50
8. National Instruments Ltd.	4	14	69
9. Nagaland Pulp & Paper Co. Ltd.	6	21	294
10. British India Corp. Ltd.	140	132	2729
11. Tyre Corp. of India Ltd.	51	24	277
12. Birds Jute and Exports Ltd.	0	13	131
13. J&K Mineral Development Corp. Ltd.	1	0	7
14. Brushware Ltd.	0	0	0
Total	558	459	6486

CPSEs Operating 1992 Pay Revision

Name of the CPSEs	Executives	NUS	Total
1. Heavy Engineering Corp. Ltd.	839	998	3457
2. Vignyan Industries Ltd.	19	9	226
3. Braithwaite & Co. Ltd.	69	42	544
4. Bengal Chemicals and Pharmaceuticals Ltd.	22	104	816
5. Instrumentation Ltd.	269	815	1715
6. Bharat Wagon and Engg. Comp. Ltd.	42	44	948
7. Bharat Pumps and Compressors Ltd.	229	38	1233
8. Triveni Structurals Ltd.	60	50	311
9. Richardson and Cruddas (1972) Ltd.	23	14	74
10. Bharat Refractories Ltd.	203	0	1690
11. Hindustan Vegetable Oils Corp. Ltd.	41	0	160
12. Hindustan Flurocarbons Ltd.	35	0	207
13. NEPA Ltd.	4	2	1208
14. Praga Tools Ltd.	93	28	554
15. Hindustan Salts Ltd.	13	4	111
16. Bharat Heavy Plate and Vessels Ltd.	295	189	1453
17. HMT Bearings Ltd.	53	40	339
18. HMT Ltd.	295	177	2429
19. HMT (International) Ltd.	48	10	68
20. HMT Chinar Watches Ltd.	12	0	580
21. HMT Machine Tools Ltd.	1022	458	4386
22. HMT Watches Ltd.	390	72	2180
23. Sambhar Salts Ltd.	13	4	111
24. Tungabhadra Steel Products Ltd.	102	0	342
25. Hindustan Steelworks Construction Co. Ltd.	348	0	1843
26. Hooghly Dock and Port Engineers Ltd.	65	100	718
27. North Eastern Handicrafts & Handloom Dev. Corp. Ltd.	7	0	137
28. Hindustan Prefab Ltd.	33	0	431
Total	4644	3198	28271